BLACK BOX

BLACK BOX

The air-crash detectives – why air safety is no accident

Nicholas Faith

Motorbooks International
Publishers & Wholesalers ®

Contents

Acknowledgements

This book is the result of the confidence of both Peter Grimsdale and Susanna Yager of Channel Four that I could write a book to accompany the television series of the same name in no time at all. That I managed this was largely thanks to the team at Boxtree, Susanna Wadeson, Katy Carrington and Caroline North, most professional and scrupulous of editors.

But an even greater contribution was made by the producers and researchers on the television series it complements. In a sense I was a member of a team, except that the other members were focusing on the television programmes. In fact, I don't believe that those involved – David Darlow, John Smithson, Jeremy Llewellyn-Jones, Philip Jones, Katherine English, Andy Weir and Emma Bowman – are fully aware of the extent of the contribution they made. This book is largely based on the eighty or so interviews they conducted which were transcribed with extraordinary speed by Daphne Walsh.

I have made very free use of these interviews and have obviously had to trim them, edit them and insert punctuation, since normal people do not talk in complete and rounded sentences (I have always suspected the few people I have ever met who did). I have tried to be scrupulous in retaining not only the sense of what the interviewees said but also their inflections, their tone of voice, their particular ways of expressing themselves. I hope I have succeeded in doing so: I would hate to be accused of betraying the trust of these admirable people.

Introduction:
Fear of Flying

Nearly every accident contains evidence which, if correctly identified and assessed, will allow the circumstances and the cause to be ascertained so that corrective action can be undertaken to prevent further accidents.
                                    – ICAO Annual Digest of Aircraft Accidents, 1974

To the investigative journalist there are only two valid headlines: 'We name the guilty party' and 'The arrow points to the defective part'. Air crashes, and the search for the causes of them, provide plenty of opportunity for using both, for the reasons behind such disasters are many and various. Nature, in the form of freak, or simply bad, weather has always been a major factor, but most crashes are traceable to some flaw in the human chain, either among those most directly involved – aircraft designers and manufacturers, maintenance engineers, pilots and crew, air-traffic controllers and airlines – or among more shadowy figures, such as the authorities who control the development of new aircraft, flight patterns and the discipline imposed on pilots.

This book is not a history of air crash detection: it is an unprecedented attempt to analyse the principal reasons for the aircraft accidents – or more precisely, those which have happened since the war to commercial airliners – and to relate them to each other, to construct a comprehensive framework which, I hope, will provide a deeper understanding of individual disasters. For air safety is no accident, it can't be in a world in which the smallest detail, of design or maintenance, the smallest error by the pilot, can destroy the lives of hundreds of innocent passengers. Just remember how it took only a tiny bomb to bring down Pan American Flight 103 over Lockerbie in southern Scotland. Like the television series it has been written to accompany, it differs from previous works on the same subject, in that it does not concentrate on the events leading up to a crash. Here these merely form the prologue to a series of stories which move outwards and forwards from the crashes themselves, focusing on the work of the air-crash detectives who piece together, sometimes literally, the evidence of the causes, human, mechanical or natural, of disasters the world over. Every death in every air crash tells a story. It is the job of the air-crash detectives to make sense of the events that led to the disaster. Consequently it is their inquiries which provide the very varied lessons to be learned from every single accident, lessons which they, helped by the press and public opinion, try to ensure are not brushed aside by airlines or aviation authorities. Over the past five decades, such painstaking work has played a crucial part in the enormous progress made in aircraft safety. Indeed it is thanks largely to the problems pinpointed by these investigators that the skies are remarkably safe compared with the land or sea. Statistically, if you were to board a jet aircraft at random every single day, it would be 26,000 years before you were involved in a major crash (less than one fatal accident every million flights), although you would be involved in an 'incident' which did not threaten life, limb, or indeed the aircraft, much more frequently. For crashes are the tiny tip of an iceberg composed of hundreds of thousands of less dramatic incidents involving an aircraft or its environment.

Indeed, the progress made over the past three or four decades in reducing the probability of air accidents is in marked contrast to the much slower advances made in sea transport, which is theoretically much safer. Back in 1854, Isambard Kingdom Brunel ensured that everyone on board his pioneering steamship the *Great Britain* had a seat in a lifeboat. Fifty-eight years later, only a third of the passengers could be accommodated in the lifeboats of the *Titanic*. More recently, innumerable studies have pointed to the inherently unsafe designs of most of the world's roll-on roll-off ferries, yet there have been no fundamental changes, even after the loss of the *Herald of Free Enterprise*, which cost 193 lives in 1987, and the *Estonia*, which went down eight years later, drowning over 900 wretched souls. Yet people are still prepared to travel in vessels like these, which would be instantly banned if ships were subject to anything like the same regulations as apply to even the smallest plane and its crew.

Yet despite the relative safety of flying, the level of air traffic is increasing all the time and on average, there's a major fatal plane crash every week, year after year. Around 1,500 airline passengers are killed annually, and the Flight Safety Foundation* foresees that '23 hull-loss accidents can be expected in the year 2000 if the rate of 1.5 per million [departures in 1992] is maintained. A continued rate of 0.98 fatal accidents per million departures [the rate for 1988–92] would result in sixteen fatal accidents in 2000.'

Both this book and the television series are based on the unprecedented access granted to the work of air-crash detectives on both sides of the Atlantic, the investigators of the Air Accident Investigation Branch of the Department of Transport in Britain and the National Transportation Safety Board in the United States. Because of the historic American dominance of civilian aircraft construction, the density of air traffic within the United States and the unique openness of American society, many of these stories concern American aircraft flying on domestic flights, though statistically, American aircraft and American airlines are among the safest in the world.

* *Flight Safety Digest*, October 1993.

The task of the investigators is made difficult not only by the inevitably fragmentary nature of the evidence but also by the multiplicity of potential problems. The Flight Safety Foundation analysed all the accidents among commercial airliners in 1992 and attributed the sixty-two accidents to thirty-seven different causes. There were nine hard landings and six 'controlled flights into terrain', but none of the other causes, which ranged from loose cargo to engine fires and 'nose gear torn off', were responsible for more than four accidents. To complicate matters further, while most accidents have a principal cause, very often there are any number of secondary factors which have a bearing on them. In its own analysis, Accident Prevention Strategies, Boeing reassessed 232 major accidents from 1982 to 1991 and identified thirty-seven individual links which could have contributed to them. As Macarthur Job says in his book *Air Disaster* of the worst crash in the history of aviation, that at Tenerife in 1977 between two Boeing 747s, it 'was the final outcome of an unfavourable coincidence of a whole class of circumstances that individually were relatively insignificant'.

The veteran investigator Chuck Miller recently wrote a paper which he called 'Downward Probable Cause'. 'I was so sick and tired of people taking that one thing and missing all the other lessons that I'm ready to tell 'em, forget what caused the accident – report it all. Of course, the people in the media and the lawyers won't like that. The idea of the single cause is a fixation of the media, that's true, but I think you can almost go back to the lay public, who don't like to have complicated stories told to them.' This encourages me, because I found it extremely difficult to try to classify many crashes. Indeed, pernickety readers could well quarrel with some of my classifications, or the fact that I have treated some crashes (notably that of United Airlines Flight 232 at Sioux City in 1989) in two separate chapters.

The history of air accidents is, as Lord Acton said of human history in general, a 'seamless web', and thus any attempt to pick it apart is inevitably bound to result in some rough edges. Sometimes, then, the allocation of the major share of the blame may seem rather arbitrary. But an attempt to categorize the accidents must be made to avoid giving the impression that they resemble another, less pretentious definition of history – just 'one damn thing after another'.

The vast majority of accidents studied by the Flight Safety Foundation occurred while a plane was taxiing, taking off or on its initial climb; or, at the other end of its flight, approaching the runway, landing or taxiing after touchdown. This vulnerability to problems on approach and landing was emphasized in a more recent study by the foundation which analysed the causes of crashes and how they had changed by comparing the ten years from 1985 to 1994 with long-term figures dating back to 1959. The foundation found that: 'Half of all worldwide commercial jet accidents between 1959 and 1994 with known causes occurred during final approach and landing, a phase representing only 4 per cent of total flight time. Of the 439 final-approach-and-landing accidents with known causes, 383 (78.1 per cent) included flight crews as a primary causal factor. This percentage was far in excess of any other primary causal factor.' The second most frequent cause remains the plane itself, while maintenance has replaced air-traffic control and airport problems as the third most important cause of accidents.

It is important to look at the pattern over long periods because the figures for individual years can be sharply affected by a single major accident, such as the Tenerife tragedy in 1977, which claimed 583 victims. According to Airclaims, the specialized insurance information service, 1985, a notoriously bad year, showed a record level of 1,866 fatalities for commercial airliners compared with the exceptionally low level of 319 deaths the previous year. Both are extreme deviations from the average of 911 deaths annually during the 1980s. The number of accidents varied equally wildly, from a single one in 1984 to twelve times as many in both the previous and following year.

Even today, even after so many advances in detection techniques, mysteries remain, leaving the haunting fear that unexplained accidents may recur. As we see in Chapter 11, even the experts of the National Transportation Safety Board were unable to define precisely what caused two major crashes, both involving the world's most-flown aircraft, the Boeing 737, first at Colorado Springs in 1991, and more recently US Air's flight 427 from Chicago to Pittsburgh in 1994. In the second tragedy the tape on the black box didn't help, since all that could be heard was an expletive followed by the words: 'Emergency! Straight down.' The Boeing 737 dropped 6,000ft and nose-dived into a ravine at 300mph, killing all 132 people on board. This accident has still not been satisfactorily explained.

Despite the problems and the mysteries, passengers on commercial airliners can feel infinitely more secure than those flying in light aircraft. Their behaviour is so erratic that professionals describe the airspace below 10,000ft as 'Indian Country', because of the small aircraft flying around and the very special dangers they pose. The pilots, especially those on the west coast of the United States, are known as 'the NRA of the skies' after the gun-happy members of the National Rifle Association. Owners and pilots of private planes, particularly in the United States, assume that they have an absolute right to use the skies, just as members of the NRA believe that they have an absolute right to carry even the most dangerous of weapons.

The far greater dangers posed by light aircraft, and not only in the United States, were dramatically brought home to me while I was writing this book. I was driving past a tiny French aerodrome on a peaceful country road totally unsullied by signs warning of low-flying aeroplanes (or planes of any sort, for that matter) when a small aircraft flew across the road some 10ft in front of the car, low enough to be visible through the windscreen. That sunny afternoon I very nearly suffered a fate which would perhaps have been entirely appropriate for the author of this book.

4

One final question: why are people so much more fascinated by plane accidents than by the regular drip-drip of deaths on the road, or indeed a shipwreck, which can claim just as many lives? Partly, of course, this is because flying remains a fundamentally unnatural act for most of us. But Jim Hall, the chairman of the NTSB, provides a better answer: 'Most of us can walk, most of us can drive and most of us can swim, but most of us can't fly, and I think there always will be a fascination with flight, and with the average person, I think there is that little sinking feeling in the stomach when they're at 30,000ft and they're not in control.'

1
The World of the Tin-Kickers . . .

Kicking tin has become a term that's used to describe accident-investigators and it's more prevalent in aviation. If you watch TV or you see a picture, typically you see a bunch of investigators, and the little caption says 'investigators looking at a piece of the wreckage'. Usually on the news you see somebody shuffling around or kicking something with their foot to turn the piece over. That has just progressed into the term tin-kicker. I am a professional tin-kicker, I go out there hunting down the clues, and the only way to do that is to roll the wreckage over and rummage through it to see what it's going to tell us.
– Gregory Feith, senior air safety investigator with the NTSB

Air-accident investigators, or 'tin-kickers', are a very special breed. In one sense they're detectives operating in a very specialized field, but, at a senior level, they have to be capable of co-ordinating, and thus of comprehending, a far wider range of professional skills than their equivalents in the criminal field. Typically, Tom Haueter, deputy chief of major investigations for the NTSB, doesn't 'think of myself so much as a detective, but as an engineer who's trying to solve a problem'. Obviously, they have to have an interest in aviation, and this natural inclination finds its most obsessive form with Gregory Feith, a senior investigator with the NTSB.

I began this love affair with airplanes when my mother bought me a plane ride for my fifth birthday and gave me an opportunity to see the world from 2,000ft. That day changed my life. I started building model airplanes. I spent lots of hours doing that, I mean, literally all night long, and it taught me two things. It taught me about airplanes, because I had to understand where the parts were and what they were, but it also taught me a lot of patience. In high school I began to fly radio-controlled airplanes and now this airplane was in the air and I was in command of it.'

He trained as a pilot, studied aviation law and managed to wangle a summer job with the NTSB during his last year at university. 'I knew that this was where I wanted to be, this was where I should be, and I'm still here sixteen years later.' Today Feith, like many of his fellow investigators, flies only for relaxation.

Feith voiced a theme that emerged repeatedly in interviews with the tin-kickers: their obsession with the job. 'I work seven days a week, twenty-four hours a day. Thinking, that's my problem. I think too much, and the reason I think too much is because I have a job that wants me to think or makes me think.' Fortunately for those of us who want to believe in the essential sanity of the tin-kickers, they don't lose all sense of perspective. 'I can't enjoy my job per se because I'm seeing the bad side of aviation. I'm seeing a disaster, one that, while it is sad, is intriguing. It's a challenge. When I go out to an accident site and all I have is 10 acres of bits and pieces of airplane, my challenge is to go out there and try to put all those pieces back together again and figure out what actually happened . . . As bad as it is, I have the greatest job in the world.'

'We're trying to make order out of chaos,' is how Feith's colleague, Robert McIntosh, the acting chief of the major investigations division of the NTSB, sums up his job.

Inevitably, the obsession affects the lives as well as the personalities of the tin-kickers. As McIntosh puts it: 'The life of an investigator does have some ups and downs that certainly affect our personal lives. I'm one of those type A personalities who involves my job with my family life and my hobbies, and consequently I tend to live and sleep aviation. It does affect our families. I think most of our investigators here are of the same mind set.'

Like all his colleagues, McIntosh is often asked what makes a good accident investigator.

He's certainly a persevering individual with a good bit of aviation knowledge, inquisitive mind and so on. The International Civil Aviation air-accident investigation manual chooses to say such things as inquisitive nature, dedication to the kind of work, diligence, patience, integrity, humility – I'm not too sure about that one! We have to have some aeronautical experience, and it has to be specialized aeronautical experience, depending on the subject that we're looking at, whether it be helicopters or fixed-wing airplanes. We also have to have some feel for engineering, but it's personalities that make things work. The lone-wolf type of person doesn't do well in solving accidents. A persevering person who is not so persevering as to be a lone-wolf type personality is the person that we're looking for. They also have to be able to communicate.

Investigators the world over work in a team in a set-up first established by British investigators after the war, with the operations inspector in charge and at least one engineer. 'We're a team of sixty or seventy investigators, and most of us are pilots or pilot engineers or ex-airline personnel,' says Bob Nelson, the veteran British investigator, who was a graduate engineer turned pilot before he became fascinated by the black art of investigating aircraft accidents. At the NTSB today, the investigators are organized into a number of 'go teams', one of which is on standby twenty-four hours a day. They include not only a chief investigator, but also specialists in systems, structures, maintenance, operations and 'human factors', which includes the delicate task of interviewing witnesses and survivors among passengers or crew. The emphasis is on team-work, not on individual egos. 'A member of the team', says Ron Schleede, the deputy director of the Office of Aviation Safety, 'has to be ready to go at a minute's notice to any place in the world; has to be able to skip Christmas, anniversaries, birthdays, work long hours and keep an open mind, not become personally involved in what's happened, and just gather the facts, document 'em, and then later let the conclusions fall out.'

Air safety investigators are curiously reluctant to be described as detectives, though they admit that the two professions have many aspects in common. 'It's detective work in many ways,' says Tony Cullen. 'It's different from clinical medicine, where one is trying to determine what the pathology is from the patient's symptoms. In this work we're trying to determine, among other things, what the patient's symptoms might have been from the pathology.' And they share one other trait: an insistence on approaching each case separately. 'The main thing you must not do in an accident investigation,' says Bill Houghton, one of the team that solved the Comet mystery in the 1950s, 'is to guess what the possible cause is and then act upon it.' Investigators also have to look for every possible solution, frequently, as in the Comet case, one that would never have occurred to the plane's designers. This involves a lot of nagging questioning which can appear irrelevant to the people they're interviewing. 'The engineers from the manufacturers often ask you why you want to know that, and we say because we think it might be important. When we find that it was the cause of the accident, they say, "We would never have thought of that."'

Yet the hesitation over the comparison remains, perhaps because the tin-kickers feel it makes them sound too glamorous, or that it provides too one-dimensional a view of their job. And it is true that some aspects of their role are not normally associated with the traditional concept of detective work. For example, they are often engaged in preventative investigations, and much of their less publicized work is centred on incidents which have not resulted in an accident. Typically, Ron Schleede says:

I don't personally think of myself as Sherlock Holmes or Dick Tracy, but we do have a goal, we study the methodologies of the criminal investigators, and I guess we are akin to them. The criminal people have a different methodology but we follow the same path as them: we gather facts, we try to avoid making early assessments or conclusions . . . we've just got to keep our eyes wide open and just keep gathering the facts, and hopefully, when we get done, everyone will agree with our conclusions, because the facts will be so clear. No one has gone with a preconceived notion and ignored some other facts . . .But in all practical senses, a lot of our business is logic and experience from the aviation industry. The good investigator, the metallurgist, the person who really goes after that small bit of detail, that one hanging word in an air-traffic communication or what have you, may be necessary, but on the other hand many of our investigators go out and look at the four corners of the airplane, the nose and the tail and the two wings, and say, 'Now, this isn't right, something's missing here from the outset.' They're looking at the overall picture. So we have both kinds of people, including the person who opens up a computer chip and counts the zeros and the ones. It takes all kinds of people to make it click.

Even the training required can assume a rather ghoulish aspect. While Greg Feith was working on small general aviation accidents he acquired the nickname Dr Blood and Guts which, as he says, 'is not a title that I wear on my chest proudly'. He got it because he used to go to autopsies on those killed in air crashes 'because I could learn a lot from the pathologist telling me what kind of damage was done to the body. That helped me in determining how that airplane struck the ground, and then I could put the pieces together, he explains. 'It was just one more piece of the puzzle I could use to figure out what happened. So I've been able to emotionally remove myself from that accident site and now I look at everything as a science. While it's a cold and callous type of position, I think I do my job, I do it very well and I do it very effectively because of that attitude.'

By definition, says Ron Schleede, they never know when the call will come or from where, since American-built aeroplanes are flying the world over.

It could be any place in the world and so you're not quite prepared. You get the call and you have to make your mind up whether we're going to go on this one, and what kind of clothes you're going to have to take, what kind of logistics you're going to have to arrange. We have a pretty well-oiled machine to organize getting hotel rooms, transportation, and our goal is to leave Washington two hours from the time that phone call comes – and that can be to Alaska, it can be to Miami or it can be to the Middle East or some place like that. So we have to get our team together and you're thinking, OK, I'm going to be gone for ten days or more and I've got to get going, and of course you start thinking about the accident, grab a couple of suitcases and throw things together and get on an airplane going to wherever it is. Then we start thinking about the accident and what we're going to do now.

Despite the existence of a well-oiled set of procedures, 'the immediate notification of an accident does produce a bit of controlled chaos around the office,' says McIntosh.

We don't get just one notification, we probably get fifteen or twenty. They're coming from the operator, they're coming from the FAA, they're coming from the news media, they're coming from the local law-enforcement people. Meanwhile, I've reached in my back pocket, where I always keep my go-team sheet, and I've looked at the go team and remembered the personalities I've seen walking in the halls this afternoon or this morning, whenever it is, or in the middle of the night. I recall, yes, I saw him in the office at five o'clock. I want to make sure I've got lots of people on the notification system. We're going to have to call the FAA, find out if there's a government airplane that we can take, just where this place is. Is it near an airport? Is it a major airport? Can we easily fly there with scheduled airlines? What's the best way to get there? When we get there? What kind of a reception can we have for a place to go and meet? Can rental cars get out to the immediate scene? Are weather conditions such that we need snowmobiles, or can we walk right out on the runway? What kind of media are going to be there to meet us? What's going to happen with the public-relations aspect? Is this a major town where the helicopters are already circling over the wreckage and we're going to have to deal with a whole lot of media interest immediately, or is it a more remote location? We've got to find somewhere to assemble; we've got to tell the manufacturer and the labour unions, it's now midnight, get your people and all the collateral teams that are going to be helping us – we call 'em the parties to the investigation – moving toward the scene, reassuring the emergency services at the local location that indeed we are coming. They're going to be very eager to see us, more than willing to hand over to us. They've very well stabilized the situation from looters, scavengers and so on. They have a hundred people out there, all of a sudden – who's going to pay those people? They get concerned about things like that. We get a lot of strange calls – 'What about the dog that was shipped on the airplane? My mother is shipping a dog.'

Complications are endless and sometimes surprising. At the site of the Boeing 737 crash at Pittsburgh in 1994 Haueter had problems finding hotel rooms and a conference room and transportation for all his people. 'US Air had blocked all the hotel rooms around the airport for the families of the passengers, so we had to negotiate with them to free up a few rooms for the accident investigators,' he explains. 'So I was up all night long. We finally left for the airport around three in the morning . . . I have two phone lines at home, both with call waiting, so in total I have about four phone lines available to me, and they were all tied up for about six hours. It was a madhouse.'

Not surprisingly, as Schleede admits, the early hours can be chaotic:

As the investigator in charge I know that I've got to organize this investigation. I know I'm not organized – I'm totally in turmoil – but I make up a check list. I sit down and I practise my speech. It starts out:

'Let's everybody be seated. My name's Ron Schleede, I'm the investigator in charge of this accident. What we're going to do here is organise the team. We can't do a major investigation without organizing the team – we're not going to run off to the accident site and start picking up pieces, we're going to get in the room and organize it.' So I practise that, I sit in the airplane someplace and I write down little notes so I don't forget the words and get out my little crib sheet. One of the guys who trained me said, 'Look like you're organized. You're not; you're never going to be organized, because you can't predict what's going to happen and who's going to be there. But you can be in charge if you look like you're organized.' So you have this list of things, and you go through it.

For the NTSB, the focal point for a major accident is often not the site itself but the command headquarters. One of the tasks of the investigator in charge is to ensure that there is a command post with a number of phone lines, fax lines, copying machines and all the equipment people need to do their job. Robert McIntosh:

> Our people aren't often moving toward the scene of the accident, they're moving into the general vicinity of the accident so that we can form the investigative teams properly to do our job. So we need to set up a command post someplace adjacent to the scene – a hotel meeting room, ballroom, basketball court, gymnasium, some location, convention centre with some meeting rooms – we need a place where we can put fifty to 100 people and start to organize our teams with group chairmen to investigate the accident, together with some local personnel from our ten regional offices around the United States.

But no rehearsal, no amount of experience or careful preparation of an introductory speech can ever prepare an investigator for what he finds on the site. As even the hard-boiled Feith admits: 'The actual arrival at an accident site is probably the most traumatic thing anybody could ever experience.' He goes on: 'I've conditioned myself over sixteen years of doing this business, but it still bothers me when I get there, only because you have a sense of an adrenaline rush – you get there, you're pumped, you're ready to go to work, but you have to step back for a moment because you're looking at death and destruction in magnitudes that are sometimes incomprehensible.'

For of course, the investigators are not confronted by a whole aeroplane, but by a series of bits and pieces. It therefore takes them some time to absorb the whole scene, especially the fact that the accident has cost lives. 'One of the first things I always notice at an accident scene is the airplane parts,' says Greg Phillips. 'I somehow shift into a mode where I don't see the passengers. I see the airplane parts – wheels and tyres and wings and cockpits – and sometimes it takes a little while before I start seeing that there are also people in the accident.'

All the investigators commented on the pungent, unmistakable smell of an accident site, like veterans of the First World War recalling the smell of poison gas. 'Once you've smelled an accident site,' says Feith, 'you never forget it. They have a distinct smell. You could put me in the woods, turn me around in circles, and if I'm downwind I can smell my way to an accident site. While I wish I could forget it, I can't, and so getting out there, you take a step back, adjust yourself to what you're about to do, and then you go forward and do it.'

'There are always similarities', says Ron Schleede. 'There's the smell of the fuel if there's been a fire; there's the bad smells in airplane accidents – the insulation and all the other things. You get it on your boots, on your clothes; you get it in your hotel room. It sticks with you. Your nose gets used to it for a while, but it's never quite gone. You leave your room and come back in and it smells like an airplane accident. That brings back bad visions.' Nevertheless, as Greg Phillips points out, it is worse for the rescue workers 'the people who are there that day – the safety workers, firemen, – have a much tougher job than I do.'

Among the most appalling accident sites ever was the one faced by Bob Nelson after one of the first Comets crashed near Calcutta.

> The scene was absolute devastation. The plane had crashed in small pieces in paddy fields. It was the monsoon season, so there was heavy rain and thunderstorms and the whole area was a quagmire. It was not accessible by road, either. Of course, there were bodies in the wreckage and in some cases small pieces of bodies. Working in the wreckage was very unpleasant, and there were a lot of snakes around, too. Conditions were very difficult and rather dangerous. We set up a camp there but our tents were blown away in a nor'wester storm.

But whatever the conditions, the accident site is their workplace, and they have to make the best of it. 'It's like a surgeon going to the theatre,' comments Eddie Trimble. 'Confronted with a scene of absolute disaster, whether it be Lockerbie or Kegworth, the average reaction is, Jesus, where do you start?' Like detectives, they start by having a general look around the site and taking everything in. 'You give yourself time to absorb all the information – that is critical,' explains Trimble.

> So you take your time, look at everything and record it, photograph it, and that way you're kind of programming the computer with the necessary data. And on a major accident they'll look at the site, they'll look for ground marks to try to give an indication of how the aircraft is impacted. Was it upright? Was it inverted? Has it been in on a wing? That can immediately begin to tell you something about what has caused the problem. They look for indications of the gear being down,

wheel marks, indications of power on propeller-driven aircraft, propeller slash marks – or, if it's gas turbines, they'll be looking for evidence of compressor damage; of, for instance, tree debris going through the compressors into the turbine area and becoming charred, which is a sign that it was still turning and burning. They'll look at heading information on impact, the configuration of the aircraft. Were the flaps down? Was the pilot trying to land? If the aircraft has slats or spoilers, trim on the stabilizers, rudder trim – if you've got an isometric problem – the balance of the rudder trim. They'll look at the completeness of the aircraft. Do we have the whole aircraft here? Maybe something's fallen off it a couple of miles south. It sounds a simple question, but it's one that you've got to ask, particularly with a high degree of disintegration.

Like any professionals dealing with tragedies, the tin-kickers have to develop a thick emotional skin, a sense of detachment.

We're a bit fortunate in that frequently the macabre side of accidents is dealt with before we arrive on the scene. Simply because accidents don't occur in our front yard, we're blessed with some travel time. I've been in the business about twenty-nine years, and I can recall the first couple of years . . . it certainly did affect me, and it was something I had to recognize that I was going to have to overcome, the personal aspects of losing people. In the military, of course, it's worse, because you tend to investigate accidents where you may know the people very closely. Consequently it's something you have to climb over in order to do a good job. But you have to remember that you're going to preclude the next one from happening, and you're going to deal with usually engineering or operational subjects, and this allows you to get by. There are people who it affects to the point where they really shouldn't be in the business, and there are people who need a lot of counselling because they get too closely involved. We try to spot that propensity early on and do something about it with counselling for our personnel, and it has become routine now to ask people or to observe people and recommend some counselling on the large accidents.

'Some of us handle it better than others,' agrees Feith.

I work with people from varying backgrounds. Some, when they get to an accident site, can't handle it because they can't comprehend what they're seeing out there – the death, the destruction. When you look out the window of a terminal at the airport and you see a big beautiful 747 which weighs 800,000lbs and can carry 500 people and then you get out to an accident site and the biggest part of that airplane left is a rudder or maybe an engine, it's very hard to comprehend sometimes.

The capacity to distance themselves does not necessarily reduce the depth of the tin-kickers' emotional reactions to incidents outside their work, it's simply that they can divide the two parts of their lives fairly satisfactorily. 'I regard going to aviation accidents as work,' is a typical reaction from the forensic pathologist Air Commodore Tony Cullen. 'For the most part I don't get desperately upset by it. However, if I come across a motor accident in which there's been a fatality, I find that terribly distressing and I suspect it's because I'm not at work there.'

All the interviewees emphasized the need for tunnel vision. As Tom Haueter put it:

> I've coped with the tragedy of the events by focusing on the technical aspects, on solving the puzzle, on taking a look at what caused the airplane to arrive at this accident. I try to stay away from the human elements of it. You see that around, obviously, and you see people's lives suddenly changed dramatically, either through death or injury. If you tried to concentrate too much on the personal aspects, you couldn't do the job very well.

Detachment is required even when listening to evidence on the cockpit voice recorders in the tranquillity of a laboratory. Frank McDermott, a veteran specialist, says that he has 'listened to thousands of tapes, and I've heard the final words of a lot of pilots and the final words of controllers talking to these pilots. You take a clinical detachment to all this. You're there to use this as a tool, to try to find out what happened so you can prevent it from happening the next time.'

Inevitably, as with any job involving death, the investigators develop their own special brand of black humour. As McIntosh describes it:

> Sometimes I've heard it said, 'Whoops, there's an accident, that's job security for us!' That's not exactly the way we think, but we are motivated to be prepared and there's a sense of anticipation when you're on duty. I wonder what will happen, where will it happen and how will I handle it. We're not out looking for something to happen – indeed, we do lots of incident investigations where no one is injured but we can make a safety improvement – but indeed, when a big case comes, for us it's an opportunity to do what we've been trained to do, and consequently I think every one of us looks forward to it . . . this is what I came here to do, this is what I want to do; it's a tragedy to some, but it's an opportunity for me to do my best to solve the case and bring up some recommendations.

Yet in spite of the investigators' professional detachment, personal reactions are inevitable. Ron Schleede admits: 'A lot of things are very hard to take, hard for anybody. No one could take going to an accident site knowing that people had died, and seeing the results for themselves, not just reading about them in newspapers or seeing them on TV.' Some accidents affected him more strongly than others. He cites the Eastern Airlines accident in New York in the early 1970s as one of the worst. 'I was the human factors investigator, survival factor, and I had to interview a father and two daughters, seven or eight years old, who had been severely burned. They were in a hospital, all in the same room. The two little girls died about a week later. I had daughters about the same age. That was the toughest one I can recall, but all of 'em are tough.' When Greg Phillips walked on to the site of the DC10 accident at Sioux City he found a small backpack that evidently belonged to a child. 'As I walked past it I stopped and looked at it and I started to see the backpacks we had prepared for our kids. I have two boys, and when we used to travel we would put together a backpack with coloured crayons and cookies and crackers and things to keep 'em busy in the airplane. I had to sit down because I really couldn't take another step. It really felt like someone had hit me between the eyes with a board.'

The obverse of the angst can be a considerable degree of professional satisfaction. Ron Schleede sees the dichotomy very clearly.

It's hard to say you enjoy a job where people die to put you to work, but the rewards of preventing accidents and getting to the bottom of them are very considerable. I've loved my job for the whole time I've worked for the Safety Board, and I don't want that to be taken wrong. We do feel we make things better. I can get on airplanes, I can look at airports and see things that I personally was involved in fixing or I know the guy who did it, and that's very rewarding.

As he says, the satisfaction comes in two forms: solving the immediate problem, the cause of a particular crash; and then, more fundamentally, seeing the acceptance of a recommendation for change resulting from their findings.

'When we're looking at a situation, we're looking at how could we have done this better, how could we have equipped people with more knowledge to avoid it?', says McIntosh. 'And in looking back two or three years past on what we've done, we say this situation is now much more clear than it was the day we were standing in the field, or the day we returned to the office, and we do feel much better about it. Consequently there are a lot more ups than downs to our business, and that's what keeps us going.'

Experiences are passed down from generation to generation of investigators, but the skill of coping with emergencies which are by definition unforeseeable, similar only in the horror they create, can only be learned on the job. Ron Schleede's first exposure to a major accident was in 1972, when he was a new employee at the NTSB. A Boeing 737 operated by United Airlines crashed in Chicago.

I was a trainee in the human factors section. We got there late at night, and had what we call our organizational meeting in a big hotel room
The airplane had been en route to Washington DC, and because E.

Howard Hunt's wife [one of the Watergate conspirators] was on board and had been killed, there was a lot of interest. There were well over a 100 people in this room. A man named Bill Lamb, investigator in charge, stepped up to the microphone and asked people to leave – the media, lawyers – and then organized the team. These progress meetings went on for about a week, and I saw this investigation come together so quickly and so thoroughly that I decided, that's the job I want. It's very rewarding to be able to pull all these people together at a big tragedy, people with different interests; to get 'em organized, and see it all come together in about ten days. We have what happened generally figured out in about ten days, and then we go on and dig into why.

For Greg Feith, the first crash of which he was in charge, that of a DC9 at Charlotte, North Carolina, turned out to be a nightmare.

I was put on duty about two weeks before the accident. We hadn't had a major commercial airplane accident in over two years, and it was totally unexpected. Given the fact that this was my first big accident here in the States, there were going to be a lot of eyes focused on this investigation not only in house but in the industry . . . Going out to the accident site was pandemonium – lights, sirens, TV cameras, every TV station around. There were probably fifty TV stations – local, national – the whole accident scene was lit up with floodlights. There were police, fire departments, ambulances. We arrived on scene and they had not begun the body-removal process because it was dark. They'd recovered all of the survivors, but they couldn't get into the body removal because they wanted to document with a grid system, so the on-scene commander had decided to wait for daylight. People were asking, why are you going to let those people stay out there?

It was a joint co-operation with the Safety Board and all of the people on scene. It was the first major decision-making process I was involved in as an IIC [investigator in charge]. That's how the night started, and progressively it went downhill after that, because there were a lot more decisions to be made. We had a gathering of over 200 people initially who began the investigation process. I'm standing up there getting the organizational meeting started, very nervous. It was not so much that I couldn't do the job, but trying to make sure that I had everything covered, because I was the focus, I wanted to make sure that I did it right the first time.

It began to unravel a little bit because of the press coverage, because of the politicians who got involved. While I tried to maintain a semblance of sanity in the investigation, it was hard not to get caught up in some of the politics which led to a situation where we, as the NTSB, determined the parties and who would participate.

It did not help that there were problems with the blood samples from the crew required for routine testing, and, far worse, with a senior official from the FAA, whom Feith was forced to order back to Washington.

> While I'm working on this issue I have five other issues I am trying to handle at the same time. There's only one of me, and I'm managing 200 people and trying to manage my time. You start at seven o'clock in the morning and you work a full day – my days were ending at midnight and one o'clock because of the press briefings and the after-meetings. You're tired at the end of the day but not tired physically, you're just tired mentally. Well, you do that for nine days on scene, and on the tenth day, when you finally come home, you just want to sleep for a week to recover.

The question of fatigue is one that is always at the back of the organizer's mind. 'One of the key things when you're running an investigation is to pace your personnel,' says Eddie Trimble. 'The next day they'll be of little use unless they get some sleep. About six o'clock I might decide to pull the team from the site to go back to the hotel to get a one hour's rest, before we start the next day. And so we'll the receptionist to give us a bell at half-past seven, and have one hour's sleep, which makes a big difference'.

Very often the investigation at the scene of the accident is devoted to one crucial end: the recovery of the 'black boxes'. One of our main concerns is that somebody is thinking about the boxes at the scene, explains Robert McIntosh. 'If the tail section, the normal location, is intact, we're going to be asking for it to be sterilized in a secure way. If we've used a government aircraft it's really lovely for us to be able to turn that aircraft in a couple of hours and get the boxes back to our laboratories.' But that's another story.

2

... And the Tools of Their Trade

The most frequent last words I have heard on cockpit voice-recorder tapes are, 'Oh shit,' said with about that much emotion. There's no panic, no scream, it's a sort of resignation: we've done everything we can, I can't think of anything else to do and this is it.

– Frank McDermott

The most powerful image in aircraft detective work is that of the 'black box' which holds the secrets of the crash. In fact there are two boxes, neither of them black – they're generally painted orange for better visibility. The oldest established is the flight-data recorder (usually now digital, and therefore abbreviated to DFDR) which records as many flight parameters as possible, including the altitude, air speed, and heading. FDRs are the best single source of information for the investigators. Not only are they objective, but also, and crucially, they provide data on the long series of events that lead up to an accident.

By contrast, the cockpit voice-recorder, which, as its name implies, captures the conversation in the cockpit prior to an accident, is a much more contentious idea. For a long time pilots fought shy of the CVR, sharing the lorry driver's fear of his tachograph as a potential 'spy in the cab'. Eventually – though in Britain only in the 1970s after the terrible crash at Staines, discussed in Chapter 14 – a compromise was reached whereby the CVR would record only thirty minutes of conversation (and also, usefully, the ambient sounds such as engine noise). At the end of this period the recording would be automatically erased and the machine would start again, and after a safe landing the whole recording would be wiped off by the pilot (an agreement which caused some problems in the much-disputed case of Captain 'Hoot' Gibson reported in Chapter 13). But the pilots' hesitations remain. In Australia the CVR cannot be used in evidence in a crash which any member of the crew has survived.

Both black boxes can hold the key to the cause of a crash, and naturally, therefore, they feature in many of the episodes related in this book. Sometimes their recovery, swift dispatch to the NTSB's laboratories in Washington (when American aircraft or airlines are involved) and their immediate decryption can in itself create great excitement. One such occasion was when a Boeing 757 plunged into the Caribbean in early February 1996, with the loss of 189 lives. It was an ill-starred flight. The 176 passengers – German tourists returning from a fortnight in the sun – should have flown on a larger Boeing 767, but for reasons that remain unclear, the airline involved, Alas Nacionales ('national wings'), from the Dominican Republic, switched to a 757 leased from the Istanbul-based Birgen Air.

Financing the rescue and assembling the equipment required to salvage the boxes was a truly international effort. The money to contract the US Navy was raised by the United States, the Dominican Republic and the German and Turkish authorities, as well as Rolls–Royce, who had manufactured the engines.

This story has everything – except, of course, a happy ending. The aircraft climbed to around 7,000ft and ended up 7,200ft below the surface of the ocean, so finding and recovering the black boxes required the use of some very specialized equipment by the US Navy. Luckily, they were able to bring up the recorders on their first dive. The aircraft had disintegrated at the precise point where the recorders were located, which freed both of them and made them easier to extract than would have been the case had they remained attached to a much larger piece of the wreckage. It also helped that the DFDRs were mounted at the back of the plane and had underwater locater beacons attached to them which emitted audible signals that could be detected from equipment in the salvage ships.

Amazingly, the whole operation took only a single day, albeit an exceedingly long one. The vessel arrived on site off the Dominican coast at around 1am. By 9.30 the flight-data recorder had been located and by noon it had been raised slowly and carefully to the surface. The recorders were dropped into a cooler filled with fresh water to prevent them from corroding further. This was sealed and carried ashore on a Zodiac-type rubber speedboat alongside the ship. A Lear jet was waiting at the airport to fly the precious container back to Washington.

The man who carried the boxes back to Washington was Dennis Grossi. He worked through the night, and before 4.30am, when he finally got to bed, he had extracted all the information relating to the accident and had a fairly clear understanding of what had happened, The Navy were therefore able to call off the recovery operation.

> The flight-data recorders gave us a complete time history of the aircraft's flight, and in particular of the airspeed indications on the aircraft, which proved to be critical in understanding the accident . . . We could see, as the aircraft was rolling down the runway, that the air speed was not increasing as it normally would. This was corroborated by the cockpit voice recorder, on which we heard a conversation between the crew members stating that the captain's airspeed indicator was not increasing as it reached 80 knots, which is a normal checkpoint . . . This gave us a clue as to the cause of the problem airspeed. The flight-data recorder told us early that we had an anomaly in the airspeed indications that were being seen by the crew; the cockpit voice recorder also revealed that the

crew members recognized they had a problem. The crew elected to continue the flight even though they had noticed this anomaly: they had three airspeed indicators, and only one of them was behaving erratically.

The pilot was comparing his airspeed indicator to the co-pilot's, and they noticed the difference and recognized that the captain's indicator was incorrect, so they took off using the co-pilot's indicator. There's also a third indicator in the cockpit to give you a vote – if you get two out of three right, you disregard the bad one. In this case, the captain's. The behaviour of the airspeed indicator showed the investigators that the crew had a blocked pressure tube. This is a tube that's stuck out in the airstream. The air goes down the tube and impacts on a pressure sensor which tells you how fast you're going. But if the tube gets blocked, then you trap air pressure inside it, and as the aircraft climbs the air that is trapped in there at sea-level relative to the lesser pressure at altitude expands and pushes against the sensor, telling it – falsely – that it's receiving airspeed information. The higher the aircraft climbs, the higher the airspeed.

There's a period when the airspeed is low; then there's another period of time when the airspeeds match, and then, as the altitude increases, the co-pilot's airspeed would have been correct but the captain's airspeed just climbed and climbed and climbed and eventually set off an erroneous overspeed warning. The normal response to an overspeed warning is to slow down. The crew did so, but the erroneous overspeed warning continued because they were still at altitude. Eventually, the airplane slowed down to the point when a stall-warning indication came on, so now they had two conflicting warnings. In the confusion, the crew chose to concentrate on the misleading overspeed warning set off by the captain's faulty airspeed indicator; eventually the aircraft stalled, they lost control and the aircraft plunged into the ocean.

This was not the only case of an apparently miraculously quick recovery of the FDR and an even more miraculously quick diagnosis of the problem. Another was the accident at Cali in Colombia at the end of 1995. Dennis Grossi again:

It was very difficult for our people to get in and out of the crash site, so once the recorders were recovered they were flown back to the United States for a read-out as quickly as possible. We got the recorders here in the evening and we worked through the night, putting in a twenty-four-hour day, and by the end of that time we had a great deal of information about the operation of the aircraft. With information from other sources, such as the air-traffic control tapes, we quickly got a fairly clear picture of the sequence of events that led up to the accident, which allowed us to pull out our on-site investigation team after less than a day up on the accident site.

Grossi cites other cases in which, as he says, 'it was crucial to know in great detail that sequence of events, to give us some insight into the human performance'. In one case, involving an accident in Central America, the operator has already re-evaluated its training programme as a result of the investigation. Before the use of flight recorders, 'you were pretty much confined to that impact area and gathering information from the wreckage itself,' says Grossi. 'That can only give you a good snapshot of what was happening in the last seconds of a flight. It doesn't give you much in the way of the events leading up to it.' The latest recorders can provide information on up to 200 parameters, including such factors as autopilot modes.

The need for flight-data recorders was first recognized as early as the 1930s. As aircraft started to carry increasing numbers of passengers, the authorities realized that they required a device that would give them a little more insight into the causes of accidents. Unfortunately, the war delayed the introduction of flight recorders until the late 1950s, and even then the first instruments used recorded only the altitude, airspeed and heading and vertical acceleration, as more advanced technology was prohibitively expensive. Originally they were placed on the wing to enable them to survive the impact of a crash and any subsequent fire. That turned out to be a bad idea, since in some of the early accidents the recorders were crushed, partly because they were rather delicate – the information was etched on to a very fragile foil by styli. The early boxes carried their own pressure and altitude sensors for altitude and airspeed. By today's standards, they were what investigators call a 'smart box' – one both registering and recording information. Today's flight recorders are 'dumb boxes', so called because they only record information provided by the aircraft's systems. The next generation of recorders used a more robust recording medium – tape – but were still limited to a mere five parameters: altitude, airspeed, heading and vertical acceleration, and microphone key.

With the introduction of wide-bodied jets, the industry went over to quarter-inch magnetic tape as a better recording medium. Another box, called a flight-data acquisition unit, acted as the smart box. It took in signals from different sensors throughout the aircraft, processed them and then sent out a serial data stream which was then recorded by the 'dumb' flight-data recorder. With the eventual elimination of the old foil flight recorders, the airlines ended up with digital smart boxes which captured the information on a digital recording medium. The current recorders have solid-state FDRs where the information is recorded on a magnetic chip. Obviously, these are more durable. Grossi was able to show one that had been terribly damaged in a fire; all the information was retrievable, whereas a comparable tape unit would not have survived. The very latest recorders, some of which are being flown over the North Sea on helicopters, combine both the cockpit voice recorder and the flight-data recorder in one unit. The next step could be to record the information on video in a single box that would divide the digital information into segments of the crash memory, containing CVR, flight-data recorder and video evidence.

Over the years, the FDRs have got stronger, as Grossi explains:

> The original specifications for crash-fire survivability were very inadequate – and that wasn't anybody's deficiencies, we just didn't know any better. The latest standards require that recorders withstand 1,100-degree centigrade temperatures for thirty minutes, or 250-degree centigrade tests for ten hours. They can also survive impact much better.

With the introduction of a solid-state recording medium came hydrostatic testing. When the magnetic chips were at the bottom of the ocean the forces were so extreme that they were cracking, so today they have to be able to withstand the pressures found at a depth of 20,000ft. The combination of the new standards and the possible introduction of solid-state memory is going to dramatically reduce those cases where the investigators are not able to recover any information.

What matters is the survival, not so much of the recorder itself, but of the recording medium. Grossi demonstrated a classic example of a high-impact accident in which the recorder's chassis had been distorted and the circuit cards had all been destroyed, but the cavity where the recording medium is normally housed was intact and could be extracted from the damaged recorder and played back. In another case, the recorder was extensively damaged but the investigators had managed to extract a portion of the magnetic tape. This revealed that the crash was the result not of an accident, but of a murder-cum-suicide. A disgruntled employee had killed his former boss on board the plane before entering the cockpit and shooting both pilots. He then committed suicide and the aircraft hit the ground at high speed. The recorder was extensively damaged, but Grossi was able to splice in the short piece of tape which was salvaged because it was wrapped around the capstan near the recording heads. The last eight seconds of the flight gave him the impact speed and the attitude of the aircraft (i.e. whether it was climbing, descending, or in level light), which were used in some other studies as part of the basis for the new crash-fire survivability requirements.

European airlines tend to have more modern recorders than domestic American carriers. This can problems, as it did in the two accidents to 737s at Pittsburgh and Colorado Springs analysed in Chapter 11. The two second-generation flight-data recorders were using digital recording but covering only the same five parameters as in the early days of the device. And these simply did not furnish enough information to provide a definitive understanding of the very complex series of events resulting in the crash. Even before the Pittsburgh accident, the NTSB had mandated that planes be upgraded to record six additional parameters relating to the attitude of the aircraft: whether the nose was pointing up or down, whether the wings were banked left or right, the elevators, the control services that made the aircraft go up and down, the thrust for both engines and longitudinal acceleration and how fast the plane was moving forward.

The difficulty of meeting this requirement was economic: the expense of retrospectively fitting the new FDRs into older aircraft. The NTSB tried to keep changes to an absolute minimum, but unfortunately, as Grossi admits, 'in the case of the Pittsburgh accident, it was not enough. We cut our absolute minimum a little bit too low.' The FAA has promised to introduce recommendations to increase the amount of information recorded, but the NTSB is keeping up the pressure. Happily, since the Pittsburgh accident, crews have become more aware of possible problems with the 737 and are reporting all sorts of anomalies in the controls. So anytime anybody even thinks that they have a problem, Grossi has a look at the FDRs, even though they may not give him the full picture.

In most crashes, the information from the FDR is complemented by that from the cockpit voice recorder. The veteran British investigator Ray Davis emphasizes the need for both recorders. 'There are some accidents where the flight-data recorder provides the vital evidence; there are others where the cockpit voice recorder sounds like it could be better. But in fact in every case you do need the two, because we never like to take one piece of evidence in isolation. We like to correlate it with another. If you've got both you can begin to believe what is recorded.'

When Davis's American counterpart, Frank M. McDermott, now a youthful seventy-five, started in the aviation accident investigation business nearly fifty years ago, there were no CVRs.

> Since the CVR has been introduced, it's given us tools we never had before. Instead of guessing and supposing what happened in the cockpit, we now have the conversation of the crew. It's always been known that if an emergency's going on in the cockpit, the pilot is not going to pick up a microphone and calmly dictate to a controller on the ground that the wing is on fire. He's going to be saying, 'What was that? What was that?' But more than that, you hear ambient noises in the cockpit that provide very vital clues. You can hear circuit-breakers popping, you can hear the aural alarms. You know what these mean and you know what the response of the crew will be, so it's an invaluable tool.

Today all commercial airliners have CVRs, but other aircraft can slip through the net. McDermott found that 'an American Air Force plane which crashed killing the US Commerce Secretary, Ron Brown, in Bosnia was hauling civilians all over the place, including the First Lady and her daughter, without a cockpit voice recorder or a flight-data recorder' – an omission which gave rise to enough publicity to ensure that military planes carrying civilians are now properly equipped with CVRs.

Investigators now take it for granted that they will be able to reconstruct the conversation in the cockpit. 'Sometimes we're disappointed when they break open the box and find that maintenance hasn't been performed and the box is there intact but the tape has stopped long ago,' says McDermott. 'The audio tapes, combined with the information that we get from the flight data recorders, allows a very accurate reconstruction. In addition the radar information captured by the FAA on the ground is also digitized and saved and can be retrieved, so you've got a very complete picture of what went wrong, and the real purpose is to apply all this to the future, to try to avoid future accidents.'

Of course, McDermott, like all the other investigators, remembers cases in which the CVR has proved invaluable. Some, like the Air Florida crash described in Chapter 9, are analysed in detail elsewhere in this book. Others include a TWA jet which, while making an approach to Dulles Airport several years ago, missed the top of Mount Weather by about 50ft. 'The cockpit voice recorder played a very, very important part in the reconstruction of that.' Both McDermott and his son, Mike, who works with his father in their consulting firm in Washington, are disgusted with the lack of progress in installing better recorders. 'Today, even a highly sophisticated technically advanced aeroplane can be equipped with outdated CVR,' says Mike McDermott. To him, this is a matter of economics.

> Right now the average cockpit voice-recorder unit is in the neighbourhood of $15 to $20,000 [£10,000 to £13,000]. For the all-digital it's about twice that, and if you're outfitting an entire fleet, by going with the old analogue versions you can cut your costs in half. There's still a lot of work to be done in the digital, but there are many, many improvements they could make to the analogue right now that they're not doing, and I believe that's all due to economics.

Newer aircraft have 'hot mikes' on the pilots themselves as well as an area mike capturing the cockpit sounds. On an aircraft with a single microphone, says Mike McDermott, 'the dynamic range, the quality of the sound itself, is very poor, because frequently the only record of the conversations is from an open microphone in the cockpit, which is generally placed behind the heads of the pilots. So they are speaking in the opposite direction of the microphone, and that makes it difficult to hear.' With a hot-mike system, the pilots wear a boom microphone that is always active and linked to the tape, so the pilot's words are no longer missed because he has turned his head and is looking over his shoulder when he says something critical. Ray Davis, playing back a demonstration tape of a VC10 taking off from Kennedy Airport in New York (which some crews find so realistic that they say it sounds like an exercise on a flight simulator) adds:

> Another benefit with the hot-microphone system is that you can hear individual breathing in each of the individual microphones. So, with total

crew incapacitation, you can detect that. You can't with any of the other systems. On that [VC10 flight] we had a three-crew operation and the flight engineer's voice was a little bit lower in volume than normal because the CVR had a fault on that one track. But one of the beauties of the hot-microphone system is that his voice was still picked up, albeit at a lower level, on the other two tracks, so there's a form of back-up mechanism built in there. We then use the cockpit-area microphone track for doing all the analysis of the systems operation, engines and what have you. It becomes a very, very useful tool.

All aircraft registered in the UK and some other countries now have hot mikes. At one point a ridiculous situation prevailed whereby some aircraft (especially the early TriStars) were fitted with two systems, the more sophisticated one required by the British CAA and the less advanced one which was adequate for the FAA and other regulatory bodies. But today, as matter of course, Boeing and the other manufacturers fit the more advanced system – one instance in which the industry has been ahead of at least some of the world's regulators. This represents a considerable advance. As Davis says, 'Even in the noisy environment of a helicopter flight deck, the quality from the hot microphone is superior to what we got, say, off a Pan-Am 747 a few years back.'

But the tape-readers are still looking for improvements. Mike McDermott points out that the tape 'still goes to an analogue tape-recorder on a thirty-minute loop which is just rerecorded over and over. After a while, these tapes don't hold up very well'. In any case, as demonstrated by the Sioux City accident involving United Flight 232 (see Chapters 8 and 12), even a thirty-minute tape may not always be long enough. The McDermotts see a whole host of advances being possible – at a price – with modern equipment. These include longer recordings – you can have a two-hour loop with an all-digital recording system – 'anything to improve the sound quality so that we can do better in ferreting out the engine sounds, the warning-horn sounds; in detecting whether is this a flap-handle sound or a gear level sound. Anything at all to increase the fidelity'.

Ray Davis describes the procedure involved in properly reading the CVR.

When we replay the cockpit voice recorder the first thing we do is to run through the whole tape – it's of thirty minutes' duration, roughly, and there are four channels. We listen to all four to get an appreciation, a picture if you will, of the accident. Then we will probably listen to just one track of the cockpit-area microphone and one of the pilot's tracks with the RT, ATC communications and so on. And then we will go through to the individual tracks and write down a transcript of all the speech. This is normally accompanied by an awful lot of pausing, because these are not hi-fi and they record all the background noise as well as the speech. Then we measure the background sounds.

Indeed, interpreting the voices, and the ambient sounds, picked up by the CVR is something of an art. 'I find it fascinating to be able to sift through the recorded audio and pick out various parameters of an accident, or causes,' says Mike McDermott. 'The fact that you can go into the recorded signal and hear the engine sounds, translate them to the performance of the aircraft, and piece together the sequence of events and how things could have been done differently. Fortunately for me, I deal with the audio tapes and radar data, and I don't have to go to the accident sites. This is just the analysis of the audio. I enjoy playing with the audio'.

> CVRs from planes involved in less serious incidents are often analysed as part of the preventative element of the investigators' work. And whatever the level of concern felt by the crew at the time, the tape-readers are far enough removed from the incident itself to allow themselves a good laugh at the pilots' expense on occasions. Ray Davis remembers listening to the CVR of one 737 which was coming down in poor visibility in Africa. The co-pilot was telling the pilot all the way down that they weren't going to make it, and the captain was saying, 'Oh no, it's all right, it's all right. I can make it.' They touched down with loads of witnesses watching, I think well over halfway down the runway, and promptly ran off the far end. The captain turned to the co-pilot and said, 'Why did you let this happen to us?' There are always some at which you can have a chuckle, and others with some very bad swearing, which can be quite comical. We investigated one incident in which nobody was hurt, and replayed the CVR to the crew. The captain was most upset because it was a very relaxed operation up until the moment things went wrong. He had been sitting there singing to himself as they were flying along. Nobody else could hear because they'd got their headsets on, but because it was a hot mike, we could hear this singing. He was shocked, because he had a terrible voice. He said, 'I'll make a conscious effort never to sing again.'

But of course, the relative distance of those listening to the recordings cannot shield them from the effects of the real tragedies. 'Some of the CVRs are pathetic – very, very nasty,' says Davis. 'They're unpleasant and a little bit off-putting.' And after hearing the tapes of the last few minutes of the ill-fated Air Florida flight, even the hardened Frank McDermott had to admit: 'It's never easy to hear that. I can listen to almost any movie on television and watch people getting shot and falling off horses and crashing airplanes, and that doesn't bother me. This you never get used to listening to. But it's something I consider necessary. It's providing a service that will eventually increase the overall safety of flying, and that makes it tolerable.' Father and son have accumulated an un-enviable record of hearing pilots' last words: Mike McDermott says that, judging from his experience, professional pilots cope very well.

In the vast majority of the tapes I've listened to where professional pilots are encountering difficulties which result in a crash, they are working very hard to prevent that crash all the way down to the ground. It could be that they're going straight down and at 35ft from the ground they're still looking for something to do to save the aircraft. Generally, they do not panic. I encounter occasional panic in the general aviation pilot, but very, very rarely do you find it in a professional pilot. Usually the last words you hear on a cockpit voice-recorder tape – and this is after the pilots have done everything they can think of to save the aircraft, and there comes a point when they resign themselves to the fact that there's absolutely nothing more that they can do – are just some form of statement with very little emotion, just sort of giving up. These are not the type of individuals who panic at that point.

For the father-and-son team, light relief from air accidents comes mainly from the other analytical jobs they are asked to do as a result of their expertise. The techniques of sound-and-frequency analysis employed in interpreting CVRs can be used for other purposes, and over the years Mike McDermott's help has been sought in matters unconnected with aviation, though he protests that he has not really gone out of his way to look for this kind of work.

When you identify sounds in the cockpit you use a certain technology and frequency-analysis programmes to identify whether it is a gunshot going off, or a circuit-breaker, or the gear handle – or, in the case of the Air Florida, is he saying on or off? That translates very well to voice identification. We also do work in the area of tape authentication, detecting whether a tape has been altered or edited in some way. We have the technology here to determine how it was done and to recreate that and show the edited parts. Fortunately, in those circumstances, most of the people I come across who have edited the tapes are not very sophisticated and don't do it in a professional manner. So it's not very difficult to determine. We also do quite a bit of sound-enhancement, not just to improve the quality of the audio on cockpit voice recorders, but on surreptitious recordings of various kinds, either on the telephone or in criminal investigation matters. The work encompasses clients such as law-enforcement organizations, and I've also worked on the defence side, for major corporations and people like that.

In other non-aviation cases I have been asked to identify voices. In one instance I worked for the Texas State Police to help them distinguish between identical twins in a drugs case. The police were confronted with the problem that one of these two individuals had made telephone calls to set up a drugs deal, and by supplying me with samples of their voices and comparing them to the recorded telephone calls, I was able to tell them which of the two twins made the calls, resulting in a conviction.

In another, non-criminal, matter I was asked by a major news organization to see if I could determine whether a voice on a recording, allegedly of a conversation between Gennifer Flowers [the most news-worthy of the President's alleged former mistresses] and Bill Clinton, was in fact Mr Clinton's. We were able to provide them with that information – and yes, it was.

3
Death in the Forest

I have seen many aircraft impacts. I have seen some aircraft torn up as much as this one, but I must say I have never seen any airplane torn up as much as this over such a large area. The pieces were extremely small, very fragmented, and it was scattered over an area half a mile long by 120yds or so wide.
– Chuck Miller, former director of the Aviation Safety Bureau, NTSB

Inevitably, air-crash detectives operate within very different political and institutional frameworks. Even the NTSB, generally held up as a model of its kind, has not, in the past, been able to escape from the consequences of the 'turf wars' so characteristic of the Washington environment – with tragic results, as we shall see later in this chapter. But in general, the NTSB functions in a more relaxed environment, and is freer to publish its findings, than its British equivalent, the equally respected Air Accident Investigation Branch, which, as part of a the Department of Transport, is slower to issue its reports and tries to avoid attaching specific blame. Other countries, especially Germany and the Netherlands, have their own highly professional bodies, but all rely heavily on the expertise of the NTSB, if only because so large a proportion of commercial airliners were built in the United States. When there is an accident, under ICAO rules, the 'interested parties' include not only the country in which the crash occurred, but also that of the manufacturer and that where the plane was registered. If an accident happens on the high seas, more than ten miles offshore, then the country of registry takes precedence in terms of the investigation and the country of origin, the victims.

By contrast, the French have their own investigation branch, the Bureau d'Enquêtes Accidents (BEA), but in addition, in the case of major accidents, they usually set up individual inquiries under an examining magistrate rather than rely exclusively on the expertise of their professional investigators, a procedure also followed in other continental European countries. The French also dislike apportioning any blame to any French institution or aircraft, and thus tend to point the finger at the pilot as the most obvious suspect in any crash. Indeed, if he survives he will often be arrested. In extreme cases they go into a state of total denial which can make it much more difficult to establish the cause of the accident. This cult of secrecy is particularly relevant today because of the problems of the Airbus A320 discussed in Chapter 7 and the story of the Franco–Italian ATR72 outlined in Chapter 9.

Even the NTSB has had to battle to achieve its present status and independence. Its history dates back to 1926, when the Commerce Department was given the authority to determine the causes of aircraft accidents, a task carried out by a small unit called the Aeronautics Branch. By 1940 the branch had evolved into a bureau of safety within the Civil Aeronautics Board, which had been set up only two years earlier. The NTSB itself was established in 1967 to cover all types of transport accidents as an independent agency, albeit one within the Department of Transportation. In theory, the Safety Board was responsible to its sponsoring government department for 'housekeeping purposes only', but the relationship was always rather artificial. It was asking for too much restraint on the part of the department, so it lasted only a few years. After the 1974 crash of the Turkish Airlines DC10 near Paris, the US Congress finally gave the NTSB total independence, and its investigators greater authority, the same year. But there is a price to be paid for independence. The Board's budget, a mere $38 million (£25 million) is tiny, and its staff of only 350 has to cover all types of transport. So it has to rely on what it calls the 'party system', calling in experts from all the interested parties to help. Moreover, as so often in the United States, some form of political control remains in that the five members of the Safety Board, who serve five-year terms, are nominated by the President and have to be approved by the Senate. To be fair to the American political process, most of the Board's members over the years have been reasonably qualified for the job.

The political nature of the board members can be an advantage. As Bob McIntosh says:

> They can handle the press, and they will actually be talking about the facts as they emerge on a daily basis, which is, I think, a little different from the UK. Then, when the report is prepared, our board members sign it. I think there are some differences in how we approach the situation. Our board is a non-technical, non-aviation oriented group of people. I think it benefits us to recognize that when we're talking to the board. We bring technical explanation to a level they can understand and then they can articulate to the Congress and the general public. It allows for a more general explanation than we might get if we were simply talking ourselves in a very, very technical way. The investigator in charge is largely independent of any of the political pressures, although information can be a bit filtered by our managing director, who will looking at the organization's health, respect and independence.

One theme that recurs in studying air accidents is how well, in general, the NTSB's investigators work with their foreign counterparts. This is partly because they are all professional investigators rather than status-conscious bureaucrats, partly because of the NTSB's acknowledged technical authority; but another important factor is the tact shown by its investigators. The case of JAL 123, described in Chapter 8, was not an international flight, as Ron Schleede points out, so the rights of the USA to get involved were limited. It was up to the discretion of the Japanese, who were happy enough to learn from the NTSB team, but worried about the presence of engineers from Boeing, the manufacturers of the crashed aircraft.

The NTSB's investigators' memories of working with their foreign colleagues are inevitably bitter-sweet. Typically, Tom Haueter remembers 'a makeshift morgue in Bangalore, India. To this day if I smell sandalwood I can remember that morgue quite vividly. But then, I also remember sitting on the wing of a wrecked 747 in the middle of a jungle with a chief investigator who was Malaysian, discussing the differences between Christianity and the Muslim faith and the meaning of the world.'

The NTSB and the AAIB have the most regular links. Ron Schleede says that he has worked closely with the AAIB since the early 1970s.

I've got personal friends there, colleagues. I've had them to my home, I've been to their homes, I've met their wives, they've met my wife. It goes way back. One of the first major accidents I went to overseas was the Lufthansa 747 in Nairobi – I believe it was in 1975. It was the first fatal 747 accident to occur. Now, the AAIB was there because of Kenya's connection with the UK. We were there because we built the airplane. A guy named Dave King came from the AAIB. He was a very young, fairly new engineer, and I was a young, new investigator. Dave still works very closely with me. He's working currently with us on an investigation. We exchange faxes weekly, sometimes daily, on ongoing investigations, and telephone calls. The AAIB work with us but they have a slightly different role from us in that they do a lot of military investigations. But that gives 'em a lot wider experience. Their investigation techniques are very similar, their methods of organizing their teams slightly different. They don't have this big mass of people like we do – they work with a smaller group and then with the other people a little bit on the outside, but their methods are excellent. We learn from them and we hope they learn a few things from us.

Robert McIntosh points to another contrast between the American and European ways of operating. Although they are similar, 'the staff of the AAIB, and indeed, of other European agencies, consider themselves more all-rounders,' he says. 'Their investigators would describe themselves as generalists, whereas in the United States the investigators are much more divided into different types of specialists in certain areas. They include experts in power plants, aircraft struc-tures, systems, operations, meteorology, and human factors. As Dave Miller points out, the AAIB has only one major advantage:

> The AAIB is one of the few investigating authorities in the world
> whose pilot investigators also have first-hand experience of active line
> flying. I think that is a tremendous advantage.

Because they are so conscious of their international status, the NTSB's investigators can afford to be generous to their foreign counterparts. Schleede worked closely with the AAIB on the crash of Pan-Am 103 at Lockerbie and tells how he went to see the mock-up of the forward section of the 747 in a hangar at Farnborough. 'It makes every investigator proud to look up at that, to see how the airplane came apart and how they proved it – how they put it together to show what happened. Any investigator in the world can be proud of the job he did.' This is not mere empty praise. When the NTSB was reconstructing the remains of US Air Flight 427 (see Chapter 11) they called in Dave King from the AAIB to help because of this work at Lockerbie.

But there is a problem in both the British and the American set-ups. In both countries separate agencies, the Civil Aviation Administration in Britain and the Federal Aviation Administration in the United States, have to decide whether to implement the investigators' recommendations in collaboration with the manufacturers and airlines – both of which are involved in the organization of the CAA and FAA. This involvement is bound to slow down the process of implementation. Indeed, in one dramatic case, the FAA balked at the investigators' findings, allowing DC10s to continue flying even after it had been found that the cargo door had a fundamental flaw. It was this interagency tension – a typically American phenomenon – which failed to prevent the crash of a DC10 in Paris in March 1974.

The scale of this disaster – at that time the world's worst ever – shocked even a veteran investigator like Chuck Miller.

> Of course, I'd been investigating accidents for many years before this,
> and I've literally picked friends of mine out of wreckages, so it wasn't
> surprising in terms of the damage to the people or the damage to the
> aircraft. But the size of this thing was incredible. The trees were what
> really tore the airplane apart, it was just like putting a piece of cheese
> into a shredding machine. There were some fairly healthy-sized trees
> there – maybe 8ins, 12ins in diameter in some cases – and they just
> acted like a whole series of knives.

Captain Jacques Lannier, then commander of the Senlis district of the Gendarmerie Nationale, was the first senior officer on the scene of what remains one of the worst accidents in airline history involving a single plane. The crash of the DC10 belonging to Turkish Airlines in the Forest of Ermenonville, thirty miles north-east of Paris, on Sunday 3 March 1974, was not only appalling in itself – though it was certainly that, all 346 souls on board losing their lives – but it remains the classic case of what can go wrong in the design of a plane, and how the smallest fault can become responsible for mass slaughter when combined with factors such as the commercial pressures involved in aircraft production, the sale of the plane to an airline ill equipped to cope with its complexities, and, above all, a political failure, that of government authorities to work together to ensure that the proper precautions are observed.

Although the television images made the crash sickeningly familiar to the whole world, the way Lannier described the scene to the authors of the standard book on the crash, *Destination Disaster* by Paul Eddy, Elaine Potter and Bruce Page, remains unforgettable, bringing to life the sheer horror behind the statistics and the dry details of technical problems which inevitably dominate any serious book on the subject.

> Everywhere the scene was nightmarish; the forest of Ermenonville had been turned into a battlefield, it was Verdun after the bloodiest battle . . . On my left, over a distance of 400 or 500m, the trees were hacked and mangled, most of them charred but not burned. Pieces of metal, brightly coloured electric wires and clothes were littered all over the ground. In the front of me, in the valley, the trees were even more severely hacked and the wreckage even greater. There were fragments of bodies and pieces of flesh that were hardly recognizable. In front of me, not far from where I stood, there were two hands clasping each other, a man's hand tightly holding a woman's hand, two hands which withstood disintegration.

Lannier caught sight of a brain, resting whole and unmarked on a bed of moss and could not prevent a photographer from accidentally stamping the soft mess into a pulp. Not one body was complete. 'Although a few heads were still attached to chests, a great many bodies were limbless, bellies were ripped open, and their contents emptied. I noticed a woman's chest had joined a man's pelvis'. A dislocated doll brought into his mind a picture of a little girl going through a departure lounge. Nearby, his companion stepped on a fishing rod with a football boot beside it.

The effects of the catastrophe were felt more widely than might otherwise have been the case, for that Sunday some of the staff of British European Airways were on strike. Consequently, many passengers of many nationalities who would normally have flow on a BEA plane had found their way on to the alternative flight offered by Turkish Airlines. Among them were a number of English rugby supporters homeward bound from the international match between France and England the previous day.

Behind the human tragedy lay a story which involved fatal laxity, not only on the part of the manufacturers, but also by the normally vigilant American authorities. Its long-term importance lies in the way the authorities' faults were cruelly exposed by the crash and in the changes that resulted, lessons that might not have been learned, let alone applied, in less open a society. The reason for the disaster was that a cargo door flew open and the hull of the aircraft simply disintegrated under the strain of the sudden depressurisation. But while other planes, including the Boeing 747, had problems with the doors of the cargo compartment, the subsequent disintegration was the result of a design feature peculiar to the DC10.

Designing a door for a pressurized aircraft should, in theory, be simplicity itself, and in the case of the doors used by passengers it is. You simply create a 'plug' door that operates on the same principle as a bath plug. If the door opens inwards and is too large for the external hole in the fuselage into which it fits, when the plane is pressurized the difference between the external and internal pressure forces the door against the fuselage, forming a perfectly airtight seal.

Unfortunately, this sort of design is not suitable for the doors of cargo compartments. Plug doors are extremely heavy, and using them here would reduce the plane's cargo-carrying capacity. Moreover, because they open inwards, they would also limit the space available in the hold. Boeing devised a solution to the problem in the KC135 tanker, which became the model for the 707, and continued to use the same principle in subsequent designs, including the 747. Its 'tension-latch' door was designed to twist and bend with the rest of the airframe and could thus be reasonably light. It is hinged outward at the top and swung down against a rubber seal before being pulled closed by a hydraulic unit. An elaborate system of latches ensures that the door cannot be shut until a manually operated lever is all the way down into its slot, and, as a further precaution, until a small vent door in the middle of the main door shuts tight. But all these measures meant that the design was not a simple one. When Lockheed used a similar device for its TriStar, it took up to 150 engineers to ensure that the door was safe while not imposing an inordinate weight penalty.

The engineers from McDonnell Douglas and the Convair division of General Dynamics, the subcontractors responsible for the doors on the DC10, adopted a different solution. In engineering theory, the idea of 'over-centre latches' was 'elegant' – the ultimate professional approval. As the authors of *Destination Disaster* explained it: 'Everyone is familiar, often unawares, with the over-centre principle. It appears in one form in an old-fashioned electric switch. Once the lever of the switch has gone past the critical mid-point of its arc, it cannot "creep" back, but can only be forced to return over its "centre" by an effort equivalent to that which moved it in the first place.' The only problem, on the DC10 door as on a light switch, was that the top part had to pass beyond the centre point of the 90-degree arc on which it travelled. For the mechanism on an aircraft door to be safe, the effort required to ensure that the door is properly closed and not simply jammed shut must be greater than a single human being can exercise. But if the mechanism is not properly adjusted, and this was the key to the whole tragedy, the door can be shut to the satisfaction of the loader involved, even if the elaborate system of catches responsible for closing it completely is not properly in place. Hence the crucial importance of the very small adjustments that should have been made to the mechanism to provide an automatic warning when the loader could not force the door shut.

The effect of an open door on a plane is multiplied 1,000 times because of the effect on the aircraft floor. In some airliners, like the DC10, this is a vital element in the aircraft's design, not so much in itself, but because through it run the control cables and thin hydraulic tubes which controlled aircraft until the advent of 'fly-by-wire' systems (see Chapter 7). In the 747 the floor is less important because Boeing attached the wires and tubes to the ceiling. The contrast was pointed out by the Rijks Luchtvaart Dienst (RLD), the Dutch equivalent of the FAA, as early as April 1971, three years before the Paris crash. 'In aeroplanes [like the DC10 but unlike the 747] where flight and engine controls, electrical cables and system lines are attached to the floor, a sudden decompression below or above the floor might not only cause damage to the floor and block the control of the aeroplane and its engines, but also the vital systems like hydraulics and oxygen lines, and can therefore endanger the safety of the aircraft.'

Beneath the design question ran a subtext: the competition between McDonnell Douglas and Lockheed, makers of a similar three-engined airliner, the L1011, or TriStar. This race inevitably speeded up the design and above all the development process. Safety consultant Bob Besco, a former pilot who declares that the DC10 'had the best handling qualities of any large airplane I ever flew', expresses the sort of doubt that emerged from the whole story. 'They had a real time war going on between the two, L1011 and the DC10. Whether that had any influence on these mistakes, or whether the design errors would still have been made even if they'd had two more years to do it, I can't really say.'

Whatever the case, proof that the locking system was not infallible came with a near miss over Windsor, Ontario on 12 June 1972. Bryce McCormick, a senior pilot with American Airlines, was flying a DC10 when the rear cargo door blew out, causing severe decompression. With extraordinary skill and nerve, McCormick managed to land the plane safely. The poor passengers were then interrogated by the FBI, who suspected that the problem had been caused by a terrorist, but the NTSB and the board of inquiry set up by American Airlines soon established the real reason. Within a few days McDonnell Douglas had tested the door and found that an average person could override the locking system and thus that the door was unsafe. Further pressure came from McCormick, who told Douglas to 'get that damn door fixed'. He received the reply: 'Mac, that's a promise.' But it was one that neither they nor the American authorities kept, at least as far as the Turkish Airlines DC10 was concerned.

McDonnell Douglas was able to delay the expensive and embarrassing changes to the door mechanism only because of confusion among the regulatory agencies involved. President Nixon had appointed as head of the FAA a solid

Republican, John Shaeffer, a former Air Force pilot with very little experience of commercial flying. In 1970, following incidents involving the 747, the FAA under Shaeffer had accused the NTSB, and more particularly the widely respected Chuck Miller, then the director of the Aviation Safety Bureau, of alarmism. The following year, the chief administrator of the NTSB was replaced by another loyal Republican, Richard L. Spears, who had no direct relevant experience. This did not deter him from harrying Miller after the Board's executive director had been downgraded as part of the Nixon administration's programme of politicizing the federal civil service. Spears tried to get Miller to produce his reports more quickly and denigrated Miller's own brainchild, the Accident Prevention Branch, which was inevitably critical of the airlines. By the end of 1974 Miller had been diagnosed as suffering from a heart problem and retired on medical grounds.

Unfortunately, the Windsor incident and the manufacturer's reaction both occurred in the first flush of the politicization of the FAA and the NTSB. In principle, supervision of the required changes was left to Arvin Basnight, head of the western region of the FAA. On looking through the airline reports (which he managed to extract from the manufacturers only after some prevarication) Dick Sliff, Basnight's deputy, found one hundred reports of doors not closing properly during the two-month period the DC10 had been in service.

At this point the the politics became decidedly murky. On direct orders from their bosses in Washington, Basnight and Sliff were prevented from issuing a legally enforceable airworthiness directive to ensure that no DC10 would fly until modifications were made to all the relevant doors. Instead the FAA relied on a gentlemen's agreement with the manufacturers, who had come up with rather a botched solution to the problem – though, had it been applied to all aircraft, even this could have prevented the Paris accident. The solution appealed to Douglas, who clearly wanted to keep unfavourable publicity to a minimum at a time when they were competing so ferociously for orders with the TriStar. It also chimed with the sunny personality of John Shaeffer, a man who, in his own words, liked 'to think optimistically about the future' – though after the Paris crash, even he had to admit that he would never have 'sat around, fat, dumb and happy' if he had known that McDonnell Douglas were still delivering planes with unsafe cargo doors.

Meanwhile, the manufacturer continued its bland response to official inquiries, insisting that the chances of a DC10 cargo door opening in flight were 'extremely remote . . . a reassessment of the DC10 design, with regard to the effects on safety, for non-plug cargo doors and small bomb explosions shows that the present standard and levels of substantiation [of the floor] are adequate'. The FAA should have been alarmed by this smug attitude, particularly since nearly twenty years earlier the agency had had to force the Douglas company to modify the design of the propeller-powered DC6. After an horrendous accident in which fifty-two people were killed, it had been discovered that fuel could spill while being transferred in flight from tank to tank, and that fuel vapour could be set alight by the electric coils of the cabin-heating system. More relevantly, a serious problem had recently emerged with the DC8, Douglas's first entry into the jet aircraft market. This related to the spoilers – flat metal plates hinged to the upper surface of each wing – which disrupt or 'spoil' the airflow over the wing and are used only when the aircraft has touched down. If they are deployed at the moment of landing, the plane loses enough speed to stall and crash. An accident caused by this fault had killed 100 people aboard a DC8 in 1970. Because the FAA failed to act decisively enough, there were two further accidents in the following year; nevertheless it took the manufacturer three years after the first crash to fit a lock on the spoiler mechanism.

Yet, despite the Windsor incident, the history of the DC6 and the more recent problems with the DC8, Basnight accepted the manufacturer's point of view and, as result, albeit somewhat reluctantly, the Dutch authorities also certified the DC10. But if the manufacturer had acknowledged the initial doubts and strengthened the floor of the DC10 in 1971, when only a handful of planes had been built, then the Paris crash could have been avoided. As it was, only the Airbus consortium absorbed the lesson and ensured that the floor of their new plane, the A300, be strengthened.

Then the engineer most closely involved with the production of the cargo door made his own plea for action. Dan Applegate, director of project engineering of the Convair division of General Dynamics, which was responsible for manufac- turing the door, had already expressed his unhappiness with some of the design features, most notably the use of electric rather than hydraulic actuators to drive the latches. This modification, made to reduce the weight, resulted in the loss of a safety feature: an inadequately closed hydraulic door would open under less pressure, even in low-level flight, than an electrically powered one. Later, Convair submitted a list of nine possible failures which could lead to loss of life, including one which was remarkably similar to what was to happen. Moreover, while the air conditioning on the first DC10 was being tested, a cargo door flew open. Incredibly, the design was approved by the FAA's representative – an engineer paid by the manufacturer. And it was approved even though five similar doors on DC8s and DC9s opened in flight during 1970 alone, and even though Convair had written that 'there were several simpler, less costly alternatives of making the failure more remote' to the method employed by McDonnell Douglas.

On 27 June 1972, only a fortnight after the Windsor near miss, Applegate went further. In a long memo, he wrote to his superiors:

> The potential for long-term Convair liability on the DC10 has been
> causing me increasing concern for several reasons . . . The airplane
> demonstrated an inherent susceptibility to catastrophic failure when
> exposed to explosive decompression of the cargo compartment in 1970
> ground tests . . . It seems to me inevitable that, in the twenty years
> ahead of us, DC10 cargo doors will come open and cargo compartments

will experience decompression for other reasons and I would expect this to usually result in the loss of the airplane . . . It is recommended that overtures be made at the highest management level to persuade Douglas to immediately make a decision to incorporate changes in the DC10 which will correct the fundamental cabin-floor catastrophic failure mode.

The memo apparently never reached Douglas, and if it had, it would have complicated the financial discussions between the companies. So the design went unchanged. Meanwhile, Chuck Miller was trying without success to get the recommendation adopted. 'I have a tendency to call 'em as I see 'em and an example of that was the recommendation having to do with the floor of the DC10,' he says. 'I'm the one who put that in the record, and I think it was known that I did that. I personally was subject to vilification because I was a civil servant, even though I was a member of the party in power in Washington.'

Turkish Airlines – known as THL in the trade – seemed an unlikely outfit to become the first airline outside the United States to buy the DC10. It was then a small company with a poor safety record and little or no experience of operating so large and sophisticated a plane. Ostensibly, THL needed the aircraft for two of its basic operations: transporting migrant workers, *gastarbeiter*, between Germany and their homeland, and carrying Muslims on the *haj*, the pilgrimage to Mecca. But there was also a hidden agenda: the Turkish armed forces, who had a considerable say in the airline's policy, needed to be able to land large numbers of troops in Cyprus in the not unlikely event of war with Greece over ownership of the island.

THL managed to acquire its six DC10s only because the Japanese, for whom they had been earmarked, failed to complete the deal and left MacDonnell Douglas without a buyer. It was unwise of the manufacturer to sell such a sophisticated plane to the Turks and then try to blame the inadequacy of the Turkish maintenance operation for the crash, though it must be said that THL did not have enough flight engineers and the training of its ground crews was so rushed that no specific individual had been entrusted with the crucial task of ensuring that the cargo doors were properly closed. Moreover, even the minimal changes finally imposed by the FAA on McDonnell Douglas had not been applied to Ship 29, the plane which crashed.

Even the disastrous consequences of the decision on the afternoon of 3 March 1974 did not have an immediate effect. A month later, at the company's annual general meeting, the chairman made McDonnell Douglas's position abundantly clear: the crash had been caused by 'human failure,' specifically that of a baggage-handler, Mohammed Mahmoudi. Official American reaction was immediate. Three days after the crash the FAA finally issued an airworthiness directive making mandatory the modifications supposed to have been carried out under the gentlemen's agreement of twenty months earlier. By the end of the month, a Senate subcommittee had started hearings into the crash. It was not long before the whole story emerged, partly because of journalistic pressure.

Pressure soon resulted in further hearings before the Senate Commerce Committee which unveiled the whole murky administrative background. Until then, says Chuck Miller, it hadn't been fully understood that the independence of the Safety Board had been under attack from both the White House and the Department of Transportation. 'This went back to the FAA not paying attention to NTSB recommendations. It had to do with who was going to be running the Board, whether it was somebody from the White House, whether it was going to be Board members, or me, or who. The Paris DC10 crash was really the straw that broke the camel's back to get this out in the open and resolved.' The result was the Independent Safety Board Act of 1974, which had two major impacts. It gave the Board more control over its budget as well as, in Miller's words, 'a much better-defined way of how FAA must answer NTSB recommendations'.

The government's response was in the hands of Alexander Butterfield, who had replaced Shaeffer as head of the FAA following Nixon's re-election in November 1972. (Butterfield is best known for letting it slip when he was working at the White House that all Nixon's conversations had been tape-recorded, a revelation which eventually led to the President's resignation.) Butterfield promptly commissioned a thorough-going investigation, and the report produced by the ad hoc committee was pretty definitive. The final design, it admitted, was safe – although it was 'an inelegant design worthy of Rube Goldberg' (the American equivalent of Heath Robinson) – but because the DC10's partitions, floors and bulkheads 'were not designed to cope with or prevent failures . . . it was therefore incumbent on McDonnell Douglas to show that [the possibility of] loss of the cargo door . . . was "extremely remote."' More generally, the FAA had been 'lax in taking appropriate airworthiness directive action where the need for ADs are clearly indicated. The situation is by no means unique to the DC10 aeroplane or to the Western region.' Indeed, as the report pointed out, foreign airworthiness authorites had complained to the FAA, which had ignored their complaints.

But the crux of the report was contained in the section on the reaction to the Windsor incident: 'The agency was not effective in attaining adequate fleet-wide action on a timely basis after problem areas were clearly indicated by the accident. Non-regulatory procedures and agreements were used in lieu of established regulatory AD procedures [and] in the long run [proved] to be ineffective in correcting design deficiencies . . . to prevent recurrence of the [Windsor] accident.' As a special subcommittee of the House of Representatives put it: 'Through regulatory nonfeasance, thousands of lives were unjustifiably put at risk.'

By 1975, the NTSB had been transformed into that rarest of animals in Washington, a genuinely independent federal agency. Not for the first or the last time, what the tin-kickers call the 'blood priority' had had its effect. It takes the loss of life to galvanize the lengthy process of adopting changes which previously seemed too expensive. 'Unfortunately, the blood priority is a very big factor in getting recommendations adopted, getting changes through,' says Robert McIntosh. 'Once you've paid in dead bodies,' agrees John Boulding, then of British Overseas Airways, 'money suddenly ceases to be a problem.' Boulding came to this conclusion after a similar clash between the priorities of the investigators and the controllers. The catalyst was the first accident ever to befall a Boeing 747, which took place in November 1974, when a Lufthansa Jumbo crashed soon after take-off from Nairobi Airport, killing fifty-nine of the 157 people aboard. The cause was simple: the leading-edge flaps, which greatly contribute to the lift required for take-off, had not been extended. The fault was traced back to the pilot's confusion over the warning lights involved, confusion compounded by changes in engine start-up drill. It soon emerged that there had been eight such incidents before the Nairobi crash, and that BOAC had warned the crews of all its Jumbos of the problem. But the message did not get through to most of the other airlines operating the 747. The need for double-checking the flaps was pooh-poohed by the FAA in the United States and, worse, the CAA in London seem not to have received three separate copies of Boulding's warning (including one delivered to the home address of the official concerned). The CAA merely asserted that it was not their responsibility to ensure that letters reached them, but that of the operators. It took the Nairobi crash to ensure that crews everywhere were alerted to potential problems.

The obstructive attitude then displayed by the CAA is now much less evident, but even today tin-kickers on both sides of the Atlantic can never be sure that their recommendations will be adopted. Even before they can convince the FAA – or the outside world, for that matter – they have first to persuade their own commissioners. These people generally have a background in aviation matters, but as lawyers, politicans, officials, not, except in rare cases, as investigators. And it is they who receive the investigators' reports and make their decisions, after public hearings that can get quite animated. Greg Feith says:

> When we work with the politically appointed board it's often difficult because of their lack of technical expertise. So when you have a very complex subject it's a trade-off between how far you get in the explanation before you lose them, or how simple you try to make it so that they get the point. It's an education process. It's also my responsibility to write the report, which I do as if I'm writing it for a lay person to read, understand and, hopefully arrive at the same conclusions as we have done. That is always a challenge.'

The next step is to convince the FAA, which has to choose whether or not to implement the NTSB's recommendations. Inevitably, given the nature of the 'turf wars' that characterize official life in Washington, the tensions implicit in the relationship between the NTSB and the FAA remained after the NTSB acquired its independence. McIntosh delicately describes the relationship as 'interesting'.

It's unique in that we're advisory – we don't make laws and we're not responsible for aviation. It's a big challenge for us to enter a recommendation process with no effect of law other than public pressure to say, 'We think you need to change this.' We tend to fly with the perfect world. We'd like to see no accidents. The FAA administrator can articulate zero accidents, but sometimes we get a letter back from them that makes us feel somewhat disappointed. But we don't stop, we just keep chipping away at our list of Most-Wanted things. If you look at the evolution of some of the regulations, they've been a long time coming. If you go back to right after the Second World War, there were almost no regulations. But we don't get discouraged very easily, we just keep coming back.

Jim Hall, the NTSB's chairman, is suitably diplomatic. He characterizes the NTSB's relationship with the FAA as 'constructive tension. We are there for the purpose of conducting accident investigation. We are, I guess, similar to an auditor in any other organization, except that we do our work essentially through accidents and incidents. We're a final filter in terms of trying to be sure that the system itself is working.'

This persistence can work, as it has done recently in the case of the 'commuter airlines', the countless smaller carriers scattered throughout the United States. The number of what were once called 'puddle-jumpers' has grown enormously since airlines in the United States were deregulated in 1978 and the rules covering these carriers (defined as using planes with thirty or fewer seats) had not been changed to cope with this expansion. Consequently the accident rate was ten times that of larger carriers. After a long campaign the NTSB has finally ensured that by the end of 1996 all airlines using aircraft with ten or more seats will be subject to the same regulations as their bigger brethren. (Technically, this means that they will be subject to regulations 14 CFR Part 121 rather than, as previously, 14 CFR Part 135). But the relationship between the NTSB and the FAA remains tense. The NTSB has now institutionalized what can only be called its nagging of the FAA in the form of its list of most-wanted improvements. This list, which also covers the other means of transport within the board's remit, is prominently displayed in the lobby of the NTSB's offices.

But the systemic problems remain. One of the things that has always bothered Chuck Miller about the FAA is that 'they tend to play a numbers game'.

They use one analysis technique or another to show that the possibility of this floor failing is 1 to 10 million, minus a tenth, or whatever it might be, and they'll call it extremely remote. They seem to have got carried away with this approach to assessing hazards without asking a more fundamental question – what if only one in that 10 million happens? What's going to be the public's reaction? Is there a reasonable way to fix it? I don't care what the odds are, and so there's a philosophical difference between those of us in the safety field as a profession and the FAA playing with these numbers.

One of the shortcomings of federal regulations, or anybody's regulations, is that you can't cover everything. Another is that they tend to classify an individual component, and that's not the nature of accidents. Accidents combine these problems with different pieces, or combine the characteristics of these different pieces into an accident. It's called systems safety, and a systems-safety approach makes sure that all the pieces fit together and that the interactions between them are adequately covered in some form of hazard analysis.

In the wake of the Paris crash we learned that General Dynamics had indeed taken a systems-safety approach, pointing out the relationship between a failed door and failure of the floor, affecting the controllability of the plane – the sort of connection the FAA still does not make.

Miller has used the DC10 disaster as an example in countless lectures.

I try to point out that it is the classic example. If you allow your attention to be concentrated on, say, the door-support structure, or the door handle, or the instructions that are on the fuselage for the baggage-handler, or the floor, or any other little item by itself, and say the cause of the accident was that the door linkage was deficient, then you forget the other lessons that are available from this accident. For instance, I know that Douglas took a wholly different look at instructions that are put in handbooks and placards on the aircraft after this crash. Why? Because there was an element of the baggage-handler not understanding English, and people didn't realize that this might come up again. If you emphasize a particular cause too much – and some of the agencies like the NTSB tend to do this – you're going to miss a lot of positive things to use in accident prevention.

British investigators suffer from precisely the same type of problems. Eddie Trimble laments:

Unfortunately, some, including myself, might say we have no leverage on the safety side in terms of having a say on whether recommendations are implemented. Historically, that has been because it's been reckoned that investigators should have absolutely no axe to grind, and therefore should come to the investigation completely free of any previous misconceptions. And for that reason accident investigation – and this is pretty well worldwide – at best only makes safety recommendations. It's then up to the regulatory authorities, and the manufacturers, to implement them. I've been in this business for twenty-four years, and by and large there's far too much wheel-slip in that area. For every twenty recommendations made as a result of major accidents, only a handful are ever implemented. Frankly, a lot of investigators might as well go and lie on a beach as conduct accident investigations as long as that pertains. They [the airlines and regulation authorities] might have very good logic-based arguments not to undertake some recommendations, but frankly we don't often hear these objections. And there's a misconception that if the airlines made a certain change, then the whole thing would become economic. Far from it. If you look at it closely, you would actually find that a lot of the real effective improvements we could have – for instance, with passenger survivability – could be implemented at a lower cost than what they're already spending on some of the improvements they've made. They seem quite frequently to back the wrong kind of solutions. I think, and have thought for a number of years, that while it's entirely legitimate that the regulatory authorities should have frequent contact with the manufacturing sector and the operators, what is missing from that whole equation is the input from the customer – the passengers who've paid for the whole thing. Everybody's salary is paid ultimately by the passengers, and yet passengers have literally no say on what recommendations are made in air transport.

4
Airlines, Airports and Air-Traffic Controllers

Did you ever hear the story of the airliner that vanished into Finnair ?
– Old pun

Fear of flying is often expressed in the nicknames given to airlines. Among the more obvious have been Air Chance for Air France, Air Fungus for Air Lingus, and Better Off on A Camel for the late lamented British Overseas Airways Corporation. Yet oddly enough, very few passengers seem to worry, consciously at least, about the safety record when it comes to choosing an airline. Passengers don't want to know about safety, perhaps because they take it for granted, or, more likely, because it's too frightening a subject to think about. In the words of Ray Justinic, the systems manager of human factors at Delta Airlines, 'People take for granted that when they buy an airline ticket they're going to have a safe flight. When we talk to a customer, they're more worried about time, possibly about the meal service on the flight. Safety is a given. They take it for granted that safety will be there.' But the airlines themselves, together with airports and their air-traffic controllers, are three of what the Americans would call 'unindicted co-conspirators' responsible for air crashes along with the four major guilty parties: the planes themselves, the way they are maintained, weather and pilots.

In theory, passengers can shop around for the safest airline. In practice it's difficult. All the airlines serving a particular route might have similar safety records, good or bad, and for many air travellers a competitive price is the priority. Moreover, the statistics can be pretty misleading. One fundamental reason for this is that the vast majority of accidents happen on the ground, or in the first minutes after take-off or on the approach to landing. Airlines and aircraft which run busy short-haul routes, which involve more take-offs and landings, therefore inevitably suffer a higher accident rate than long-haul airlines operating relatively few flights. Qantas, the Australian carrier, which falls into the second category, often leads the rather arbitrary league tables so far as safety is concerned.

In any case, since the sample of errors, omissions, accidents and the much greater number of near disasters is relatively small, statistically, conclusions can only be reached from what frequently amounts to a series of coincidences. Delta

44

Airlines, for example, had been renowned as one of the safest carriers in the United States before it accumulated six incidents within a single fortnight, including a near miss, a landing on the wrong runway, a landing at the wrong airport, and a case of the crew shutting down both engines. United Airlines, too, had a run of problems, even though the safety record over the decades of this, the world's largest airline, has been remarkable. It preserved its fleet of twenty Caravelles for twelve years, even though, in the words of one aviation insurer, other airlines 'crashed Caravelles with monotonous regularity'.

Interestingly while airlines eager for maximum profits are sometimes responsible for accidents through lack of maintenance and imposing too great a strain on their employees, there is no correlation between profit and performance. If anything, efficient airlines tend to be safe as well as profitable – the managers know that nothing is as costly as a crash.

Yet in spite of the misleading figures, there is no doubt that some airlines are safer than others. The analysis of jet losses in 1995 made by the specialist insurer Airclaims shows a typical year (insofar as there is such a thing in so wildly fluctuating a run of statistics). Only one major western airline was involved in a crash which involved the loss of the aircraft. The remaining twenty-one accidents occurred among a wide variety of airlines. The only common factors were that none had had more than one such accident and that they came primarily from the Third World. African airlines were particularly susceptible to accidents in that particular year.

There is a vicious circle operating here. Small, unprofitable, marginal airlines, only too common in developing countries anxious for their own airline as a symbol of national status, are unlikely to be able to afford new aircraft. The older aircraft they therefore tend to operate are likely to be safe in themselves, but will require much greater and more expensive maintenance than newer planes. But, by definition, these airlines are likely to be undercapitalized and underorganized, and thus less capable of keeping their fleet up to scratch than larger, better established, more successful operators.

Such problems are by no means confined to the Third World. You have only to look at the record of smaller airlines within the United States, supposedly the country with the most effective airline policing system in the world. Perhaps the worst example recorded in post-war American aviation history emerged from the crash of a flight of Downeast Airlines in May 1979. It turned out that the chief pilot had been given so much work that he was suffering from 'chronic fatigue', which was not surprising, given that he had had to do everything, from training the crews and organizing the schedules to hiring pilots and maintaining the necessary files on them. The NTSB discovered that the airline was ignoring most of the regulations as a matter of course and pressuring pilots to fly regardless of the weather. If employees objected, they suffered everything from humiliation to coercion and, in some cases actually lost their jobs.

Five years later, in August 1984, came the crash of a small commuter plane operated by Vieques Airlink on a busy island-hopping schedule round the US Virgin Islands in the Caribbean. A Britten–Norman Islander piloted by a twenty-one-year-old 'captain', Miguel Garcia, plunged into the sea shortly after take-off, killing all nine people aboard. The grisly reality unearthed by the investigators and recounted by Patrick Foreman in his book *Flying into Danger* beggared belief. The airline, its planes and pilots were all accredited for passenger operations by the Federal Aviation Authority, yet the certification hid a can of worms.

Young Garcia was not blameless. He had claimed to have flown twin-engine planes for over 400 hours instead of the 145 hours' experience he actually had. And as he held only a commercial pilot's licence, not one for an airline pilot, he was unqualified, both in theory and in practice, to pilot a passenger-carrying plane. Indeed, when he hit trouble he fumbled the controls so badly that the Islander stalled once it had slowed to its unbelievably slow stalling speed of a mere 45mph. But there were mitigating circumstances: the plane was more than 600lbs overweight and the load was badly balanced; there was water in the fuel tanks above the normal safety limit (indeed, when the first investigators arrived they found water and mud in the airport's fuel-storage tanks and in the tanks of another plane nearby). The airline had cheated with its paperwork, claiming that the plane was not on a scheduled flight but an 'on-demand' charter flight, a change which, legally anyway, allowed Garcia to fly the plane. The NTSB slammed the FAA for its inadequate supervision of the airline, and finally, ten long months after the crash, its operations were suspended because of 'careless and reckless behaviour which endangered the lives and property of others'.

The problems of American-owned airlines have greatly increased in the eighteen years since the industry was deregulated. This provided smaller airlines with extraordinary opportunities to compete on routes new and old, a pattern which is now being repeated in Western Europe as the skies are, painfully and gradually, wrenched from the monopoly of often incompetent national flag–carriers. Inevitably, most of the newcomers rely on old aircraft and second-string pilots and, at best, their maintenance is less effective than that of larger carriers. They might also farm out their maintenance to outside companies which may not be competent and are certainly unlikely to be properly supervised by an airline desperate to reduce its costs.

The case of Valu-Jet shows what can happen. This super-cheap airline was already being closely supervised by the FAA – in particular because of its poor maintenance record – before the crash of one of its jets in the Florida Everglades in May 1996. Inquiries revealed the usual host of problems, ranging from potential – and uncorrected – electrical faults to the carriage in the cargo hold of 144 oxygen generators, which, against the regulations, were full of the gas which is thought to have ignited and caused the accident. Even then it seemed that the airline would get away with its laxity – on the stockmarket its shares rebounded after an initial drop when news of the accident broke. However, a few weeks later, clearly realizing that the FAA was going to shut it down, Valu-Jet 'voluntarily' suspended operations, although it was later allowed to start flying again.

Since planes are at their most vulnerable at take-off or on landing, airports and air-traffic controllers are obviously an important element in the safety equation. And no element has shown greater advances in safety in the past couple of decades than airports. There was ample room for improvement, if only because many airports had been designed to handle only small propeller-driven planes and so were totally unsuitable for the greater space needed by jets, especially with the larger ones, not only on the runways themselves but also on the approaches. In the late 1950s the British built the Vickers VC10 on the assumption that runways would remain relatively short, but Boeing assumed, rightly as it turned out, that they would be lengthened because every country and major city would want to be able to cope with the latest aircraft. This assumption gave Boeing a considerable commercial advantage, since obviously a plane like the VC10, designed to take off from relatively short runways, especially in hot climates, is bound to be restricted to carrying a smaller load than one designed for a longer runway.

Early airports, such as Croydon in London, Templehof in Berlin, and Le Bourget in Paris, were naturally sited too near the cities they were serving for modern conditions, although Templehof is only now being replaced, as is Kaitak, the airport serving Hong Kong, where the planes seem to land between strings of washing. The National Airport in Washington remains busy, although it would surely have been shut down long ago if it had not been so conveniently placed for members of the US Congress. National is one of many airports designed for the smaller and slower aircraft of the pre-jet era and is simply too small and too cramped to handle the jets that use it today. Most of these airports, however, are at tourist destinations. Funchal in Madeira, its dauntingly short runway poised on a cliff edge by the seashore, is only too typical. Patrick Foreman records two incidents there, both involving British pilots, in 1987. The first resulted in a virtual crash landing. The pilot of the second plane, a Boeing 767, preferred not to land, but, in Foreman's words 'slammed on full power and took off over the cliff's edge to disappear like a fighter from the deck of an aircraft-carrier'. Mystified, the Portuguese telephoned the chief pilot of the airline in Britain to ask if one of their pilots had made this dashing manoeuvre. 'Yes,' answered the chief pilot. 'It was me, and I'm going to cancel the route.'

By definition such airports tend to be located by the sea, and, more particularly, between mountains and the sea. Malaga and Alicante, the gateways to southern Spain, used to be among the worst, but in their day Rhodes and other Greek airports also had pretty bad reputations. Vying for the wooden spoon with the airports round the Mediterranean coast are those of another popular holiday destination, the Caribbean, where there are a lot of them, and where the local governments are neither rich nor efficient enough to keep them up to scratch. A typical result was the 1976 crash of an American Airlines 727 at St Thomas, the capital of the US Virgin Islands, which killed thirty-five passengers and four flight attendants. St Thomas was one of only three US airports given a 'black star' rating by the International Airline Pilots Association as 'critically deficient'. The *New York Times* declared at the time: 'In the eyes of numerous air-safety experts, Tuesday's plane crash on St Thomas is deemed a textbook example of a crash that was almost bound to happen. The reason? Conditions at the Caribbean airport – the short runway and dangerous hills at the eastern end – provided little safety cushion in case of trouble, even though they met official criteria'. The *Washington Post* added that the airport had been the subject of 'discussions, plans, reports and controversy for twenty years'. The lack of action was largely due to the fact that legislators from St Thomas's bigger neighbour, St Croix, opposed any improvement to ensure that all jet traffic passed through their own airport.

The danger implicit in an airport location close to high mountains and susceptible to strong winds, as is the case with Teheran, is exacerbated if the airport and, more particularly, its aircraft-control system, is underequipped or simply badly run, or both. A classic case was Columbo in Sri Lanka, where a succession of near accidents in 1978 revealed that a series of power failures had cut navigational aid transmissions at vital moments. It was only as a result of the efforts of a local reporter with links to foreign newspapers that the truth emerged. It led to immediate and dramatic improvements.

Inadequate, or faulty, or simply incompetent air-traffic control is a major, and unfortunately relatively unpublicized, cause of plane crashes. The stories of disasters or near crashes caused or complicated by the inadequate linguistic skills of controllers in many countries are innumerable. The problem has been exacerbated by the almost casual way in which English has been assumed to be the lingua franca of the skies without any concerted attempt to ensure that controllers are properly taught the version of the language used in communicating with pilots. This cavalier assumption, which could be construed as linguistic imperialism, has bred a natural reaction, particularly among Spanish-speaking controllers, who often deliberately embarrass Anglophone or German-speaking pilots by addressing them in Spanish.

It makes matters much worse that, as David Beaty explains in *The Naked Pilot*, 'It is considered a sign of efficiency to understand and read back your clearance first time. It is also inbuilt in cultural mores that to ask people to repeat something indicates defective hearing on your part and is considered slightly rude, specially to a foreigner speaking your language'. Beaty was describing the events which led up to the crash of a Dan Air Boeing 727 in Tenerife in 1980, which killed everyone on board, but this was not the only incident in which a tragedy was exacerbated, if not caused, by mutual incomprehension. The collision of a British Trident and a Yugoslav DC9 over the beacon at Zagreb in 1976 can be directly traced back to the fact that the air-traffic controller was speaking Serbo-Croat.

Despite repeated proof that clear communication is vital, the problem remains unresolved. Nearly twenty years after the appalling crash on the runway at Tenerife between two Jumbos, nothing much seems to have been done.

Even within Europe, air-traffic control is by no means perfect, partly because there is no fully effective pan-European air-traffic control system. National jealousies ensure that the skies continue to be controlled at national level. This imposition of the territorial imperative to the airspace above countries is not only a source of confusion, it also artificially limits the capacity of the air to carry planes, since central control would ensure a much more even flow of traffic.

According to Paul Roitsch, who represented ALPA's pilots during the Tenerife investigations:

> Hardly any of the recommendations that the human factors study group made have been implemented. Perhaps the most important of those was that all air-traffic control communications between aircraft and controllers be conducted in fluent, unaccented English. Now this is the ICAO, but throughout most of the world the tendency is still to have locals in the tower whose English is questionable, to say the least. I can recall one European capital, which I won't mention by name, at which you could tell how close you were to the airport by the way the controllers spoke English. When you were some distance out you could hardly understand them; when you were a little closer in their English was much better, and by the time you got on final approach, they were perfectly fluent. That is true in much of the world today; in fact in much of the world today even on the final approach it's difficult to understand. It's a rule that should be implemented and enforced. It would save lives.

No better illustration of the fog that can be created by the lack of control of the controllers can be provided than the crash over Nantes in north-west France in February 1973. The French air-traffic controllers were on strike, and their duties had been taken over by the military, a situation which led a few cautious airlines to avoid French airspace. The collision involved an Iberian Airlines DC9 bound for London from Majorca, which crashed, killing all sixty-eight people on board, and a Convair Coronado belonging to Spantax, a Spanish charter airline, which miraculously managed to land at the military airport of Cognac 100 miles further south, even though it had lost a large chunk of wing.

Yet rather than being hailed as a hero, the pilot of the Coronado, Captain Arenas, was arrested. In the resulting furore, the French authorities, led by the transport minister Robert Galley, blamed everyone except themselves. They claimed that the air-traffic controllers had been completely exonerated by an examination of the tape-recorded exchanges between them and the pilots. These were not released. Further investigation by a team from *The Sunday Times* in England, which included Patrick Foreman, proved that the two pilots had been forced to listen to separate controllers on different radio frequencies, resulting in total confusion which rendered the crash almost inevitable.

Some months later it emerged that the French air force was trying to suppress a report by the chief aviation inspector, which had pinpointed elementary errors by the controllers as the cause of the crash. Even when the report was finally published, two years later, it had been filleted and lacked the text of the crucial radio conversations normally included in such reports. But it did admit that the military control system had 'created a source of conflict' and mentioned 'difficulties' in radio comunication which resulted in 'a complete failure of the crews and controllers to understand each other'. The French press finally got their teeth into Galley, who had to resign, but it took five years of legal action before the relatives of those killed in the DC9 received financial compensation.

The French are by no means the only guilty authorities. The American politics which had had such a terrible result in the Paris DC10 crash covered in Chapter 3, also prevented the skies over the United States from being as safe as they ought to have been in the late 1980s. When President Reagan fired 11,400 air-traffic controllers who went on strike in 1981, it initially seemed that even these most skilled and specialized of technicians could be replaced without ill effects. In the four years after 1980 accidents fell by a third and killed 74 per cent fewer people. But, as we have seen, you need to look at statistics over a longer period to find the true trend. And deaths jumped from 54 in 1984 to 561 a year later. Moreover, near collisions – a far better indicator of the safety situation because they are more numerous – rose from 589 in 1984 to 777 in 1986. This prompted a warning from the General Accounting Office, the US government's watchdog, that 'the present system does not provide the same level of safety as before the 1981 strike'.

The situation did not improve with time. A near miss over Seal Beach in California in February 1989 revealed a disturbing state of affairs. The NTSB found that the air-traffic control centre concerned had made eight operational errors, breaches of the minimum safety margin between planes, in the previous year alone. The causes were inadequate staffing – fifty-one instead of the authorized sixty-six controllers – and the resulting excess overtime.

In the 1980s the problems in Canada seemed even more deep-rooted and even more political. In 1983 an Air Canada Boeing 767 ran out of fuel at 41,000ft on a flight from Montreal to Edmonton. The problem was eventually traced to pressure placed on the airline to order the aircraft to metric specifications. As a result the fuel for the new 767s was weighed in kilogrammes while that for older aircraft was measured in pounds. The inevitable confusion led to this incident, which the airline tried to blame on the pilots. (Someone had confused volume measurements for weight – so the pilots and/or the ground staff had to be responsible for it.) They were exonerated only after a public outcry and the establishment of a committee of inquiry.

Six years later, muddle in the Canadian administration was again high-lighted after the crash of a Fokker F28 belonging to Air Ontario. The accident was the culmination of a series of problems, including the fact that the airport from which the plane took off – and one, moreover, well known for its freak weather conditions – did not have its own control tower and so the aircraft had to rely on instructions from another airport eighty miles away. In addition, and fatally, the aircraft had not been de-iced. Again, public opinion forced the abandonment of the official inquiry by the Canadian Air Safety Board, which clearly lacked any form of credibility. As so often, the subsequent Commission of Inquiry found a whole litany of faults. The airline had a record of sloppy maintenance and the authorities had tried to cut down on the airport's firefighting equipment, resulting in chaos at the scene of the crash. And if the Canadians had such difficulties so recently, it is not for us to be too severe on the authorities, airlines, airports, and air-traffic controllers in poorer, supposedly less civilized countries.

5
Catch a Falling Star

The Comet was a pilot's dream. It was fast, comfortable and smooth. Everyone who flew the jet fell in love with it.
— Group Captain John 'Cat's-Eye' Cunningham

A handful of accidents involving faulty designs have changed aviation history. The first of these occurred in the 1930s at the dawn of regular passenger travel by air. Even in the United States, then as now at the forefront of air transport, travel depended on primitive tri-motor planes made by Fokker, Ford or Boeing, which carried small numbers of passengers at a maximum speed of around 120mph. On 31 March 1932, a TWA Fokker tri-motor broke up and plummeted to the ground at the tiny town of Bazaar in Kansas. The two pilots and six passengers were killed instantly. The subsequent investigation revealed that the crash had been directly caused by rot in the wooden spar of the wing. At a time when accidents were fairly frequent, this one proved to be historic: one of the passengers was Knut Rockne, the legendary coach of the all-conquering football team of Notre Dame University. The whole country went into mourning and the reputation of the tri-motors was destroyed overnight.

The disaster was a crucial fillip to Douglas and Boeing, which had been working on top-secret all-metal single-wing aircraft appropriate for the industry's financial mainstay: the air-mail contracts granted by the federal government. Such designs would also be suitable for the airlines' next target: a regular service from coast to coast. After the Kansas crash the new aircraft seemed, indeed were, the only solution to the problem created by the failure of wooden wings and the clumsy tri-motor configuration. In February 1933, Boeing's revolutionary 247 made its first flight and Douglas's DC1 followed five months later.

By March 1939 Boeing was ready and launched the Stratoliner, which took the next step in the aircraft revolution. Its pressurized cabin enabled the plane to fly at far higher altitudes than could be reached by the non-pressurized competition. The aircraft was demonstrated to its 'launch customer', KLM, in Seattle, but as it headed towards Mount Rainier it stalled and the wings were torn off. The investigation revealed serious structural and aerodynamic problems. Plane-makers were learning the hard way how to build the increasingly sophisticated aircraft their customers demanded. But the accident provided the DC1's successor, the DC3 Dakota, and its successor, the DC4, with a clear flight into aviation history, and they dominated passenger air transport through the war years and right through the 1950s.

But the accidents that had the most profound effect on aviation history and by no coincidence laid the foundations of the science of air-crash detection were those involving the pioneering jet airliner the De Havilland Comet. Despite its tragic history, the Comet remains the most significant single development in civil aircraft history. At a stroke it doubled the speed of air travel to 500mph, and introduced a simultaneous quantum leap in the comfort of travel, so much smoother were jet engines than their propeller-driven predecessors and so much higher did the plane fly. It is difficult now to recapture the extraordinary nature of an achievement which, however flawed, introduced the term 'jet age' to the world.

The Comet was conceived in 1946, for the British people one of the gloomiest of the many depressing years immediately after the war. It came to symbolize the dream that Britain could remain at the forefront of aeronautical progress as she had been with radar, the Spitfire, and latterly, with the development of the jet engine. De Havilland, the Comet's manufacturers, already had experience in building jet engines and fighters, most recently the Vampire. It was three years before the Comet made its first flight. It was a dream. As the pilot, John 'Cats-Eyes' Cunningham, recalls: 'It flew extremely smoothly and responded to the controls in the best way that De Havilland aircraft usually did. I assumed that it would change aviation, and so it has proved. It was a bit like Concorde.'

Before the first aeroplane had been built, the Ministry of Supply and BOAC had signed orders for sixteen aircraft. The first scheduled flight for the aeroplane was on 2 May 1952. Crowds filled the public enclosure at London Airport to watch G-ALYP Yankee Papa take off for Johannesburg, carrying thirty-six passengers who were paying £315 (around £7,500 today) for the return trip. But within two years, triumph had turned into tragedy.

The first sign of trouble came with a minor accident on take-off from Rome's Ciampino Airport on 26 October 1952, which seriously damaged the Comet's undercarriage. De Havilland had warned pilots about the dangers of lifting the nose too high before reaching the correct airspeed, and the incident was unfairly blamed on the pilot, Captain Foote. Then, on 3 March 1953, there was a more serious accident in Pakistan. A Canadian Pacific Comet on a delivery flight to Australia for the airline's trans-Pacific route crashed on take-off from Karachi, killing the pilot and the crew of ten.

Bob Nelson, an air-accident investigator, was called at home, told of the accident, and sent by the Air Accident Investigation Branch on the next flight to Karachi. He found tyre marks on the runway suggesting that the pilot, Captain Pentland, had tried to correct his mistake. The marks then disappeared, which indicated to Nelson that the aeroplane had become airborne. The undercarriage hit a low wall which dragged the airliner down and it burst into flames. The pilot had been briefed by Cunningham on the take-off problem of the jet, but was attempting to break a record for the flight from London to Australia. He was under pressure to take off in darkness and fatigued from the previous legs of the journey. These were thought to have been major contributory factors to the accident. Nelson says of the Rome and Karachi crashes: 'Both were take-off accidents, and the take-off was at night. One of the problems with the Comet was that it had a very short nose, and when there wasn't a very clear horizon it was possible, especially at night, for the aircraft to get into a steep attitude and then not build up sufficient airspeed for take-off. That occurred in both incidents.' As a result of these crashes De Havilland changed the shape of the leading edge of the wing, and as Cunningham says, every single transport aeroplane since then has had to 'demonstrate that it can put its tail on the ground and continue to fly off even with an engine failure', itself a major development in aircraft safety, but one that was totally overshdowed by the Comet's later troubles.

Two months later disaster struck again, and the first sign of a more fundamental flaw was seen. On 2 May 1953, a BOAC Comet landed at Dum Dum Airport in Calcutta to refuel. It took off again in heavy monsoon weather and six minutes later, as it was climbing to its cruising altitude, the pilot lost control. The plane went into a steep dive and disintegrated. Six crew and thirty-seven passengers lost their lives in the catastrophe. Nelson was dispatched to the crash site. It was a horrific scene, one that haunts him to this day. 'The remains of clothing and bodies were strewn around the mangled, burned out wreckage.' Despite the conditions, he and the Indian investigator, Shri Ram Malhotra, worked meticulously at the site, piecing the evidence together. The Indian public inquiry found that the Comet had suffered structural failure in the air and it was recommended that the wreckage should be sent back to Farnborough for expert analysis to determine which part of the aeroplane failed first. Nelson, who had flown out to Calcutta in a Comet, says that after seeing this crash he began to lose his confidence in jet travel, and he returned to London in a Constellation.

Ten months later, on 10 January 1954, a Comet left Rome en route to London. As it reached its cruising altitude it exploded in mid-air, and the wreckage fell into the sea ten miles south of the island of Elba. Six crew and twenty-nine passengers died. Nelson was sent out to Italy and arrived in Rome early the next morning. He immediately seized the initiative, realizing how important the accident investigation was, not just for British aviation, but for the whole country. He argued with the Italian air force general involved that the investigation should become the responsibility of the United Kingdom air accident investigators. The wreckage had been found at least ten miles off the Italian coast, so the accident had occurred over international waters.

Nelson contacted the minister for transport and civil aviation, Alan Lennox-Boyd (the Embassy started to take him far more seriously when he received a personal cable from the minister) and informed him that the investigation would involve a very costly salvage operation. Lennox-Boyd said that that he would call on the services of the Royal Navy and that he would come out himself to lend Nelson some moral support. Nelson received very little help from the Embassy. He had been told that the ambassador was away in Sicily, showing the flag. Lennox-Boyd is said to have reported this to Winston Churchill, the prime minister, who replied, prophetically, 'We had better sort out this Comet business or there won't be a flag to wave.'

Nelson's first and most unpleasant task was to attend some of the autopsies being carried out by the Italian pathologists, basically to see if there were any metal fragments embedded in the bodies – in an explosion, some form of fragmentation is inevitable. There was no sign of this, which led Nelson to believe that the accident had occurred as a result of sudden decompression of the aircraft. He was then called back to London for a high-level meeting to look into the airworthiness of the Comet. The aeroplanes had been grounded, and this was costing BOAC £50,000 ($120,000) a week. The first meeting of what came to be known as the Abell Committee (after its chairman, the engineering operations director at BOAC) looked at a number of possible causes and suggested fifty modifications to the airliner. On 23 March 1954, a few weeks after the committee's second meeting and after the modification programme had been completed, Alan Lennox-Boyd gave permission for the Comet to take to the air again.

This decision has been attacked as dangerous and politically motivated, and accusations have been made that lives were put at risk for the sake of British glory and commercial gain. This case won't stand up, however: no pattern had been established, since all the previous accidents appeared to have logical causes – operational problems in the cases of the Rome and Karachi crashes, appalling weather in the case of the Calcutta disaster.

Meanwhile, Nelson had returned to Elba to help co-ordinate the start of the salvage operation with the help of the British Mediterranean fleet, then a powerful force. Commander Gerald Forsberg, who was in charge of the naval operation, had suggested that they enlist the help of the local fishermen to trawl for pieces of the wreckage. Nelson was authorized to spend £5,000 (then $12,000) to charter Italian fishing boats to search for the debris. This was a considerable sum at the time, but a trifle compared with the sums subsequently spent on the inquiry. This work had to be paid for in hard currency, so Nelson was obliged to travel across Elba through bandit country, carrying several million lire, to get the cash. The navy used the most modern salvage gear, including heavy lifting equipment and even television cameras to recover the wreckage, which was lying in 500ft of water. The Royal Aircraft Establishment even launched a model of the plane, which it then exploded to provide the searchers with some idea of the pattern in which the debris would have fallen. In the event, however, the crucial pieces were recovered by the Italian trawlermen. As the wreckage was brought ashore it was washed down in fresh water to prevent further corrosion, although they weren't unable to remove all the traces of its sojourn on the seabed, photographed by the team of engineering inspectors on the spot and sent back, 'like pieces of a jigsaw puzzle', in Nelson's words, to the RAE's headquarters at Farnborough.

The final Comet disaster which marked the end of this tragic episode in British aviation history came with the loss of another plane and its seven crew and fourteen passengers as it was climbing after take-off, again from Rome, on 8 April 1954. Nelson admits they were in the dark. As both aircraft had crashed immediately after leaving Rome, some speculated that sabotage was the cause. There had been considerable fire damage on the fuselage around the centre section, and this, coupled with concerns about pressure refuelling, gave rise to the idea that one of the engines had exploded on one or both of the crashed aircraft. At the time, the public knew so little about flying so high and fast, an experience hitherto confined to a handful of fighter pilots, that there were even more far-fetched suggestions that the aircraft had come into contact with flying saucers, or even gremlins, at high altitude.

After the Elba crash it was inevitable that the government would call for the services of the RAE, the major British centre for aeronautical research and air-worthiness and investigation of the frequent accidents to which military aircraft in particular were subject. Uniquely in the world, it combined all the facilities required, from well-equipped laboratories and workshops to runways, including, critically, the specialist expertise required for research into stress and metal fatigue. According to Ken Raithby, one of the engineers working on the matter, 'We soon came to the conclusion that there was a potential problem there and so the work was stepped up.' Unfortunately, the aircraft industry thought that the RAE 'were mad boffins dreaming up crazy ideas, that they were the people who knew how to design aeroplanes, and that their aeroplanes never suffered from any problems'. The investigators at the RAE had also worked on a number of mysterious accidents, the results of which have never been publicized. John Cook, one of the team, confirms: 'The basic accident-investigation techniques were already in place before the first Comet broke up.'

Since 1951 the RAE had been directed by a brilliant young engineer, Arnold (now Sir Arnold) Hall. He got on the telephone to Duncan Sandys, a junior minister and former son-in-law of the prime minister, ensuring that the investigators were given financial carte blanche and that the Comet had total priority over the RAE's other work. Sir Arnold designed a combined programme to filter the information. There would be four main strands to the investigation. They would fully reconstruct as much of the wreckage from the Elba crash as they could recover, and at the same time they would build a water tank to pressure-test the fuselage. Flight tests of a Comet fitted with strain gauges to measure movements inside the cabin would be conducted, and they would use evidence from the postmortems and tests on guinea pigs to back up their results.

The postmortems were important not only in themselves, but also because they emphasized, for the first time, the importance of forensic pathology as applied to the victims of crashes. At the outset of the investigation, the bodies were the only physical remains of the crash recovered, and as much evidence as possible of the causes had to be established from them. In fact, as Air Commodore Tony Cullen points out, the pathologists found three crucial pieces of evidence: first, that the lungs showed evidence of explosive decompression; secondly, that the presence of 'fat embolism' in the lungs indicated that the victims had been 'injured in the air before they hit the sea'; and thirdly, that the burns the passengers had suffered occurred while the bodies were floating on the sea, which meant there had been burning fuel on the surface of the water. From this evidence it became apparent that recovery of the wreckage was urgently required to establish the cause of the 'explosive decompression' which had resulted in the injuries and the fire that had caused the burns.

Even the RAE had only four permanent members in the accident section. One of them, Arthur Almond, remembers that it was soon decided that 'two would do the wing and two the fuselage' in the joint effort to reconstruct the aircraft from the dribs and drabs of pieces, mostly fragments, as they arrived from the Mediterranean. For six months this quartet of unsung heroes worked long hours seven days a week to crack the problem. All the director could do was to drop in, discuss the technical aspects of their inquiry and encourage them. According to Bill Houghton, another of the investigators, it was very frustrating because 'we had to wait for the bits of the fuselage to trickle in, and there were great long gaps when we received nothing'.

The engineers had special frameworks built to help them to recognize from which part of the structure the bits of the 'jigsaw' had come and they spent five or six hours a day under floodlights perched perilously on scaffolding on top of this 'skeleton'. They faced problems of size and fragmentation which they had not encountered before, but which were to become familiar to future investigators. 'The scale of it was something new for us', says Almond. 'We hadn't had such large aeroplanes to deal with that had been broken up like this.'

A possible line of inquiry became apparent almost immediately. 'If the wings were to fail under normal loading', says John Cook, another of the four, 'they would break upwards. But we found that these wings had broken off by bending downwards, and what that meant was that something catastrophic had happened to the aircraft.' Cook then came across some vital evidence on the wing when he was wiping it clean which proved that a large part of the top of the fuselage had been the first part to fail. There had been some indication from the earlier crash at Calcutta that the rear end of the fuselage had been the first to separate. The RAE team found what Cook describes as 'very heavy and distinctive impact marks' on the left-hand side of the wing, 'part of a pattern of smears and scratches which ran across the whole surface of the wing, right across the fractures'. They could now say with confidence that the wing failures were secondary to the failures in the fuselage. 'The score marks on the wing suggested that it had been intact when the objects from the fuselage had been jettisoned by a cabin explosion across their surface.' The groove was full of silicone, which could either have come from the aircraft's paint or from the seabed. Sir Arnold insisted that they dug deeper to establish the source of the silicone, which was, in fact, the paint.

They soon pinpointed the exact position of the original fracture. 'Very soon after the crash', says Arthur Almond, 'we received small portions of interior furnishings and fabrics which had very clearly come away from the aeroplane at high altitude. There had been a complete structural failure. It was very soon found that before any of the failures occurred in the rear fuselage, there had been an opening of some sort at the front.' Bill Houghton then found the impression of a one-anna coin on the tail, a clue indicating that everything behind the rear fuselage of the aircraft had been in place when the cabin had ruptured.

Late in August in 1954, the crucial piece of evidence arrived at Farnborough. It was a large section of the top of the fuselage that housed both the automatic direction-finding aerials. 'I had already drawn conclusions that a certain part of the fuselage had caused the impact marks', says Cook, 'but had to wait for confirmation which could come only from part of the pressurized cabin. The crack split fore and aft of the ADF window, and under close examination we found that there was evidence that work had been done at these points during manufacture.' To this day Cook remembers his excitement when this piece of wreckage came in. 'It was hanging from the crane, still dripping seawater, and I could see from a distance that what I wanted was there: the distinctive shape of the fractured edge.' Once it had been slotted in to its place in the jigsaw, 'There it was. Eureka. That was the end of my story, really. It proved beyond all doubt that the wings were secondary and that the primary failure lay in the fuselage.'

The discovery gave the team enormous satisfaction, not only in solving the mystery itself, but because their findings demonstrated the importance of the accident section. of the RAE. 'There was certain elitism about the place in those early days', says Cook. 'It was very much full of high-degree types from Oxford and Cambridge, and we did rather laugh at those who were flying around with lots of high-minded theories and trying to prove them by various abstruse calculations. But the answer lay in the wreckage. We knew that.' The others didn't, not at the outset, anyway. And in the longer run, the quartet have carved their names in the history of air-accident investigation. In a very real sense, they were the ancestors of today's tin-kickers, who, like them, do not start with theories or hypotheses but rely solely on the evidence. This was not only the first, and most significant, triumph for the pragmatic tin-tickers, technicians rather than academic engineers. Within the framework of the then pretty hidebound British class system, it was also a triumph for what one might call the noncommissioned officers over the toffee-nosed officer class represented by the academics at Farnborough.

Nevertheless the breakthrough had to be validated. They got together a group of people 'with specialized knowledge of applied testing and applied loads', explains Raithby, who initiated a programme to simulate the stress cycle applicable to normal flights. 'They started with the aeroplane fully loaded on the runway ready for take-off, taking off, the lift being transferred to the wings as it climbs up to cruising altitude' – over double the normal height attained by the pressurized propeller airliners of the time – 'a period of cruise and then a release of pressure on the descent, eventually landing with a reduced weight. This involved a completely new method of testing. We were really starting from scratch with nothing more than sketches on the back of an envelope.'

To test the theory that it was metal fatigue that had caused the accident they required a totally new type of structure, a tank filled with water in which a fuselage could be immersed and subjected to stresses similar to those suffered in flight. It had to be water because, as Sir Arnold explains, air is compressible, and if you fill such a chamber with air, at some point it will explode. 'Water, being much less compressible, stores much less energy when it's pumped in, and so you don't destroy your specimen if it fractures.' The tank, 'a pretty master-piece of quick design', as Sir Arnold rightly calls it, was not a simple affair. Nevertheless, it was built, on a deserted corner of the airfield at Farnborough, in the amazingly short period of three weeks and filled once Sir Arnold had managed to persuade the local suppliers to provide him with enough water.

The new tank could simulate the effects of a three-hour flight in a mere ten minutes. In the days before electronics, there had to be a team in place all the time, twenty-four hours a day, seven days a week. Raithby recalls:

> In the first two and a half weeks we had got to the stage of simulating about 1,900 separate flights. I was resting in my bed when my colleague phoned at about two o'clock in the morning. He said, 'You'd better come in. We've got a failure.' I said, 'You've what? A failure? Not already, surely. He said yes they had, so they sent a car for me. By the time I arrived, they'd got the tank drained down and it was a failure allright. The fuselage was split more or less from end to end.

The tank test, the most glamorous part of the exercise, merely provided confirmation of the solution being simultaneously worked out by the four engineers in another hangar. The cabin had lasted the equivalent of 3,060 flights – three times the number for either of the Comets involved in the Rome crashes.

Scientifically, the test was eminently satisfactory. Sir Arnold Hall says, 'The specimen in the tank showed a serious fracture in one of the windows close to the nose of the aeroplane after a relatively short period, the equivalent of 3,000 hours of flying.' The stress was magnified by the shape of the windows, which were square with rounded edges, a design chosen to allow passengers the best possible visibility. As the former attorney-general, Sir Hartley Shawcross, remarked at the subsequent inquiry, it was a 'kind of fingerprint', since metallurgists could state that the pattern of the fracture had been caused by fatigue as opposed to stress. It was the first time a whole fuselage had been tested for metal fatigue using a water tank, but although it was by far the most widely publicized element, it was only one of the innovations in investigatory techniques brought about by the Comet work.

By the time a court of inquiry under an eminent doctor, Lord Cohen, sat in October 1954, and after a mere three months of investigation, Sir Arnold Hall was in a position to present a definitive report on behalf of the RAE. He was cross-examined by Shawcross, a famously aggressive lawyer representing De Havilland, but Sir Arnold was one of the few people during Shawcross's long career to have bettered him. The court concluded that the crash had occurred because of a fatigue crack which had started at the top of a window, where the stresses were greatest and that the compression–decompression process had been repeated every time the plane took off or landed.

Nevertheless, Sir Arnold points out, 'In their first design, De Havilland did everything that any designer at that time would have done. but they didn't know enough.' When the Comet was being designed, observes Bill Houghton, 'they had done it in small sections, which they had pressure-tested, and considered that the stress levels and everything were satisfactory. At the time there was, says Raithby, 'an insufficent understanding of the effects of metal fatigue of highly localized stresses that you can get round cut-outs, round rivet holes and windows'. Lord Cohen cleared De Havilland of any blame for the accidents. He concluded that they had been working at the furthest edge of knowledge into aerodynamics at that time; that the RAE's investigations had identified a number of modifications which needed to be made to the aircraft, apart from those to strengthen the fuselage and replace the square windows with smaller, round ones. The new Comet IV which resulted from the findings never enjoyed any great commercial success, although it managed to beat its great rival, the Boeing 707, in commercial service across the Atlantic by a week, but its longevity was enormous. The Nimrod maritime reconnaissance aircraft based on a Comet fuseleage are still flying forty years later.

In the four years between the investigation and the arrival in service of the Comet IV, Boeing and Douglas had learned from the problems experienced by De Havilland and went on to dominate the world's aviation market for over three decades. As usual, the British were foolish enough to share their discoveries with their American rivals. John Cunningham says: 'They were fully informed and admitted that if it hadn't been for our problems, it would have happened to one of them.' As Raithby says, 'The investigation introduced a new concept in structural design, which was aimed at looking in much more detail at the localized conditions in critical areas of a structure.' It also led to the concept of what became known as fail-safe design – a sort of belt-and-braces principle whereby the designer has to try to assess where the weakest part of the structure is located and deal with any problems that could result from any potential weakness. This is a philosophy that has been applied to pretty well every aircraft design since.

For all the might-have-beens, it is highly probable that Boeing's success was inevitable. The American market was the largest in the world and the local manufacturers had the immense support of the US government – the military–industrial complex ensured that the designs for the KC135 tanker built by Boeing for the US Defense Department provided a superb platform on which Boeing could base the 707. Moreover, the Comet – inevitably, given that there were no civil jet planes at the time – was the product of a design team brought up on military aircraft, and their mentality involved designing to the very limits of the possible. In particular, De Havilland's chief designer, John Bishop, who had designed the Mosquito and the advanced fighter the Vampire, had a reputation for going to or beyond the edge. With the Mosquito the wings kept falling off, and he could only use a sixteenth-inch aluminium skin on the Comet because the engines were simply not powerful enough to lift the extra weight which would have been created had he increased the thickness even to a more reasonable eighth of an inch.

There was another factor which would almost certainly have proved decisive in the long run: Boeing always thought big, while the Comet, even if it had not been subjected to the traumas induced by its design flaws, could never have been developed commercially to compete with the 707. The same phenomenon could be seen with Britain's other entrants in the civil-aeroplane race: the superb VC10 was relatively uneconomic, and shortsightedness on the part of British European Airways ensured that the Trident was smaller than the manufacturers intended – too small to cope with the American competition.

In one sense the Comet story could be said to be a case of life imitating art. In 1948, *No Highway*, a very successful novel by Nevil Shute, himself an engineer, had been published. The story revolves round a typical 'mad scientist', Theodore Honey, and his boss, Dr Dennis Scott, the newly appointed thirty-four-year-old head of the structural department of the RAE, who found Honey, with the features of a sallow frog, 'one of the ugliest men I have ever met'. Honey had developed the theory that the Reindeer, the great white hope of British aviation, would break apart from metal fatigue after precisely 1,440 hours in the air, and had built a test rig to prove the point.

Three years later, the book was filmed with an all-star cast, including James Stewart as an improbable Theodore Honey, Marlene Dietrich and Jack Hawkins as a decidedly convincing Dennis Scott.

Unfortunately for those looking for parallels, Honey's ideas were based on the theory that 'when a structure like a tailplane is vibrated, a tiny quantity of energy is absorbed into it, proportionate to the mass of the structure and the time that the treatment goes on for and a certain integral of strain.' The idea sounds loopy, but the end result – metal fatigue, caused by repetitive strain – is what happened to the Comet. Shute spins a magnificent yarn about this plane, which was carrying all Britain's transatlantic air traffic; how one crashed after 1,393 hours in the air; how the evidence was removed by the Russians (a Russian diplomat had died in the accident); how the crucial port tailplane was found near a Canadian lake called Dancing Bear Water following a seance in which Honey's daughter (he was a deep-dyed nutter who believed in parapsychology) had written that the wreckage would be found 'under the foot of the bear'. In retrospect, the investigators can only claim that they took seriously Shute's disclaimer at the end of the book, that the Reindeer was 'not based on any particular commercial aircraft, nor do the troubles from which it suffered refer to any actual events. The scrupulous and painstaking investigation of accidents is the key to safety in the air and demands the services of men of the very highest quality. If my story underlines this point, it will have served a useful purpose.' We can all say amen to that.

6
A Question of Survival

Douglas built this ship to last, but nobody expected
The bloody thing would fly and fly, no matter how they wrecked it –
While nations fall, and men retire, and jets go obsolete,
The Gooney Bird flies on and on, at eleven thousand feet.
Chorus: They patched her up with masking tape, with paperclips and
   strings,
And still she flies and never dies – Methuselah with wings.
   – Song celebrating the Gooney Bird, the airmen's name for the DC3

The most surprising fact about new types of aircraft is not that they are liable to accidents, but that, given the complexity of their design and the unpredictable strains to which they can be subjected after the weather, maintenance engineers and the pilots have done their worst, they have so few. Problems can occur with any manufacturer, with any airplane, despite the best efforts people give it from time zero,' says Chuck Miller. 'I know of nothing in life that starts out functioning perfectly, and this applies, as I like to tell my wife, to her golf game or to somebody building an airplane. You must recognize that you're not smart enough to catch everything, even though you try your damnedest to do it.'

When it comes to designing and building new planes the authorities are relatively helpless. As one Boeing engineer says in *Destination Disaster*: 'I could build you an aeroplane which fitted into every one of the federal airworthiness regulations, and you still wouldn't fly in it if you knew what you were doing.' By contrast there are many examples, and not only the DC3 of the rhyme quoted at the head of the chapter, of aircraft surviving strains and stresses far greater than those they were designed to cope with. In Chapter 8 you will find the story of the Boeing 737 belonging to Aloha Airlines which managed to land after the roof had been removed as if by a tin-opener, with the loss of only one unfortunate flight attendant.

Rudi Kapustin, a former investigator of major accidents with the NTSB, was amazed that anyone escaped from the crash at Dallas Fort Worth detailed in Chapter 10. He also remembers 'an accident on a DC10 in Mexico City where the airplane landed on the wrong runway, went out of control and ran into a warehouse. The airplane actually disintegrated and the middle stayed intact. There were survivors in that – and they had quite a few survivors from the 747

Lufthansa accident at Nairobi.' He adds: 'The DC10 in Sioux City had survivors, too. You're surprised, when you see wreckage like that, that anybody could walk out alive.' It is the Boeing 747 which appears to have the greatest capacity to continue to fly even when it has been ripped apart. Until the Nairobi crash in 1974, the Jumbo, which represented the biggest leap in aeroplane size in the history of aviation, had enjoyed four years of unblemished service with a dozen airlines, a total of over 2 million hours in the air. With the 707 it had been assumed that there would be a crash of some description once every 200,000 hours of flight, and the working assumption for the 747 was a crash for every half a million hours.

In February 1985 a China Airlines jumbo flying from Taipei to Los Angeles underwent an extraordinary series of convolutions. It rolled until the wings were vertical, then nose-dived, turning upside down. This created appalling stresses, not only on the plane but also on the crew, who were pinned helplessly in their seats by the centripetal forces unleashed in the dive – stresses reckoned to be ten or twelve times the force of gravity. When the plane finally landed, chunks of the tail had been torn off, the wings were permanently bent upwards and the auxiliary power unit (APU) had been torn from its mountings on the tail. Remarkably, the aircraft and those aboard survived.

In July 1971, following problems with the wing flaps, a Pan-Am Jumbo bound for Japan from San Francisco managed to crash land after ploughing through 30ft of the pier-like structure which extends out from the runway over the bay. As the authors of *Destination Disaster* describe it:

> The damage to the 747 was comparable, perhaps, to a hit from an anti-aircraft shell . . . 'Missiles' of angle iron ripped through the hull. Undercarriage bogies, wing flaps and fuselage bulkheads shattered on impact with the light gantries. The cabin floor above the wheel wells sprang up 2ft in front of the passengers' eyes and split open, spraying metal fragments . . . Large parts of the 747's undercarriage had been carried away or driven up into the hull, and wreckage was embedded in the tailplane and elevator system.

Yet the sheer brute strength of the 747, helped by the duplication of the crucial hydraulic systems (three of the plane's four hydraulic systems were knocked out) enabled it to survive.

Of course, however carefully planes are maintained, they are going to become more dangerous, more fragile, the older they get. This is not only because of wear and tear, but also because, by definition, older planes do not include the increasing number of safety features introduced to newer models. Even so, in good hands modern jets can remain astonishingly safe for a long time. Despite some disturbingly inexplicable crashes in the early 1990s, Boeing's 737–100–300 series is now statistically safer than it was twenty years ago, partly, one suspects, because pilots are so familiar with its characteristics and have lived with it so long. The pattern with the 737's great competitor, the McDonnell Douglas DC9, is very similar.

What is called in the trade 'controlled flight into terrain,' – in lay language, hitting an unexpected obstacle – used to be a major cause of accidents. One particular crash, that of a TWA Boeing 727 which hit a mountain near Washington DC in December 1974, killing ninety-two people, led to immediate action, if only because a couple of months earlier another plane had nearly crashed into the same mountain. The result was the introduction of the GPWS (ground proximity warning system). A Boeing official told Patrick Foreman, author of *Flight Into Danger*, 'Nowhere in the safety statistics has one change so clearly showed up.' The reduction in such accidents was indeed dramatic: numbers fell from thirty-three in 1969 to a mere eight in 1984, though investigators believe that even this figure is still far too high.

The enormous improvements in the safety of planes when they are actually aloft stands in marked contrast to the lack of progress when it comes to actually surviving a crash. The veteran British accident investigator Eddie Trimble quotes Frank Taylor, the head of the Cranfield Aviation Safety Centre, as saying:

> Although the rate of accidents had reduced quite appreciably since the old piston-engine days, we were still killing just about as many people per accident as we always had. In other words, although we'd reduced the number of accidents, we hadn't actually addressed the question of how to protect people in these situations. And it's still largely like that. There's a lot that should be done to improve impact survivability in terms of floor design, seat design, overhead design, and in terms of protecting people against smoke and toxics and fires.

Trimble makes the obvious comparison with car seatbelts.

> If you look at the restraint systems you have in your car, they're far better than what you've got on your average public-transport aircraft. You've got shoulder restraints, not just a lap belt; padded fascias, padded steering wheels, collapsible steering wheels; you have airbags, crumple zones in cars. There is no equivalent on an aircraft, because the whole question of what happens to an aircraft in a crash is given much less consideration than it is with cars. People will say to you, we design aircraft to fly, not to crash. Fair enough. I dare say car manufacturers would respond that they design cars to be driven, not to crash. But they know they're going to crash, and they take sensible precautions based on modern technology. It doesn't seem to stop cars selling – in fact there is an argument that safety increasingly sells cars. And some of us would like to see the same sort of arguments deployed on the aviation side.

Nora Marshall, of the survival factors division of the NTSB, emphasizes:

> People don't realize the importance of seatbelts. Once they take off they sort of relax, like they're in their living room, and take their seatbelts off. I've done a couple of turbulence accidents and the upsetting part is that if people had worn their seatbelts they wouldn't have had an injury. I'm working on one right now where a passenger became a quadriplegic following a turbulence encounter. He broke his neck and won't be able to walk again. In non-fatal accidents, turbulence is the leading cause of injury to passengers, so it's a simple, cost-effective solution. I did an accident over the Pacific where there were two fatalities and 157 injuries as a result of people being thrown around the cabin because they didn't have seatbelts on. In some accidents, passengers are so confused that they try to release the belts as though they were in a car. Aeroplane belts are different, and in some cases people have actually had to have other people release their seatbelt for them.

Marshall and other experts become even more passionate when it comes to child restraint. 'The interviews that have affected me the most,' she says, 'have been with mothers who've lost their children in an accident. It happened in Sioux City and it happened in Charlotte.' In the course of such interviews she has often thought that if the children had been restrained there would have been no need for the interview. As far back as 1978, the NTSB had been trying to get the FAA to do some research on the best way to restrain children. Following the Sioux City accident, the NTSB recommended that all children up to the age of two be restrained. But still they can be carried on the mother's lap. Marshall is amazed 'that you can't hold your laptop on your lap for take-off, but you can hold a 30lb child. It puts the child at great risk.'

Marshall interviewed a mother who lost her grip on her baby during the impact. Fortunately, the baby was found by someone else and survived, but the woman was very adamant that from then on that she would not travel with her children without restraints.

> Before they got on an airplane to leave Sioux City they went out and bought a child restraint and strapped their little girl into it for take-off. When they got on the next flight they took they strapped their baby into the child restraint again. A flight attendant came along and said, 'You can't use that.' The mother refused to take off unless her child was strapped into the seat and the captain came and told her that they would go ahead. At that time the FAA regulations allowed the airlines to decide whether a child restraint could be used. Following our recommendation, they didn't make it mandatory, but they did change the rules so that an airline could not prevent a parent from using an approved child restraint.

Jan Brown, a flight attendant who was one of the heroines of the Sioux City crash (her story is told in Chapter 12), is even more vehement. One of the passengers, Sandra Michaelson, was unable to keep hold of her child. 'The child flew through the air and an overhead compartment opened. She flew into it, and that's what saved her. I saw Laurie Michaelson in the cornfield afterwards.' Another mother had become hysterical before the final crash.

> When I finally had to leave the wreckage because the smoke was so unbelievably thick, the first person I met was the mother of this little boy. She was heading back into what was left of the cabin. I stopped her, and she said, 'I have to go back and get my son. I said 'You can't go back.' She said, 'You told me to put my baby on the floor and I did, and he's gone.' To this day that gives me chills. My first thought was that I'd have to live with this for the rest of my life. But I told her that it was the best thing to do, it was all we had – and it was. But it shouldn't have been that way. That little boy would be alive today if he'd been in a seat. Because the FAA says children under two can fly for free and sit on a parent's lap, her boy was killed.
>
> If life is worth anything, and if we're going to talk about family values, parents should be aware of this. If the FAA are now going to focus on safety then I would expect one of the first things they attend to is to ensure that every passenger is safe on an airplane, with a restraint. Why should it be necessary to have a bill in Congress to mandate safety? It's pure common sense. If it's required by law in a car, then it's definitely required in an airplane. I do not believe that the cost of the extra seat will force parents to drive instead. We have unbelievable numbers of children over two years old whose parents bought a seat, and they're still flying. When we buy children all these expensive toys, their own TVs, CDs, VCRs, Nintendo games and everything, who can question spending money to make a child safe? None of these toys will mean anything if that child is no longer there to enjoy them.

The lack of public pressure on the airlines, and thus on the manufacturers, could well be due to a fatalistic attitude: 'The public tends to believe that if you're involved in an airplane accident, you're goners; there's nothing they can do,' says Marshall flatly. 'But in fact there are a lot of things that people can do, and a lot of accidents are survivable. It just requires quick action once the airplane stops. To get out of the airplane, you have to take responsibility for your own safety and get going.'

Only a handful of airlines, among them the Scandinavian company SAS, even try to limit the amount of hand baggage. 'We're always struggling with it. It simply is not safe to have all of that luggage,' declares Jan Brown. 'We have cargo compartments for luggage – the cabin should be for people, and maybe lightweight objects, but it certainly should not be jammed to the hilt with heavy baggage. It's hazardous if we get into severe turbulence, overhead bins open and objects fall out and injure people.' Yet, says Marshall, 'Even with fire and smoke in the cabin, people will still stop to look for their possessions. What we want to teach people is that you've just got to get out. In the accident in Los Angeles where the smoke was in the cabin immediately, one passenger told us that her evacuation was slowed down by somebody reaching into the overhead compartment to get out their luggage. Twenty-eight people lost their lives because they couldn't get out quickly enough.'

When accidents do occur, the passengers' behaviour often depends on the degree to which they have been prepared for a crash. 'At Sioux City, the passengers were prepared for an emergency landing, although not for the full horror of what they went through,' says Marshall. 'They were braced, their seat-belts were done up tightly, and two thirds of them survived a truly catastrophic accident.' One of the things she noticed at that scene was that a lot of people helped others.

> There was an eight-year-old boy who was travelling by himself, and a passenger seated nearby moved over when they had the emergency to be with him. And there was a seventy-seven-year-old woman on board in a wheelchair. People helped her, because she couldn't get herself out. The difference was that it was an accident they were prepared for, whereas Manchester and Los Angeles happened without warning. Then the survival instinct kicks in. There are a limited number of exits, and they will fight to get out them, but research has shown that if they co-operate more, people can get out faster.

Four fifths of all accidents involving passenger planes occur within a single kilometre of an airport, so firefighting teams should (and generally are), be on hand within a very few minutes. As a result, 95 per cent of passengers survive a crash if there is no fire. If there is, only a third come out alive. Nevertheless, efforts to reduce the impact of fires have been, at best, spasmodic. No licensing authority giving permission for the construction of a public building, a cinema, say, would ever have allowed the use of the polyurethane foam regularly present in aircraft seats until very recently. It has been known for decades that, as Patrick Foreman wrote 'foam cushions become near-explosive when they are massed in an enclosed tunnel of metal and exposed to the high temperatures of a fuel fire'.

Aircraft fires are invariably dramatic events. A Boeing 707 of the Brazilian airline Varig crash-landed safely in an orchard near Paris in 1973. Thanks to the pilot's skill, the plane was hardly damaged and the fuel tanks remained intact, so there was no external fire. But when the crew opened the cabin door, as Patrick Foreman relates, 'they were met by billowing smoke and silence. Precious little life was left aboard . . . A blaze in the rear lavatory had spread to the seats in the last few minutes before touchdown and turned the cabin into a gas chamber in which 123 passengers out of 134 had been rapidly asphyxiated.'

It was after this tragedy that smoking in aircraft lavatories was forbidden. Foreman records another accident in September of that year which cost fifty-five lives. 'A DC10 was about to take off at Malaga. A nosewheel tyre burst on take-off and the pilot chose to abort, although he could have taken off quite safely. He overran the runway and the plane crashed through a perimeter fence. In the subsequent fire most of the passengers died in the choking black smoke from the toxic fumes inside the cabin.'

Over the past twenty years major manufacturers, like Boeing, Airbus and McDonnell Douglas, have applied their own criteria to try to limit toxic emissions from materials. Yet such developments can only help to a certain extent. Every plane, after all, is already carrying very large quantities of highly flammable material: its fuel. Eddie Trimble elaborates.

In the past people believed that you could develop materials that could resist fire for longer. But the tests did not allow for the enormous heat of a real aircraft fire. There are no materials currently available which can do this kind of job. A lot of fibreglass materials are pretty good in terms of reducing toxic emissions, and they tend to be used in cabin compartments. The fire-blocking material brought in after the Manchester crash will delay the combustion of the foam constituents of the seat cushions for about a minute in test conditions, but that's all it really buys you. At the same time, the rest of the cabin materials – the overheads, the side walls, curtain materials, whatever – will be combusting and giving off gases. Side walls quite often have a polyvinyl fluoride finish on them, which flashes off hydrogen fluoride very quickly. Any wool or nylon will produce cyanide; they all produce carbon dioxide. We've had accidents since Manchester with aircraft that had fire-blocker, but we still find that the passengers are suffering and in their accounts are making the same kind of remarks as they did previously.

If fire breaks out while the plane is still in the air the situation is critical Robert Kadlec, an aircraft failure analyst, explains.

It takes time to land, and during that time the fire can continue to grow and perhaps interfere with flight-control systems or the propulsion system. Aircraft have to be designed to be strong, light and compact, and when the materials aircraft are built of burn they generate smoke. Further, because of the high airspeeds, depending on where the fire develops, at times it can be fanned by the effect of aerodynamic forces on the fire itself.

In addition smoke creates complete disorientation. As Bob Graham says of the Manchester crash:

People would probably have had a sense of direction based on where they were sitting, but visibility would have been nil very quickly. They might have been able to see some light at the end of the gangways, but irritants in the smoke can stop you from keeping your eyes open. I have inhaled smoke on many occasions, like most firefighters. The particular smoke you get from burning plastics and oils and the like is very acrid. As soon as you take a breath, you cough or retch, and that causes you to take another breath, usually a much deeper one. That disables you, and thereafter you're overcome by the toxicity of the smoke.

The Manchester accident referred to by Eddie Trimble and Bob Graham was the single most influential event in the story of air-crash survival. On the evening of 22 August 1985, a Boeing 737 belonging to the British Airways subsidiary British Airtours was taking off from Manchester Airport on a charter flight to Corfu with 131 passengers and six crew members on board. As Eddie Trimble describes it, the plane accelerated normally, and after about thirty-six seconds there was a thud. 'The captain, who wasn't handling the aircraft at that point, thought it was a tyre failure or bird strike, and called for the co-pilot to abort the take-off. He then notified the controller, who replied that they had a fire. Just as the captain was speaking to the controller, the fire bell went off. He identified the left engine as the problem and decelerated. About fourteen seconds before pulling into a taxiway, he called for emergency evacuation on the right side of the aircraft.'

The cause was simple. On the take-off run the head section of the number nine combustion chamber had been jettisoned through the combustion casing, had struck a wing tank access panel and ruptured it. Immediately, there was a vast release of fuel in the vicinity of a hot engine. The passengers, at least those behind the over-wing exit, were immediately aware of the fire in the left wing. Several stood up; others called for them to sit down, an instruction repeated over the public-address system by the purser, when he saw what was happening. 'The Purser acted very quickly,' says Trimble 'and being aware that the fire was on the left side of the aircraft, he went to open the forward right-wing door. He hit it fairly forcibly, as you would appreciate. But the door jammed.'

Ironically, this apparently dangerous failure may have saved a lot of lives. Chris Protheroe of the AAIB points out:

> Any opening will encourage the spread of smoke by sucking it out of the aircraft, so had they been successful in opening the forward right-hand door, then arguably that could have drawn the fire into the forward part of the cabin. Instead they opened the door on the upwind side, the effect of which would have been to keep the fire down the back end of the aircraft. The flow induced by that action would actually have been beneficial.

When the purser couldn't open the right-hand door, with commendable quick thinking, he immediately went to the front left door. 'He cracked the door open and had a look,' says Trimble.

Fuel was beginning to flow forward from under the left wing, with some associated fire. But the purser judged that it wasn't sufficiently near the L1 exit to prevent its use. So he opened the door fully and applied the slide, and the evacuation started under the control of the forward hostess. As she started her evacuation, she had to unblock people from the 22½in aperture between the forward bulkheads and the door. She had to grab the first person from the wreck in order to free the floor, and they started evacuating down the L1 slide.

By this time, less than half a minute after the aircraft had come to a halt a rapid intervention vehicle was already beginning to apply foam to the engine, and the first people off were almost knocked down by it. It was shortly joined by another couple of fire tenders. The purser then returned to the right-hand door to try to overcome the problem. Meanwhile, the aft right door had been opened and the slide had been deployed, presumably by one of the two aft stewardesses, neither of whom survived. But that exit was almost instantaneously unusable because the wind was blowing the fire and smoke on to that section of the aircraft.

The wind direction proved fatal, as Chris Protheroe explains.

The wind not only affects the way the fire attacks the outside of the aircraft, it also affects, through the aerodynamic processes, what is going on inside and the way the toxic gases, the smoke and all the nasty materials under high temperatures are actually carried through the fuselage. People tend to think in terms of a howling gale, but we're not talking anything like a howling gale. At Manchester the wind speed was about 6 or 7 knots, which is nothing in terms of normal aircraft operation. But any wind that is badly orientated will tend to produce a bad scenario; any wind, however slight that is, that is well orientated will in turn enhance the prospects for survival. So a windspeed of even 2 knots can be critical. If the wind had been coming from another direction, I think probably everyone would have survived.

By this time the fire was also coming up through the air-conditioning grilles and the windows were beginning to melt. As soon as the aircraft stopped, the back end of the cabin was covered in thick, black, hot smoke. 'This caused a mass movement forward of the rear passengers, and the aisle quickly became blocked,' says Trimble. A lot of passengers had to climb over seats in order to get forward. Then there was pressure on the passengers seated at the over-wing exit on the right-hand side to open that door.

Two young girls seated next to this exit tried to open it. One pulled the handle of the emergency-pull placard at the top. The door, which weighed 48lbs, pivoted about its lower edge and fell inwards across the first girl, effectively trapping her in her seat. A passenger immediately behind them grabbed the hatch and manhandled it over, and people began to escape. The first two girls got out and off the wing without any problem, and a few others managed to extricate themselves before the smoke reached the exit. As a result, says Trimble, 'there were people lying half in and half out of the exit. One of the passengers reported looking back and seeing a mass of people just locked together, almost incapable of movement. Another survivor said that he took one breath of the smoke and it felt as though his lungs had solidified. A man who collapsed from the effects of the smoke told Trimble later that his mouth and nostrils and ears were clogged with carbonacrous debris 'with the consistency of Oxo cubes'.

Trimble was reminded of a survivor of another crash who fought his way to a door. When he took a breath of fresh air, he said he felt like Superman – with the added energy, he was able to open the door properly and get out.

Meanwhile, the purser had attacked the front right door again, identified the problem and, within seventy seconds, had managed to open it and deploy the slide. As soon as he did so, hot thick smoke rolled forward. He was grabbing the passengers as they came through the bulkhead aperture and then pushing them towards the slide. But there was a bottleneck, the 22½ gap between the bulkead and the door, which could really only take one person at a time. Eight passengers were overcome by smoke before they got out. Two of them were young women who collapsed in the forward vestibule area and were dragged out by the forward stewardesses and thrown on to the slide.

'In the end something like eighteen got out of the front left-hand door, thirty-four, I think, out of the right-wing door, and twenty-seven – including two infants – out of the over-wing,' says Trimble. Fifty-five people lost their lives in the accident, fifty-four of them on board. It took thirty-three minutes to locate the last survivor, who later died in hospital. One survivor, a young boy of about thirteen, had a lucky escape. He was rescued by a fireman who saw his hand moving above a body jammed in an exit. The fireman was the driver of a fire engine and therefore had no breathing apparatus, but he jumped on to the wing and managed to get the boy out unharmed, which was amazing considering that the child had been in the burning aircraft for something like five and a half minutes after it came to a halt.

'Manchester is typical of what happens when an aircraft cabin is seriously affected by combustion products from cabin-interior materials,' says Trimble.

The main problem is one of debilitation, a rapid reduction in your mobility, which increases your time of exposure. The toxic gases – carbon monoxide, hydrogen cyanide, acidic gases, hydrogen chloride, hydrogen fluoride – affect your ability to use oxygen. Carbon monoxide combines with the haemoglobin in the blood which is the main transporting medium in the blood for oxygen. It locks up the haemoglobin and reduces the capability of the blood to transport oxygen to the tissues. Cyanide affects the tissues themselves. The more you breathe in, the more debilitated you become, and it's a rapid process. This is why you find large groups of people, as we did at Manchester, in and around the over-wing, apparently so near safety, who just hadn't the energy to make it. After the DC9 in-flight fire at Cincinnati, there were similar comments from survivors, who said that by the time they got to the exits they barely had the strength and presence of mind to negotiate them. At Manchester, people were found on the grass unable to breathe, faces black and burned, coughing up profuse amounts of mucus. Fortunately, flight attendants from a BA TriStar which had just landed managed to clear their lungs by slapping them on the back.

For once the easiest part of the investigation was determining the cause. Even as Steve Moss and his team walked up to the aircraft, they could see the main cause of the fire: the tear in the access panel on the underside of the wing and the gaping hole in the combustion section of the left-hand-side engine. It seemed pretty clear at first glance that the engine had ruptured and a part had been thrown out and hit the underside of a wing. The entire wing on most jet transport aircraft is a fuel tank, and as this aircraft was departing for a flight to Corfu, it had several hundreds of gallons of fuel in each.' The black boxes confirmed the first suspicions.

The fuel is burned in a steel combustion chamber which air enters from the front of the engine at high pressure and high temperature, exiting through the turbines at the back.

We found that the combustion chamber outer case had actually split open. There are nine combustion cans in the combustion chamber outer case, arranged in a ring around the centre of the engine, and fuel is injected at high pressure in here, ignites and comes out of the back of the can. Normally, you wouldn't be able to see them – they would be buried inside the combustion chamber outer case – but we could see virtually all the cans. The significant part of the can – and quite a heavy part, a cast piece known as the dome, or front of the can – was missing.

It was later recovered from the runway. 'It was quite clear that the dome had struck the underside of the fuel-tank access panel,' Moss continues. 'It had come out of the engine under the force of the combustion chamber rupturing, a bit like a blow-out on a tyre, and had struck the underside of the panel, causing it to fracture, and then dropped out on to the runway.' The result was that hundreds of gallons of fuel had poured out before the fire was extinguished.

'It probably would not have penetrated the normal wing structure, which is quite strong, because it has to support the weight of the aircraft in flight,' explains Moss. 'But the access panels, which are really just there to keep the fuel in, were made of a fairly brittle material which was prone to impact damage of this type. It had not really been foreseen that a part could actually come out of the combustion chamber area and rupture one of those panels.' Historically, there had been three occasions when parts, including the dome, had been ejected from JT8 engines, and in those cases take-off had been abandoned, fortunately without any damage. 'It really was just very bad luck that it struck that under-wing access panel.'

According to the official report, the resultant fire developed catastrophically primarily because of adverse orientation of the parked aircraft relative to the wing, even though the wing was lined. Major contributory factors were the vulnerability of the wing-tank access panels to impact; a lack of any effective provision for fighting major fires inside the aircraft cabin; the vulnerability of the aircraft hull to external fire; and the extremely toxic nature of the emissions from the burning interior materials.

Because of the numbers who died, despite the extraordinary quick reactions, efficiency and bravery of the rescuers, the effects of the Manchester disaster were far-reaching, prompting rethinks in every aspect of safety from evacuation procedure and the fire-resistant qualities of materials to the training of fire-fighters. The least significant changes were those made to the engine: Boeing simply reinforced the panel protecting the cans.

When aircraft crash in flight, we've all come to expect fatalities, but what shocked everyone about Manchester, says inspector Dave King, was that this aircraft didn't actually crash. It just decelerated under control, on a very well-equipped airport, and came to a halt. Yet the fire managed to gain a hold so quickly that fifty-five people lost their lives.

> That placed a focus on survivability, something that, prior to 1985, if one looks at accident reports, was not a big issue. I don't know whether it was that perhaps we did accept that if you crashed aeroplanes it would inevitably have fatal consequences. I think now we're a little more enlightened. The speed at which the fire penetrated the fuselage and threatened the safety of the occupants was another surprise, and in many respects the sort of things that we were able to analyse and deduce from this accident did not agree with much of the research material which had been produced in terms of what we should have been able to expect as a viable evacuation time for passengers within such a fuselage with a fire outside. Another clear area of focus was just how and why this fire got such a rapid hold and managed to so rapidly threaten the safety of the occupants.

Another shock arose from the witness statements, which, says Chris Protheroe, revealed that the situation the victims faced was very different from the scenarios used in the certification of aircraft to test, for example, the efficiency of exits. 'We heard stories of survivors struggling across the backs of other survivors; people collapsed in the aisles. The galley structure – the furniture, if you like – in the forward galley area restricted the opening from the cabin into the forward vestibule area, and people became physically log-jammed in the gap. A lot of these problems were really quite dispiriting.'

The inability of the victims to get to the exits was of course the central feature of the crash. It was the worst incident even the experienced Bob Graham had ever faced. When he returned to the fuselage and entered it through the front of the aircraft:

> When I got to the top and looked into the interior, part of the roof had been burned away. There was still smoke and steam, but through that I could see that there were a lot of casualties. The central gangway was impassable because of casualties and there were other casualties still in the seats. The availability of the exits was the key issue to start with, and, of course, because of the location of the fire and the wind direction, we lost half of the exits immediately. The thing is that even with only half the exits, you should still be able to get out.

As Trimble notes, the evacuation certification does not require the aircraft to be evacuated using only half the exits. 'It may be that you can't use your forward doors because of crash-induced distortion or fire in that area. You may have to get out of both rear doors and, say, one over-wing,' he says. 'Or, in the case of Manchester, both forward doors and one over-wing. And as soon as you try to evacuate using both forward doors, that kind of restriction becomes a problem, bearing in mind that in these conditions people reported going over the seats and coming up against a wall in the thick, black smoke and then having to feel round to find the aperture.'

'We didn't manage to evacuate the people quickly enough,' says Dave King, 'and so we felt it was our challenge to examine the evacuation criteria, look at all of the protection to stop fire rapidly penetrating such a fuselage, and to look at the research that had predicted that that fuselage would be better at resisting such fire penetration.'

As we have already seen, part of the problem is that passengers don't want to think about crashes. Marshall reminds us of a point we would all recognize.

> A lot of people don't pay attention to the demonstration at the beginning of a flight. They think they know where the exits are, but they probably don't, and in any case, in a lot of situations the exit you think you would use isn't usable. In Los Angeles, most of the people who didn't get out were trying to use the over-wing exits, and yet perhaps some of those who were in line there could have used the exits in the back. People appear to get fixated on an exit and not think of trying another. In another accident somebody said, 'I saw the line at the front, and I thought, well, that's crazy, I'm not going to wait in that line,' and they turned around and went back to the over-wing exit. You have to be thinking about the whole scenario, not just the exit you've decided

you're going to use. At Sioux City none of the exits were usable. People got out through breaks in the fuselage.

In the wake of the undoubted improvements since Manchester, if a similar crash occurred today, says King:

> The evacuation procedure would be similar, but it would hopefully be more successful in that some of the issues which we drew to the industry's attention have been addressed. At Manchester, the presence of a seat row alongside the exit, in our opinion, made access to the over-wing far from free. The position of the forward galleys and the jam in accessing the forward doors was an issue which has led to a considerable amount of dynamic research at Cranfield, testing the evacuation of passengers from a similar cabin environment using a variety of galley widths and configurations, and also from over-wing exits, using a variety of seat pitches and configurations around the exit to try to get some numerical measure of what is a good evacuation route. The seat configuration around over-wing exits was changed by mandate not long afterwards. There were variations in what an operator could do to satisfy the requirements, but the over-wing exits were made more accessible. And cabin configurations are being rethought, giving consideration to the evacuation requirements in getting through galley areas, for example.

Today there's a wider gap at the floor bulkheads on most aircraft. The problem is that there are so many old aircraft around that need to be retrospectively fitted (and the bigger the gaps, the fewer the passengers, the lower the revenue).

Yet Bob Graham, the outside fire expert, still believes that with this kind of fire, in those sort of circumstances, there are always going to be fatalities. 'I don't think there is the time to escape from an aircraft. I don't think you could be sure that everyone would get out of the plane if you had that identical situation again.'

One possible improvement that was not adopted was the compulsory fitting of smoke hoods. Trimble started to look at them for two reasons. In Manchester only six of the fifty-five people killed had died due to heat. The rest had generally died as a result of incapacitation and the subsequent ingestion of lethal doses of carbon monoxide. It was a typical percentage for all types of fires, not only those on planes. He felt therefore that it was not enough to tell passengers to get out as quickly as possible. 'For most, who are not near an exit, it seemed to me that your only chance was to have respiratory protection and preferably a visual aid to allow you to maintain your mobility and the use of whatever visual clues are available.' The other benefit of smoke hoods was demonstrated by a pretty thorough assessment of safety equipment sponsored by the FAA in 1980. 'Fire water sprays, fire-hardening, fire-blocker, low-level lighting, compartmentation – they looked at just about every concept you could apply to improve fire survival.' The resulting cost-benefit analysis showed that smoke hoods were the most cost-effective measure at around $450,000 (£290,000) per life saved, providing far better value than the recommendation that was adopted, fire-blocking of seats, costing $3 million.

For the first time in aviation history (it was back to the blood factor), Trimble found himself on a programme putting hoods to the test in the sort of conditions to be expected in aircraft fires. Nothing came of the programme, though Trimble himself now takes a smoke hood with him when he travels, mainly, he says, because 'you're probably more at risk in some hotels abroad' than you are flying there.

Advances were also made in the training of firefighters to deal with fires caused by burning fuel pouring out of a plane. At Manchester, says Chris Protheroe, they were not able to lay foam down over the top of the pool to dampen the fire down because there was a burning column of liquid dropping all the time.

Today in the UK, a lot of thought is given to the problem of running fuel fires of this kind, though it is still a very intractable type to deal with. But more significantly, the firefighters had no means of actually dealing with the fire once it had got a hold on the interior of the aircraft – obviously you cannot have firemen in heavy helmets and kit stumbling up trying to get on board through exits where people are trying to get out. So the fire crews have to wait till people have stopped coming out before they can make any attempt to get in. And the point at which people stop coming out is the point where they've collapsed and effectively their lives have been compromised. So the firemen had to watch impotently while they knew passengers inside were perishing. At the moment there is no means of tackling fires inside the aircraft cabin.

There has been a lot of work done on sprinkler systems – not the deluge sort of systems, but fairly carefully controlled sprinklers which will produce a properly tuned spray or mist in the cabin. These are extremely effective ways of fighting the internal fire. If some means could be devised whereby the fire-service vehicles arriving could plug into this system and pump material into the interior space, it would be an effective way of dealing with the problem, and I think it would offer a great deal of hope for improving survivability. But there are, as ever, problems associated with cost. A lot of emotion attaches to aircraft accidents, and aircraft fires in particular, and people adopt very rigid views, I think. Certainly we have not been as successful as we would wish to be in moving forward and motivating change to adopt sprinklers and other life-enhancing systems.

The effects of these changes were seen when another Boeing 737 crashed on to the M1 motorway at Kegworth near the East Midlands Airport in early 1989. When they viewed the site Eddie Trimble remembers remarking to another investigator that 'it didn't really look as though you could do too much about that particular type of accident from the point of view of survival'. When the plane hit the steep embankment of the motorway, the floor had collapsed and the seats had effectively gone through the floor. They were the latest seats which could withstand higher G-forces, but the floor was standard floor. ('One of the interesting things about Kegworth,' says Nora Marshall, who visited the site with other investigators from the NTSB, 'is that as far back as 1970 the Safety Board had been recommending increased seat strength, and this was the first accident we'd seen involving an aircraft whose seats had been designed to that higher seat strength.') 'At the time it was difficult to see how you could improve that situation, but we decided to have a look at the survival side. I was delighted that so many had survived, and I was particularly delighted that there had been no real post-crash fire – there had been a small one associated with the left engine, which was quickly extinguished by the arriving fire crew, but other than that, there was no problem. The wing tanks held pretty well. That was really a major influence on the survivability of the accident.'

Possibly the most unexpected effect has been on the treatment of survivors and the relatives of the victims, who previously felt – indeed were – excluded from the aftermath of a crash. 'At Manchester, we adopted the practice of inviting relatives and survivors down to the branch at a late stage in the investigation to spend a day with us, and I continued this after Kegworth,' says Trimble.

> To anyone who's not experienced accident situations, this might sound odd, but there is quite a strong compulsion in survivors and the relatives of those who have been injured or killed to see the aircraft. And they seem to get something out of this. Obviously, it can be quite poignant for perhaps twenty minutes or so, as you take them through and show them the aircraft, the seats where their relatives sat. But it's amazing that after half an hour or so, they do seem to get a tremendous amount out of it.

Yet for all the improvements, it still seems to people like Trimble as though safety is 'a little bit the Cinderella of the situation'. This imbalance needs to be redressed, in his view. 'A lot of people may disagree. They might prefer to have a TV in a seat back to being in a safer seat, he says. 'I think if you evaluate the options and choose the most cost-effective solutions, you end up spending less money for greater effect. It's a question of choices. But over the last fifteen, twenty years marketing seems to be leading the field in aviation, and the reasons for that are understandable. The aviation industry went through a very lean period for four or five years, and obviously marketing was very important.'

Perhaps passenger pressure might yet correct the imbalance. 'When the relatives of victims and the survivors of Manchester, who formed their Sci Safe, survivors' campaign to improve safety and airline-flight equipment, were called before a parliamentary committee on aviation safety, they were complimented on their depth of knowledge in these areas, which apparently exceeded that of a lot of the professionals who were called before the same committee,' says Trimble. 'So I think there are a lot of people among the travelling public who are quite capable of appreciating the issues involved, and of making an effective contribution to these debates.'

7
A System Too Far

There's an apocryphal story of a flight crew which put an automated airplane over Paris into a holding pattern and couldn't figure out how to change the programme to get it back out again. It's still there, three years later, with the crew trying to figure it out. On the ground they're trying to find a way to refuel the airplane and get some food to the pilots and passengers so they get it out of the holding pattern.

– Bob Besco

In the past technical improvements have served to increase aircraft safety, but now the limit in this respect seems to have been reached. Over the past few years a new generation of aircraft has emerged in which the computer has taken over much of the pilot's work: 'The computer flies the plane and the pilot flies the computer,' as Peter Mellor of the Centre for Software Reliability succinctly sums it up. Things have gone so far that the cyncial notion that instead of training pilots to operate computers, we should train computer nerds to be pilots is only half a joke.

In the past eight years the problems created by this increased encroachment by computers on the pilot's role have come to a head in the Airbus A320. This plane was introduced by the Franco–German–British–Spanish Airbus consortium in 1988 in a successful attempt to steal a march on Boeing, for the previous thirty-five years the dominant force in the world's commercial aircraft business. To reduce the cost of the aircraft, the fuel and the numbers of crew required to fly it, Airbus went much further in automating the flying process than ever before by introducing what is known as a flight management system. 'This is a kind of a machine partner,' says Professor David Woods, 'which rides in the cockpit with the flight crew and manages the flightpath of the aircraft. It's what the pilot talks to, giving instructions through a keyboard. This system is on all of the modern airplanes made by all the different manufacturers – the MD-11; the Boeing family, 757, 767 or the new 777; and the Airbus series, the A320 being the most notable. All of these flight management systems impose the same kinds of roles and challenges on the flight crew.'

But Airbus got there first, and partly for that reason, it is Airbus which has attracted the majority of the unfavourable attention accorded to modern flight systems, notably the ill-named 'fly-by-wire' concept in which the pilot has no direct physical contact with the operating systems. The A320 was the result of a long process of automating aircraft controls. Pete Mellor explains:

> On early aircraft the commands of the pilot were transmitted to the control surfaces mechanically via cables. On heavier aircraft these signals were transmitted electrically and caused hydraulic actuators to move. The important thing was that the pilot had ultimate total control over the way in which the aircraft behaved. With the A320, the electrical signals are still used to transmit the pilot's commands to the control surfaces, but in addition we now have a computerized flight-control system which oversees the actions of the pilot. The pilot's commands are still taken into account, but in certain circumstances the flight-control system will say no, you're not allowed to do that, and the pilot cannot exceed the limits set by the computer. Initially, this type of computerized flight-control system had to be used on military aircraft, because many modern military fighters simply cannot be flown by the pilot without the computer control system: either they are either aerodynamically unstable, or, when they're flying at low altitude, controlling the plane requires such quick reactions that they're beyond the reaction times of humans.

The introduction of such systems was inevitable, since only a computer can cope with the infinite number of variables involved in getting a modern aircraft from A to B. Moreover, the new systems made it possible to save weight, to make the modern planes quieter than conventional aircraft by using composite materials in their construction. Controlling the engines electronically is much more efficient than a pilot handling them manually. Maintenance is also made much easier by the automatic monitoring of all the systems on board and the recording of any minor malfunctions, which are printed out for the benefit of the ground engineers. Inevitably the systems have added an entire new dimension to the communication between man and machine which hasn't been part of aviation in the past.

The heart of the new system is the computer network which controls the plane. Mellor elaborates:

> The A320 actually contains about 150 separate boxes, each of which could be described as a computer in its own right. So in effect it's an aeroplane wrapped around a computer network. One particular problem with software is that when it goes wrong it tends to go very, very wrong very, very, quickly because software is a digital entity and the way that it behaves depends upon its logic and not upon the laws of physics, which are nice and continuous. If you make a slight change to a physical system, you expect a slight change in its behaviour, but with a computer system, a tiny change to the input can alter the output completely and totally wild things can happen.

Bob Besco makes an analogy which will be familiar to many and is hardly reassuring.

> When a pilot is flying one of the current sophisticated airplanes, it's very similar to what we do with our software programmes on our home computers. We ask the computer to complete a particular routine for us and it'll just crash and give us all sorts of problems. With an airplane, you think you've asked it to do one thing and it does another. But in the airplane you're on a very rigid time schedule. You might be about to run out of fuel. On the automated airplane we don't have the leisure that we have with the computer – put it on hold, go out and have a cup of coffee, get down the manual and read it some more.

This is not just a theoretical problem, as Mellor records.

> At Amsterdam in 1988, shortly after take-off, the pilots saw an error message displayed on their screens which indicated that they had lost most of the flight-control system. Then they got another message telling them that one of the main computers had failed, and yet another telling them that the hydraulics had failed. On each occasion they could see no actual evidence of any failures, and it was only when they got a message warning of lavatory smoke, and it turned out that there wasn't a fire in any of the toilets, that they decided they'd had enough. Then they found they couldn't get an indication that the landing gear was properly down, so they had to fly past the control tower and get the air-traffic controller to visually check that their gear was in position before they attempted a landing. This was all very alarming, even though the landing was perfectly safe.
>
> After another incident like that with a different plane shortly afterwards, it was found that there was a problem with the flight-warning computer, which filters all the error messages from the other systems.

Airbus did its best to reduce the likelihood of a software problem by providing what Mellor calls 'defence in depth against the failure of either the software or the hardware in any one of the five basic computers which make up the flight-control system.' Every individual computer is actually two separate computers, both of which are capable of performing the same function, but although the software in them is written to the same specification, it is actually written differently so that any faults in one set of software will not be present in the other. If they do not match to within a certain tolerance, the whole computer closes itself down and the other computers in the flight-control system take over the functions it was performing. In that way Airbus hoped that they had developed something which was reliable enough to be entrusted with the second-to-second flight of the plane.

'The regulations require that a system on board an aircraft can only fail in a catastrophic way, in other words, in a way which will crash the plane, at most once every billion hours,' says Mellor. 'With mechanical systems, it's possible to demonstrate this by well-tried engineering techniques, but with software, even if you test it for 100 years, you won't know that there isn't some very obscure fault still in there that is going to cause a failure shortly afterwards. The best you can do with software is to develop it as carefully as you can and then examine the process of development rather than the product itself.'

Although the design of the A320 was based on economic considerations and wasn't intended to remove the pilot from the loop, it was an inevitable result of the design philosophy. As Captain Heino Caesar of Lufthansa put it: 'For the first time in aviation history, pilots no longer had undisputed and direct access to the flight controls of the aircraft but were dependent on what the construction engineers programmed into the software of the steering computers. The pilot was in many aspects pushed out of the centre of the decision-making process.' Crucially, reducing the degree to which the pilot was – and felt – in control of the aircraft went against tradition, against the pilot's basic instincts.

The flight-management system (called the flight-management and guidance system by Airbus) has developed over the years to control the navigation of the plane. By the time the A320 was designed it became possible to programme in a route that the flight-management system would then automatically follow without the intervention of the pilot. In fact, says Mellor:

It is possible to envisage the pilot operating the plane by turning on the automatic pilot immediately after take-off, leaving the flight-management system to fly the plane through a predetermined route, taking optimum decisions to maximize fuel efficiency, and to land the plane in any weather conditions at the destination airport, without intervening at all. Of course, the pilot can always switch off the flight-management system and resume control of the plane, but even when he has so-called manual control of an aircraft like the A320, the flight-control system – the thing which, as one of my colleagues says, keeps the pointy end forward and the shiny side up – will actually prevent the pilot from doing certain things, like putting the plane into a stall attitude or a dive, or increasing the speed past the limit for which the plane has been designed.

Naturally, the less pilots have to do, the more bored they get. As one training captain described, increased computerization leads to 'a tendency to breed inactivity or complacency', which in turns leads to a sluggish grip on reality in a sudden emergency.

To complicate matters further, says Mellor, the computer systems contain different 'modes' for when the plane is on the ground, taking off, cruising or in the various stages of descent and landing. 'On descent below 50ft, the system goes into "landing mode", and below 30ft it begins to put the nose down automatically, he continues. 'As a result, the way in which the flight-control system controls the aircraft will vary between different periods of the flight. It will also vary if there is a failure on board. Then the system will automatically reconfigure itself to cope with the loss and may also change the control laws under which the plane is made to respond.'

This is the crux of the matter: the transfer of control between the human and the machine component; the breakdown in co-ordination, in team effort between the automation and the flight crew. Put with excessive simplicity the mode problem is that the computer may believe that it is set to behave as though the aircraft were landing, or climbing, while, for his own urgent reasons, the pilot wants to override this impression to ensure that it behaves in a different way. This may involve manouevres or changes of speed or direction incompatible with the computer's own mode. Of course, just as flight automation is nothing new, neither is mode confusion; for the pilot may not be entirely familiar with the limitations imposed by any particular mode. According to Bob Besco, the first mode confusion accident occurred in 1972, with the first generation of auto-mated aeroplanes. 'The flight crew of a Lockheed L1011 inadvertently switched modes and didn't realize it, because the only display they had was two adjacent lights of the same size, he says. 'One went off and the other one went on. If they didn't see the switch occur, they wouldn't be able to click out of their peripheral vision and see that they had changed modes until it was too late.'

But with the A320 came mode confusion in spades. 'If I enter the right value but the device is in the wrong mode,' says Professor David Woods, 'the automation says, "Oh, you want me to descend at this rate, not this angle." We now have a mismatch. The flight crew's expectation is that they're descending at a certain angle; the automation has taken the same input and acted on it differently.' The problem is not with either the system or with what Woods calls the human component. 'We have to see that these two parts work together as a single system, and we have to recognize that when these kinds of breakdowns occur, it is showing us that there is some kind of problem with the overall system and it requires a system fix.'

As Mellor points out, 'Because of this multiplication of different possible modes, it's difficult for the pilots to remember what the implications of the system being in a particular mode are in terms of the way that the plane will behave. So it's quite often easy for the pilots to confuse the modes, thinking that the plane is in one mode when in fact it's in a totally different one.' In some cases this can occur with only a minimal warning, in others without any warning at all, and can thus create delay in an emergency while the crew works out what mode they're in. The answer, says Woods, is the avoidance of what he calls 'automation surprises'.

The trick is keeping the pilot in the loop so that he knows what the automation is doing and is connected to the aircraft well enough not to be surprised when the machine no longer can handle what's happening. Eventually the crew notices that the automation is doing something that doesn't match their model of the situation. That's when a surprise occurs. Our data suggests that they usually pick it up when the aircraft behaves in an unexpected way – they do not tend to pick it up from displays about the state of the automation. If they only recognize it when the aircraft does something unexpected, it may be the case that they don't have the time to recover. For example, they may be lower in altitude and travelling much slower than they expected to be at this stage of an approach to an airport. Do they have the room and the time available to bring the engines up to higher power, to get the speed up so as not to impact on the ground short of the runway?

The inability of the pilot to override the computer system is exacerbated by the design of what are called 'glass cockpits' in which computer screens have largely replaced the system of dials which, however confusing they may appear to the layman, are the pilots' natural environment. In redesigning the cockpit without reference to pilots' earlier experiences, the designers may have thrown some babies out with the bathwater. Captain Heino Caesar uses the example of the old-fashioned analogue watch, one baby which has been saved. This has not been replaced by digital watches 'because they are difficult to read; they don't tell us at a glance what time it is'. However, other instruments have lost their clarity.

In earlier designs for each engine there is a row of indicators constructed so that in normal cruise, every pointer is pointing in the same direction. If one pointer is going out of the parallel, you see it immediately. But if you are descending in the A320, you see a little vertical-speed indicator which simply shows the tendency sink then the amount of sink – say, 3,300 – and you have to read it. A conventional vertical-speed indicator has the figures 0, 500, 1,000, 2,000, 3,000, and the pointer shows at a glance that you are going too steep. On the A320, you have to count the digits and say '33 – what is it?'

'We learned' agrees David Woods, 'how to design the flight instruments to allow people to get a quick assessment of what's going on – a check-read, it's called – through a quick glance or scan of the instruments. They can see if the airplane is doing what I expected it to do, or if there is a problem developing, so I know where to focus my attention.' He concedes: 'In the modern glass cockpit, as we put more and more information on the CRT screens, pilots have to read more. We have undermined their ability to size up at a glance what was going on.'

The problem of control is compounded by the absence of the mechanical linkages found in earlier generations of aircraft, which provided the pilot with the legitimate feeling that he was in charge of the plane. In earlier aircraft designs, says Mellor, 'if the co-pilot notices that something seems to be going wrong and the pilot doesn't seem to be taking action, he can move his column and the two pilots will then instantly be in communication, just by feeling that the other one is exerting pressure on the column. In the Airbus, where side sticks are in use, there is no linkage at all between the two. One of the crew can obtain control from the other by pressing a button, but there is no tactile linkage at all.'

By contrast, Boeing, which has the reputation of being much more pilot-centred, still puts the old-fashioned control column between the pilot's legs. He doesn't have to look at an artificial horizon or at his instruments, he just places his hand on the control column while he looks outside or talks to somebody else. He knows exactly what his aircraft is doing. 'In these advanced aircraft you have to pick up everything optically,' complains Caesar. 'You can't hear anything, you can't smell anything, you can't feel anything. You have to look at some instruments. Man is a 50,000-year-old piece of software, not designed to move in the fourth dimension, and we are depriving him of a very essential redundant sensory channel: the tactile one.' The whole set-up may be economical and logical from an engineer's point of view, but it is not says Mellor, 'what an ordinary, frustrated, fatigued pilot needs, understands and appreciates to make split-second decisions, especially under stress'.

In theory, increasing the automation of aircraft controls should reduce the pilot's workload, simplify his job, in effect deskill it. This creates the problem of what Professor Woods calls the 'substitution myth' – the common belief that automation eliminates the need for people. 'When we study worlds like aviation, what we find instead is that automation transforms the role of people. There is now a need for co-ordination between the people and the automation. Like any worker with his colleagues, automation needs to function as a team player.' Another part of the myth is that substituting a machine for people will mean less training. 'What in fact we've found is that it leads to different training. We need to spend less time on practising steep turns – the manual flying skills are not as critical. Instead, what we need to train is the judgement, because the pilot's role has shifted and he has become more of a manager of these auto-mated resources.' However, Mellor warns: 'There will be occasions when pilots will need their basic airmanship, and if those skills have atrophied because the computers are taking all the decisions, then they may not react instinctively by the seat of their pants when they really need to.' He likens the situation to trying to transfer to a standard manual-gearshift car when you have learned to drive in an automatic. Heino Caesar agrees. 'If a young pilot who has learned to fly on an A320 is given control of a relatively conventional plane – and we still have mixed fleets of conventional, electromechanical cockpits and very advanced automated cockpits – this will pose some problems. We will need more training, not less.'

The level of training required to fly an A320 as opposed to older aircraft has been increased. Inputting a new flightplan to the flight-management computer is a fairly complex task; it is also necessary to understand the different modes that the system can adopt and the ways in which the system, and thus the plane, will respond when one or more of the flight-control computers is out of commission.

Charles Huettner of NASA puts the most positive gloss on the development. 'Historically, the pilot's role was to physically operate the aircraft. Most of the computation, the decisions and so forth, went on in his head. Today the pilot has been elevated from the doer to the decision-maker, manager of the flight. He is controlling the aircraft, watching for the distance from other aircraft; planning the most efficient routes. He has taken one step higher in the authority level.' Woods phrases it less bullishly. 'The automation is a resource for you to manage, so we have a new skill.'

The attitude of the manufacturers towards the pilots merely exacerbated the problems involved in training with the A320. In one instance, cited by Heino Caesar, an instructor turned round in the seat, pushed in the autopilot and said, 'See, the plane is doing everything by itself. Any schoolboy can fly it.'

'Our captain stood up and said, "I'm not a schoolboy, I'm a trained 727 captain. In that case I do not need the training here. I'll go back to Frankfurt and fly your crate." And he left the simulator. It was only then that they realized how ridiculous and dangerous this statement was. Yet their own people trained pilots to operate the aircraft like that.'

In the context of air-crash investigation, the result of the dramatic changes introduced by Airbus and, to a lesser extent, by Boeing, has been to make the cause of accidents even more confusing than before. Bob Besco says: 'Today, every time we have an accident with an automated airplane, the design community will say that it was possible for the crew to have told what mode they were in. But there is a reasonable chance that a busy flight crew might perhaps have been handling other emergencies.' Woods quotes a pilot talking about a typical incident: 'Both of us were engrossed in trying to figure out why this computerized marvel was doing what it was, rather than turning everything off and manually flying the aircraft until we could sort things out.' As Mellor confirms, many of the fatal crashes involving Airbuses – and not just the A320s – have been ascribed to pilot error.

But in every single case an objective reading of the reports reveals that more than simple pilot error was involved. To start with one must always ask why the pilot made the mistake. What was it that confused him? Was he adequately trained? All these accidents also involved some element of mode confusion. In all cases it's possible to say that the plane and its systems were behaving as they should have done, but if the system leads the plane into a dangerous situation, then something is wrong with the way that system has been specified.

What Woods, like most of his fellow-experts, was too tactful to spell out was that the troubles with the A320 were exacerbated by the French habit of furiously denying the existence of a problem while at the same time working equally furiously to sort it out. This attitude is another reason why the Airbus series in particular has been the focus of criticism aimed at the new flight systems. In the eight years since the A320 was launched in 1988 it has been involved in at least five accidents, as well as numerous other 'incidents' in which man and computerized machine have clashed. In several of these the Airbus has unaccountably reared up during the approach to landing and then stalled. The trouble was that although the computer was doing what it was supposed to, the pilot was either not sufficiently trained or aware enough to work out what the plane was doing.

The earliest example occurred at Habsheim, near Mulhouse in eastern France when an A320 crashed on a demonstration run on 26 June 1988. The crew had initiated a low-speed flypast, but failed to pull up to clear trees at the end of runway. The crash was blamed on cockpit confusion over altitude, but outside observers claim that the onboard computer believed the aircraft to be landing, and thus was in landing mode. Consequently it took too much time for the engines to throttle up to avert the crash. The A320's onboard computers have since been programmed to maintain more power on the final approach.

Unfortunately, the whole investigation was marred by a series of rows involving the investigators, the French authorities and the pilot, Michel Asseline, on such points as the height of the trees into which the plane crashed, the possibility of altimeter failure, the theft of some television film of the accident, the engines' alleged poor restart rate at low altitude, and the fact that the CVF and DFDR went off four seconds before impact.

The next accident came in February 1990, when an Indian Airlines A320 crashed 4,000ft short of the runway at Bangalore after a flight from Bombay, killing ninety of the 146 people on board. This disaster spawned another clash of opinions. The Indian investigation suggested that the aircraft's sophisticated landing system was incompatible with the facilities installed in Bangalore. Airbus said pilot error was to blame. Mellor believes that the two pilots unintentionally got into the wrong mode for some reason: 'They got into a mode which kept their engines at flight idle, they were not aware that that would be a consequence of this mode, and they didn't react to it until it was too late.' A further dimension was provided by one well-placed observer who maintained that the Indian pilot was to blame, and his error was not Airbus's fault. 'He was a very weak person. We know that, because training captains had flown with him on 737s. He was far below average and he was released by Airbus on condition that he had continuous training in India. He never got that training, and he crashed because he didn't know how to operate the systems.'

The most publicized of the crashes happened on 20 January 1992, when an A320 belonging to the French domestic airline Air Inter careered into the Vosges

Mountains on a domestic flight from Lyons to Strasbourg, killing eighty-two of its ninety passengers, and five of the six crew. The tragedy highlighted problems at Air Inter over and above those normally associated with the introduction of the A320. The airline provided less training to pilots of the A320, and was the only major airline in the world operating it which at that time had no GPWS installed. The pressure on pilots was increased by what Heino Caesar calls the 'hurry-up syndrome'.

> In today's competitive conditions, airlines rely on reliability, and passengers judge reliability by punctuality. But in a domestic network with very short sectors, like Air Inter, it is very difficult if not impossible to make up for lost time. It can only be done in flight, and the tighter the airline's schedule, the greater the pressures on the pilot to arrive on time. So pilots try to fly straight in whenever possible – every circle around costs at least five precious minutes – to shift the burden. There's an old saying that it's better to be a few minutes late in this life than several years early in the next, but that is not always appreciated by the pilots – or the passengers.

Air Inter could not say that it had not been warned. A month before the crash, a confidential report by a French official body had predicted that 'a serious accident will occur with an A320 in the near future'. The three Air Inter pilots who compiled the report denounced the airline's cover-ups of earlier problems with the A320, including a 'brutal' landing at Grenoble a month earlier. The report went on to criticize inadequate maintenance and overwork of crews. The French official report after the Strasbourg crash, although predictably circumspect, gave the game away. At Air Inter the considerable problems created by the A320 had been compounded by union resentment at the linked introduction of two-man crews. By 1992 the A320s were no longer manned by volunteers and, as the report put it, many of the conscripts were 'less motivated and more reticent regarding the change', notably from the Mercures and Caravelles that were being phased out. Moreover, the airline had 'no organizational structure exclusively devoted to flight safety' and because of the tensions between unions and management, the information gathered from previous incidents involving the A320 was not widely circulated. As a result flights resulting in 'major anomalies' were not the subject of inquiries. The official bodies concerned had not been informed either, but had in any case never carried out a general inspection of the airline, and none of the fleet of A320s had been inspected in four previous years. More technical inspections were hindered by the union's refusal to allow on board inspectors who were not qualified captains.

The report also tackled the heart of the matter: the way the crew had changed their flightplan to avoid any delay to the flight. Echoing Heino Caesar's words, the report stated that Air Inter's short flight times made it 'very difficult to compensate for delays . . . Adherence to timetables is perceived as being of prime importance in the culture of the company and forms a crucial part of operational organization.' Crew members were made aware of the added fuel costs brought about by deviation from the flightplan. In the years before the crash, the competition from France's new ultra-fast trains, the TGVs, had added to the emphasis on punctuality. The report also hints at possible tension between the pilots. The pilot of the doomed plane was a little slow and had learned to fly advanced jets only at a late stage in his career, while the co-pilot could be a 'little condescending towards people he felt were slower to understand than himself'. Could this have included the pilot? Certainly, since the crash, Air Inter has made sure that the captain on all A320s has spent at least 300 hours on it, partly because there had been three previous crashes involving pilots with less than that level of experience. Moreover, Air Inter, which, until the Strasburg accident had been the airline which stuck most closely to the Airbus Industrie philosophy of depending utterly on the computers, subsequently changed their policy.

The authorities' initial reaction was far less forthcoming – astonishingly so, according to a local television journalist, Jean-Pierre Stucki. When he and his crew arrived at the nearest village, they say they saw 'hundreds of men in uniforms near the *gendarmerie* and the fire station not doing anything – just waiting'. Unable to get any official information, Stucki spoke to the villagers, who told him that people had heard the crash at seven o'clock. Others said that there was smoke and the smell of kerosene in the forest. 'By following the smell, it took us under a quarter of an hour to find the site.' They were naturally surprised at the absence of any rescuers. Just a few minutes later, 'we heard some voices calling and discovered the survivors around the fire. They were badly injured, some of them, and asking desperately for rescue.'

The first rescuer to arrive – a quarter of an hour later – was a *gendarme* whose initial reaction was to ask Stucki and his crew to leave the scene. There was total chaos. No one knew exactly where or how they could help. 'The first survivor to be taken away from the site was a little girl of eighteen months. A *gendarme* took her in his arms to an ambulance on the road and then, little by little, the survivors able to walk were evacuated.' But it took hours to rescue the more seriously injured, and in the meantime at least two people had died.

When Stucki started asking questions the first reaction of the authorities was fury, on the grounds that he was trying to denigrate the efforts made by the rescuers. But then Stucki discovered that they were lying about relatively simple facts: for instance, claiming that it had been a stormy night. He also found that the army had known the exact location of the accident for some hours but hadn't guided the rescuers there. He naturally concluded that this was the result either of administrative chaos or a desire to keep an accident to the A320, France's aeronautical pride and joy, under wraps. Stucki believes that the French administration was deeply worried about the possible commercial consequences of the crash. In addition they believed that no one could have survived it, so, in

The roll-call of 'Busby's Babes' – the Manchester United football stars killed in the Munich crash of 6 February 1958. *(Popperfoto)*

Despite the appalling weather conditions, the German authorities refused to accept that these had anything to do with the Munich crash. *(Popperfoto)*

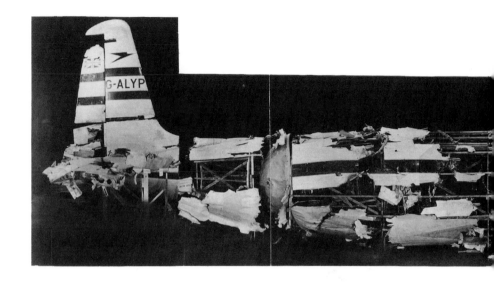

Above: The first reconstruction: Comet G–ALYP in the hangar at Farnborough, in the summer of 1954. *(Royal Aircraft Establishment)*

Below: The aftermath of the Trident crash at Staines in 1972. *(Srdja Djukanovic)*

The crumpled cargo
door on the DC10
involved in the
'Windsor Incident' of
June 1972.
(Corbis-Bettman/UPI)

Above: The tragic crash of the plane flying the Axbridge Ladies' Guild on a special outing to Switzerland in October 1973. *(Popperfoto)*

Below: Rescuers carry the body of one of the 345 victims of the Turkish Airlines DC10 crash in a wood outside Paris on 3 March 1974. *(Popperfoto)*

Above: Ice floes on the Potomac: rescue workers towing to shore the remains of the Air Florida plane which crashed into the river on 13 January 1982.
(Popperfoto)

Below: A hillside strewn with wreckage: the remains of JAL Flight 123, the Boeing 747 which crashed near Mount Osutaka, Japan, on 12 August 1985.
(Popperfoto)

Firefighters at the site of the 1985 Manchester crash.
(Eric Shaw/Press Association)

The remains of the Boeing 737 which crashed on 8 January 1989 on the M1 at Kegworth, a few hundred yards short of East Midlands Airport. *(Popperfoto)*

Above: The problems of recovering wreckage from the Valu-Jet Flight 592 plane which crashed into the Florida Everglades on 11 May 1996. *(Popperfoto)*

Below: The press in action at the NTSB headquarters in Washington after the recovery of the CVR from the Valu-Jet plane. *(AP Photo/Mark Wilson)*

Greg Feith of the NTSB examining the wreckage collected from the Valu-Jet in a hangar at Tamiami Airport, Miami. *(AP Photo/Hans Deryk)*

his view, 'The first priority was maybe not to rescue but to put a cordon around the place and control the situation, maybe with a judge, with an official inquiry, with Airbus people coming very quickly.'

Two hypotheses for the disaster soon emerged: the first, that the crew were using inaccurate charts, has now been eliminated; the second, that the crash was a result of a misunderstanding between the pilot and the computer system, merely confused the whole issue.

Subsequent developments did nothing to help. The DFDR was destroyed, and the CVR was only 80 per cent usable. The quick-access Recorder, installed by Air Inter 'for maintenance', contained no trace of the last seventeen seconds before impact. The crash was first investigated by an eleven-person commission which included a pilot only after the union threatened to go on strike. Even after the report was published, the arguments and legal challenges involving the victims and the authorities still continue.

In early 1992 IFALPA held a conference on the A320 and suggested a number of improvements, including reduction of cockpit noise, a rearrangement of certain buttons on the autopilot, better indicators on the autopilot, better cockpit lighting, low-speed warning noise, better screens, HUD during landing and more visible instruments. But still the problems continued. On 14 September 1993, a Lufthansa A320 piloted by Hans-Jorg Hansen, chief instructor on the A320 and the longer-range A340, overshot the runway and hit an embankment at Warsaw. Hansen and a passenger were killed. The crash was caused by the plane's computer failing to register that the aircraft had landed because the second wing undercarriage had come down much later than the first. It didn't help that the weather was appalling, with high winds, pouring rain and bad drainage off the tarmac. Indeed, Airbus thinks aquaplaning was the most likely cause of the accident.

The worst accident involving an Airbus, in this case one of the earlier A300s, was the crash of a China Airlines flight on 26 April 1994 at Nagoya Airport west of Tokyo following what the *Los Angeles Times* described, with journalistic licence but not inaccurately, as 'a terrifying battle between an inexperienced co-pilot and his airplane's super-sophisticated computer system'. Of the 271 people aboard, 264 were killed.

The lead-up was simplicity itself. The plane was being flown manually on approach to landing by its twenty-six-year-old co-pilot. About two minutes before touching down, the A300 went into go-around mode, for reasons still unknown. Even though the pilot had warned the co-pilot three times in thirty seconds, as witnessed by the voice-recorder, the co-pilot continued to attempt to land the plane. The upshot was that the autopilot was trying to pitch the nose up while the co-pilot was trying to pitch it down. The crew then switched the go-around mode off, but the stabilizer flaps remained set at a sharp angle. The crew, realizing that the plane was too high to land, put the go-around mode back on. This caused the plane to climb sharply and approach a stall. The A300 stall-prevention system automatically increased the engine thrust, but this merely increased the climb angle to 53 degrees. Unfortunately, the aircraft couldn't increase speed quickly enough. It stalled, the nose dropped and the airspeed increased to 150mph at an altitude of 800ft. At this point, the entire electrical system, including the flight data and voice-recorders, stopped functioning, again, for reasons unknown, and the plane crashed.

There had been four similar but non-fatal incidents before Nagoya, but in this instance apportioning blame was complicated by the fact that the pilots failed to follow normal, explicit procedure for controlling the aircraft, and that they had both been drinking alcohol. In the event, members of the senior management of China Airlines took the blame and resigned, leaving Airbus to face the biggest lawsuit in aviation history – because of the nature of Japanese law, the plaintiffs are entitled to claim $2.8 million (£1.9 million) for every passenger.

In August 1996, an official Japanese report admitted that the crew was inexperienced and lacked adequate knowledge of the aircraft's system, but also recommended that Airbus simplify its instruction manual and the design of the control lever.

Yet still the accidents continued. On 30 June 1994 an A330 aircraft crashed while testing emergency procedures, killing all six of those on board, including Nick Warner, Airbus's chief test pilot. Three months later an A310 belonging to the Romanian airline Tarom was involved in an incident at Orly Airport. It was on landing approach when it climbed sharply before entering a 4,500 ft freefall. The preliminary report by the French investigators suggested that the aircraft was approaching Orly faster than it should in theory have been, given the positioning of the flaps at the time. This discrepancy caused the automatic system to reduce speed, which in turn sent the aircraft into climb mode. The dive resulted from the crew's failure to identify the reason for the change and quickly restore the approach angle. Six months later in March 1995, another A310 belonging to Tarom crashed at Bucharest, killing sixty people. The plane was taking off manually but the engines were in automatic mode. The preliminary investigation showed that as the flight moved from take-off settings to climb settings, the right engine failed to reduce power in accordance with the computer climb model. Manual attempts to correct this were unsuccessful; in fact they made the situation worse, since the computer programme continued to reduce power to the left engine in response to overthrust of the right. This caused the aircraft to yaw to the left and fly into the ground.

In January 1995 there was another overrun at Warsaw which echoed the Lufthansa accident fifteen months earlier – even though the plane had been modified to solve the problems revealed by the previous disaster. In July of the same year an A320 had a bounced landing. Because of the bounce, the plane was in mid-air, but the computer decided it was landing and deployed the spoilers, which brought it crashing to earth, hurting nobody but severely damaging the plane.

Airbus was still struggling to amend its instructions when, on 27 April 1995 an A320 operated by North-West Airlines experienced uncontrolled roll while on its final approach to Washington National Airport. It was found that the roll was due to pilot-induced oscillation, thought to be a result of a pilot unfamiliar with the feel of the plane overcontrolling it with the sidestick controller. Other pilots of A320s had experienced similar problems and Airbus had addressed the problem in a temporary revision. The French authorities had received the revision in 1993 but had decided that no further regulatory action was needed. Since the revision was merely advisory, the FAA did not check whether it had been properly distributed and absorbed. As a result, it was interpreted and disseminated in different ways by the US operators. North-West made no changes to its operating manual, while America West put the information into the 'adverse weather' section. The NTSB, however, concluded that the information had not been effectively disseminated and was concerned that 'other useful and perhaps critical information of a similar nature is not being effectively communicated'.

Over the years Airbus had been struggling to adapt its systems to the habits of real-life pilots, but until the death of test pilot Nick Warner the company's engineers could legitimately dismiss accidents as the result of mistakes by pilots. But Warner was what the French call a 'golden boy' and the fact that even he had been unable to override a software error until the plane was too close to the ground finally brought home to Airbus the need to train pilots to be able to override the automatic systems much more easily.

Even before the Warner crash, Airbus, while not admitting its mistakes, had made changes, softening the rigorous automatism which marked the early days of the A320, and ended up with systems and training routines which should ensure that this splendid aircraft – and the other long-distance members of the Airbus stable – will continue to take a considerable share of the world market from Boeing. In the meantime Boeing, despite its deserved reputation for having a more crew-centred approach than the Airbus planes, has had its own problems with its automated aircraft.

Indeed investigators as a group hesitate before attributing problems to the A320 in particular. 'We've seen accidents to Airbus aircraft, we've seen accidents to Boeing aircraft and McDonnell Douglas and other companies,' says Dave Miller of the AAIB. 'I don't think Airbuses are any more susceptible to accidents or serious incidents than any other aircraft. It's just that sometimes the public perception of a problem relates back to the latest accident, the accident that's fresh in the press. But accidents very soon become yesterday's news.'

The Boeing automation is significantly different from Airbus's, from the ground upwards. The 777 flight-control system uses a different machine architecture and has a fundamentally different mission requirement, governed by the use of a different interface. Yet in the case of the Boeing 757 which crashed at Cali in Colombia early in 1996, the FDRs clearly revealed the same sort of problem generally associated with the A320 – confusion in the cockpit in the minutes before the crash while the pilots reprogrammed their computers. It took the captain a minute and a half – an eternity in a crisis – to enter the necessary change of direction to enable him to fly over the approach beacon, and not, as actually happened, into the hillside. But the computer was programmed to turn the aircraft slowly so as to minimize the inconvenience to passengers. When the crew tried to use a different computer they were already too low. They regained manual control a mere and totally inadequate eleven seconds before the plane crashed, killing all 160 people aboard.

For all the changes now being made, many respected observers believe that a total rethink is needed; that the pilot should be returned to the centre of what was once his universe. In Heino Caesar's words, 'The machinery must be constructed around the two men in the cockpit, so that these human beings can understand it, can handle it and feel comfortable with it. The A320 is a step too far. It overloads the human being with certain features. Of course, every man can be conditioned for every workplace, however odd it may be. It's just a matter of expenditure and how much energy and time you invest.'

Bob Besco asserts: 'We need to start by asking what the flight crew needs to have in the way of support to accomplish their mission.' Even more important is not increased pilot training, but 'drastic changes in the type of training that we've been giving'.

> We've depended on automation being learned while people were flying a line. I think that before a pilot is turned loose on the travelling public on an automated airplane, he has to demonstrate that he can accomplish all the manoeuvres in emergency conditions. It's been said many times: you're better off designing the airplane right in the first place rather than trying to correct bad or the deficient designs with extensive investments in training. There's an old adage in the design business: to err is human and to forgive is by design.

8
Diamonds in the Dust

There's been a marked increase in BFOs recently. For BFO, read Bits Falling Off.
— A (not surprisingly anonymous) engineer

Even the best-designed aircraft need maintaining, and it only takes a few casually tightened bolts, or a failure to replace a broken spar, to cause the most appalling of crashes. Possibly the biggest danger is posed, not by bad maintenance, but by the results of the vast and profitable trade in stolen or fake parts. As one engineer put it, 'I know people who quit running drugs and switched to aircraft parts because it was more profitable.' There is also a brisk trade in old parts that are simply shined and re-sold to the airlines, a practice known as a 'strip and dip' operation. Unfortunately, the responsibility for detecting the traffic is shared between the authorities, the manufacturers, and the airlines, all of whom suffer from the effects of unsafe and defective parts but prefer to keep quiet about it. Among the most recent incidents resulting from this world-wide scandal was the explosion of an engine on a plane which exploded – fortunately before take-off – because the compressor disc was cracked and corroded, the result of shoddy maintenance.

When the worst happens, however, the investigators have often been able to find the vital clue – the 'diamond in the dust' – through the equivalent of searching for a needle in a gigantic haystack which may sprawl over many miles of countryside or water.

Modern planes are so reliable that major overhauls are not deemed necessary until after the equivalent of 1,000 days and nights of non-stop use. Every sixty flying hours, however, they are thoroughly checked for signs of external wear and tear, and every 400 hours every system in the plane is examined. But the failure of a relatively minor component or inadequate maintenance can often be exacerbated by a series of errors. The results are totally unpredictable: a major crash, such as Japanese Airlines flight 123; a crisis compounded by a series of misunderstandings in which only superb flying saves the aircraft, as in the Air Canada Boeing 767 incident of July 1983; an even more dramatic crisis in which even the greatest skill can only soften the impact, as with the Sioux City disaster of 19 July 1989. In the case of the loss of a Lockheed TriStar in the Florida

Everglades in December 1972, the failure of a tiny component, together with a succession of minor mistakes, escalated into a catastrophe.

The Everglades crash was important, not only because ninety-nine of the 176 people on board perished, but because it was the first accident involving a wide-bodied jet, and one which confirmed their underlying strength as well as the problems posed by new equipment. The crash was triggered by a faulty lightbulb, or, to be precise, by faulty filaments in two lightbulbs which should have indicated that the plane's undercarriage had been successfully lowered for its approach to Miami Airport. When the lights failed to come on, the crew immediately tried to check whether there was anything wrong with the bulbs, but they couldn't get to them. So the flight engineer went below to the electronics bay – what specialists call the 'hellhole' – where he could see for himself whether the undercarriage had been lowered. In the meantime the plane had gone into a holding pattern some 2,000ft above the airport while they concentrated their attention on the possible fault.

Unfortunately, as he turned to speak to the flight engineer, the captain had pushed lightly on his control wheel and had inadvertently disengaged the altitude-hold function on the autopilot. The aircraft started to lose height without the captain being aware of the fact – largely because he and the rest of the crew were still obsessed by the undercarriage. Even then the TriStar might have been saved. The control tower at Miami was aware that the aircraft was descending away from the airport towards the swamps of the Everglades, but at the vital moment the controller was distracted by having to deal with a query from another aircraft. According to a senior investigator, the controller later explained his failure to warn the pilot with the excuse that he had intended to, but the pilot's voice was so calm when he asked him how he was doing that he figured the pilot knew what he was doing.

> The controller added that pilots resent it when controllers try to climb in the cockpit and fly their airplanes. This is nonsense, and it was nonsense then. It wasn't typical at all of the training and conduct of most controllers, who would have said anywhere along the line, 'you're descending – what are you doing?' This controller said nothing, though he must have seen the plane continue to descend below 900ft, and down to 300ft. At 300ft he's lost on radar, there's no target at all. By then he would have been within seconds of impact in the Everglades. Any words of warning would have alerted the pilot and everything would have been fine. But it was a lot of little things that just built up into a disaster.

An even more extraordinary sequence of small mishaps and misunderstandings afflicted an Air Canada Boeing 767 flying from Montreal to Ottawa and Edmonton in July 1983. And it was no coincidence that, like the TriStar, this was a new type of aircraft. A total failure of the fuel-gauge indicators was only one of the teething problems confronting the plane. In his book *Emergency*, Stanley Stewart wrote that the MEL (minimum equipment list) on the newly introduced 767 was incomplete. Many items were blank and alterations were constantly being made to it. 'In the few months since the 767's introduction, over fifty changes had been made. The list was not considered reliable and it was Maintenance Control's practice to authorize flights contrary to the MEL.'

In addition to these difficulties, there were misunderstandings between the pilot, Captain Pearson, and the mechanics over the exact condition of the fuel-measurement system and the plane should not have been allowed to take off. Nevertheless, with the gauges out of action, the fuel would automatically be tested manually using a dipstick. Unfortunately, the 767s were the first planes in the Air Canada fleet in which the gauges were calibrated in kilogrammes. The maintenance personnel calculated the quantity of fuel required in litres and converted litres into pounds instead of kilogrammes. They then measured the depth of the fuel in centimetres and translated that, correctly, into litres, but again used the wrong multiplier, converting litres into pounds, not kilogrammes. The crew, too, miscalculated the conversion factor, so the plane carried only 22,300lbs of fuel, less than half the 22,300kg he thought he had on board. The upshot was a forced landing in a disused airfield near Lake Winnipeg which, luckily, Captain Pearson's flight officer knew, having spent the previous summer there. They were even more fortunate that the nose wheel collapsed as the plane landed and thus halted it just short of the end of a runway which was at the time being used as a racing-car circuit and which housed a whole village of caravans and camper vans. Ironically, it was the very lack of fuel that necessitated the landing that prevented a major tragedy, since although the front of the aircraft continued to emit clouds of black, oily smoke for some time afterwards, there was no fire.

This is not the only example of incidents caused by fuel shortage. Four years earlier, a Boeing 747 had been forced to make an emergency landing at Newark Airport south of New York because of a discrepancy in the fuel gauges and an error in what is known as the fuel-management chart. It left the aircraft seriously short of fuel when it was diverted from Kennedy Airport because of bad weather. In another instance, mechanics had fitted the wrong type of O-ring oil seal, which had disintegrated in flight, allowing oil to be pumped out under pressure.

Over the past twenty years a handful of the crashes caused by maintenance errors have enabled investigators to throw light on specific problems (and thus to improve safety thereafter) and have also showed the art of air-crash detection at its most ingenious.

By 1979, the DC10 had recovered from its earlier dramas, and no operator was happier with it than American Airlines. The only thing that bugged them was the amount of time and man hours it took to change engines. So, on their own initiative, the airline worked out another system, with the co-operation of

McDonnell Douglas and the FAA and shared the new procedures with other airlines.

But then, on 25 May, one of the airline's DC10s crashed as it was taking off from O'Hare International Airport in Chicago. The disaster, which killed all 273 people on board, was then, and fortunately remains, the worst aircrash to have taken place on American soil. Because of the plane's previous history the news brought an immediate reaction, included the grounding of all DC10s operating in the United States. But it did not take long for a remarkable piece of detective work on the part of the tin-kickers, combined with what one can only call serendipity, to clear the aircraft itself of blame and pin it instead on the improvement in the engine-maintenance system devised by American and approved by all concerned.

By the time the investigating team reached the scene of the crash, it was pretty obvious from the witness reports that during take-off and the initial climb the engine and the pylon which connects it to the wing had separated from the left wing. Shortly afterwards the plane was seen to roll to the left and fall straight into the ground. The cause of the separation wasn't immediately apparent, so the investigators looked at the engine and the connection with the rest of the plane. They found some fractured bolts, and then discovered that the rear bulkhead of the pylon was also fractured. The part was immediately sent to Washington for analysis by Michael Marx, the NTSB's leading metallurgist.

In the meantime, Bud Laynor and a colleague had gone to American Airlines' maintenance base in Tulsa, Oklahoma. According to Laynor, they learned that there had been some previous damage to the aft pylon bulkhead which had been identified by another airline that was using the same procedures as American Airlines.

That caused us to look a little bit closer at whether this pylon damage pre-existed at the time of the Chicago accident. When we identified that it had, we noted that the fracture of the aft bulkhead was consistent with the flange on the bulkhead having struck the mating part on the wing, producing an overload crack in the centre which then progressed in fatigue until the final fracture. As soon as the FAA got wind of the problem, they immediately asked for an inspection of that particular part of the pylon structure in all the other DC10s, and they found a few that had not yet failed where they could see overload damage in the centre of the flange on that aft bulkhead of the pylon, which had been through the same maintenance procedure. Those airplanes were, of course, immediately taken out of service until they were repaired.

Meanwhile, Laynor and his colleague had made the discovery that solved the whole problem. Laynor tells it in the deadpan fashion characteristic of the tin-kicker, which somewhat removes the drama of a discovery comparable, in the context of the history of air-crash investigations, to the apple falling on Isaac Newton's head.

When we got to Tulsa it just happened that they had an airplane in the hangar on which they were performing this airworthiness directive. We knew that the AD compliance required you to remove the pylon from the wing. On the DC10 the pylon is attached to the wing and the engine's attached to the pylon. The original procedure for accomplishing the airworthiness directive called for the airlines to remove the engine from the pylon, which meant disconnecting all the umbilicals between the engine and the pylon assembly, removing the pylon from the wing as a separate unit, accomplishing the airworthiness directive and then installing it back the same way, pylon to wing first, and then engine to pylon.

We learned that some of the carriers had improvised, or come up with another procedure that they considered more efficient. This required you to remove the pylon and engine assembly from the wing without separating the engine from the pylon first. It was a considerable time-saver, because they didn't have to disconnect and reconnect all the umbilicals for fuel, electric and pneumatic systems and suchlike between the pylon and the engine. In doing this they used a forklift placed under the engine to support its weight and the pylon, and then they removed the pins from a forward and rear bulkhead-to-wing attachment and lowered the unit as an assembly, which saved a lot of time. The procedure had been approved by the FAA. Continental Airlines was using the same procedure, and they had found after removing the engine that there had been some damage to the aft bulkhead structure of the pylon. They had identified some parts that had been cracked because the engine had rocked when they removed the forward pin, and as it rocked, the aft bulkhead flange came into contact with the mating part on the wing structure.

A colleague and I went out to the hangar and saw how it was done, and it became clear that you could indeed cause this kind of damage if the engine did rock on the forklift, and that there would be some rocking involved if the engine wasn't supported directly under its centre of gravity. And it would be fairly difficult to position it so precisely that it wouldn't tilt one way or the other as you dropped the forklift.

Once they had actually seen a forklift truck handle the assembly in the way they suspected it would, the penny dropped, so they called Michael Marx in the materials lab at the Safety Board's headquarters in Washington, who had the parts from the crash for examination. 'We asked him to focus his attention on this aft bulkhead part, because we thought that there could have been some pre-existing damage which could have weakened the structure and ultimately caused it to separate.'

Until the phone call, Marx had been puzzled by the evidence, especially when he examined the faulty part under a powerful microscope.

There was evidence of a crack, as if something had impacted and caused a crack in the pylon, and then there was evidence of progression from the crack as a result of cyclic stress or fatigue. This was very perplexing, because normally when you look at a fatigue fracture, what you see is a problem that initiates in fatigue and progresses in fatigue and then grows into an overstress. What we had here was kind of the opposite – an overstress which was a large area, and then the fatigue that had progressed.

Then came Bud Laynor's crucial phone call. Laynor told Marx that if he saw any unusual damage to the aft bulkhead mounting structure, particularly in the flange area, which indicated that it might have struck the mating part on the wing hard and fractured in overload initially, he should pay close attention. 'Mike became somewhat excited at that point, because that was exactly what was puzzling him. The kind of damage that he did see on that part did indicate that there was a possibility that the aft bulkhead flange had been struck by some part or had struck some part before the failure started progress in cyclic fatigue and then became so weak that it broke,' remembers Laynor. 'So at that point we focused very heavily on that as the initiating factor for the pylon and engine assembly separating from the wing during take-off.'

In a sense it was a disaster for which no one was directly responsible. As Bob Besco says: 'At American, we felt that American had taken a point of leadership to correct a maintainability question that derived from the initial design, and so should have been Douglas's responsibility. In fact some people went so far as to say American was the only one doing it, which wasn't true. Other airlines were using that same change procedure, and cracks were appearing in the pylons of DC10s from other airlines at the same time.'

Many of the most terrible accidents arise from failures of the hydraulic control systems on a plane. The danger is well known; indeed, the hydraulics are recognized as so crucial that they are carefully protected, and indeed duplicated (or, in the case of the 747, 'quadruplicated'). But in certain unhappy circumstances they can all be disrupted, as they were when the cargo door of the DC10 flew off over Paris in 1974. Eleven years later came an even worse disaster, again caused by the failure of the hydraulics.

Until the advent of the 'super-jumbos' it is, fortunately, unlikely that any crash involving a single aeroplane will cause as many deaths as the crash of Japan Airlines flight 123 into a mountainside seventy miles from Tokyo on Monday 12 August 1985. The reason for this is very simple: the flight involved a Boeing 747 specially adapted for Japanese conditions to act as a commuter jet – capable of carrying over 500 passengers – 100 more than an ordinary 747. Indeed Flight 123 from Tokyo to Osaka, thirty-five minutes away, was carrying 509 passengers and fifteen crew, but only three passengers and one off-duty stewardess survived.

JAL 123 was twelve minutes into its flight when a bang was heard on the flight deck. In one of the great understatements of all time, the captain told air-traffic control: 'Immediate . . . ah, trouble.' He and the crew had lost control of the aircraft because the hydraulic systems were no longer working. For over half an hour they struggled, without knowing exactly what had happened or that, in the absence of hydraulic controls, they could have stabilized the plane using differential thrust from the engines (although neither they nor anybody else had been trained how to do so). Ron Schleede, the investigator sent to Japan by the NTSB, explains.

> They flew this airplane in various circles, climbing: descending and circling, out over the water, back over land. Even though they kept it airborne for thirty-two minutes, they weren't really in control. They'd add power on one side, and the airplane would turn; they'd add a lot of power and speed up, and they'd climb. We don't know how they eventually lost control, but I know that in the end they clipped the top of this mountain, and at that point the accident was inevitable. It was probably inevitable anyhow.

Yumi Ochiai, the off-duty stewardess who was one of the few survivors, was sitting at the rear of the plane. She remembers the Boeing 747 going into a *hira-hira* – literally falling like a leaf.

Bob Besco relates that the gyrations resulting from the loss of the controls were probably more extreme than you'd find on the wildest amusement park rollercoaster ride. 'They were not only up and down like in a rollercoaster, they were like some of the more modern rides, where you get turned from side to side and roll and yaw and pitch.' Finally, the right wing tip clipped the side of Mount Osutaka, and three seconds later the rest of the plane crashed on the next mountain ridge so violently that it destroyed over 3,000 trees. Although the crew did not have time to explain their predicament, many of the passengers were able to write farewell notes to their families which were recovered after the accident.

The whole country was mobilized to help in the aftermath of Japan's worst air disaster. Unfortunately, their helicopters could find nowhere to land, yet a US Army helicopter about to lower rescue personnel was told to return to base because, they were told, Japanese rescuers were on the way. The crash was at dusk. Because the US machine left the scene and no other choppers arrived before dark, operations only resumed in the morning. From Ochiai's testimony, it appears that several survivors died during the night. There was also a lot of administrative confusion among the various authorities involved, which delayed handing over some of the wreckage because it could not be moved from one part of Japan to another.

When Ron Schleede and his colleagues arrived they found the aircraft wreckage strewn over the mountainsides. 'It was very difficult getting down to the site', he says. 'We had to use ropes in certain areas because of the steepness, and there was jagged metal all over the place. The tail section was at the very bottom of this steep gully. We had difficulty getting there. Our helicopters missed the site the first time because of poor visibility and communications. Later, poor Schleede, who doesn't like helicopters at the best of times, was nearly involved in an accident himself when the one in which he was flying had to make a forced landing due to problems with hydraulic fluid.

The scene of the crash was typically Japanese – and not only because of the mountainous terrain. 'All over the site there were little religious shrines that had been built. They build them with little stones and things piled up, a keepsake – a medal or something, a ring – and a picture of the person. There were offerings there too, food and fruit, remembers Schleede. 'While we were there, they were bringing the family members in big white Chinooks and dropping flowers on the accident site. I was told there were over 5,000 people on the mountain the first day I was there.' He describes the early stages of the investigation.

> When we first got to the accident site we were escorted by Japanese accident-investigation commission people. Initially, the Japanese were reluctant to have Boeing there, but we assured them that we always worked with them and we were able to convince them that we needed Boeing's expertise. The only stipulation was that the Boeing people had to stay very close to us. They couldn't wander off. The Japanese were very courteous – there was a language barrier, obviously, but they helped us get to the bulkhead area. Besides the broken metal and everything there were hundreds and hundreds of thousands of empty film cartridges, and boxes of Fuji and Kodak film. The media had been there in tremendous force. I don't know how many pictures must have been taken.

Yet the police seemed to have relied on the work of an artist, who spent days methodically drawing the aft bulkhead with colour pencils. The investigators already knew from the survivors and the crew's radio communications that there had been a structural failure in the tail area. 'We didn't go back the next day. We were wiped out, we needed a day of rest, but we studied what we knew and some of us knew we had to focus on that tail,' recounts Schleede.

> One of our team was a fractures mechanics metallurgist, Tom Swift, who worked for the FAA. He didn't go to the accident site – he wasn't the type. When we first got to the rear bulkhead, it had been laid out slightly in its original shape, in several pieces. We knew that was the place to focus, because the surviving flight attendant had told people about this tremendous explosion, and then, she said, she looked up and out and saw the sky from her position in the aft part of the airplane. One obvious point was the way this thing had torn, virtually in a circle, from its mounts. We refer to it as a saw tooth, where it pulled out from

the rivets under tremendous force. The edges were all saw-toothed.

We didn't really know what we were looking for for sure, we just knew that that's where it had happened. The saw-tooth fractures were an obvious feature; there was another section in the seam that was a straight failure, and that raised a question right away that there might be fatigue or a problem. That's not how metal normally fails.

Seven years earlier the bulkhead had been repaired at Osaka by Boeing engineers after the tail had struck the runway while landing. The resulting bump had damaged the back half of the plane, including the aft pressure bulkhead.

Schleede and his team studied the repair documents and came up with some theories. 'One was that the rivets hadn't been put in properly. If instead of two rows of rivets taking up the two pieces of metal, there'd only been one, it would have had only half the strength.' Swift soon worked out the number of times you would have to stress the join before it would break. 'His calculations,' says Schleede, 'were within 5 per cent of what that airplane had actually flown since the repair. We just knew that if this metal wasn't put together right it would fail about the predicted amount of time this airplane flew. So the next day, when we went to the accident site, we definitely focused on the tail.'

We went down and studied the seam in the bulkhead which had been repaired in depth, but all we had was a little hand-held 30-power magnifying glass and our cameras and our eyes. It became obvious all of a sudden that this joint had been put together improperly. There was supposed to have been a splice when they repaired it, and therefore three rows of rivets.

Instead of replacing the whole bulkhead, Boeing had merely replaced half of it. In doing so, when they put the pieces back together again, they allowed a single rivet line to carry the loads, thus increasing the stress along a certain rivet line in the bulkhead. Every subsequent take-off and landing was a 'pressure cycle' which steadily increased the stress at these rivet lines. The way the repair had been carried out caused tiny cracks to form and grow. The initial design of the airplane allows for failures to occur in a portion of the bulkhead, with straps to keep it from progressing too far. But in this particular case all the cracks linked up simultaneously and blew the whole bulkhead out. This in turn caused an overpressure into the tail, which blew the tail off and severed all the hydraulic control lines into the tail. The aircraft would still have been flyable if they had had the hydraulic systems, and so the recommendations were obvious: to try to preserve the hydraulic systems in case of a catastrophic failure such as this.

Trying to explain all this to Mr Fujiwara, the chief Japanese investigator, was a problem because the interpreter was technically unqualified. Schleede drew pictures of the failure on the back of some of his business cards.

I drew for him the way the joint that was in question should have been designed, how it was put together originally – two pieces of metal lapped over with two rows of rivets holding it together. Then I took a second business card and I talked about the repair and I showed him how the repair was supposed to have been made, with the two pieces of metal that didn't quite match at the ends so that they had to put a third piece in between, a splice with three rows of rivets. On the third card I drew how it had actually been repaired. Then he understood, and we went back and looked. The bulkhead was right there in front of us. We looked at it, held it up.

The two pieces of metal didn't quite come up tight enough to put two rows of rivets in. The splice had been cut short and had not gone all the way through, so that even though there were three rows of rivets, one of them only took up two pieces of metal, and there wasn't a double taking 'em up. That joint was the one that failed.

Our senior metallurgist, Mike Marx, was on holiday fishing at my cabin up in Canada. He left the next day for Tokyo. I called him that night and told him I needed to get him in the lab early. We got there around six and I brought in the pictures I had taken. He could tell that there was fatigue on those fractures. That was confirmation: we knew that it had failed and we knew it had been improperly riveted; now we had actual fatigue of the metal that would tell us that it did in fact break and fail. Boeing's structural engineer, who was there, reacted as you would expect. He was very upset, because this repair and this design and everything was his responsibility at Boeing.

Every structure on that airplane is supposed to crack only at a certain distance, and then it hits what they call a crack-stopper. It's supposed to turn 90 degrees and then flap open; then you lose pressurization in a controlled fashion. It's called a failsafe design. In this case, because the defective joint was some 30ins long, the fatigue damage went beyond the crack-stoppers, so when it failed, rather than ripping and then turning, it shattered like a plate. It just blew up. When it failed, all the air had to escape out through the tail. The blow-out panels couldn't handle this tremendous onrush of air which travelled up the vertical fin and pressurized it. Then there was a second boom when the aft portion of the vertical fin blew off. This contains the upper and lower segments of the rudder, which is powered by hydraulic pressure. All four hydraulic systems on the 747 were plumbed back to this area, and all four of 'em came up this spar in the vertical fin. When this thing tore off it opened all four hydraulic lines, the fluid dissipated very rapidly and all of the flight controls were inoperative. So the airplane was virtually uncontrollable, ailerons – elevators, rudders: nothing would work.

To an outsider, the most amazing part of the story is not the eventual failure of the rivets, but the fact that even the bodged repair was strong enough to survive 6,500 take-offs and landings. Even then, the failure would not have been fatal but for two other unfortunate coincidences: that the weakness of the repair was undetectable, and that the repair happened to run across more than one of the bays in the bulkhead. This is shaped like an umbrella with individual ribs preventing any crack or split from blowing out more than a small single bay of about a hand's width.

Although Boeing immediately took full responsibility for the accident, the chairman of JAL offered his resignation, which was accepted. Boeing later settled all the liability cases, which satisfied a peculiarly Japanese sense of fitness and retribution. Bob Besco had gone to Japan to work with the law firm representing the victims some three or four months before the trial came up. 'The father of one of the young girls who had died in the airplane had been waiting in the office to talk to me and thank me for helping him put his daughter's soul at rest. He felt that it was his responsibility to make sure that things were set right so that his daughter would go to his religion's equivalent of heaven, because she had died an unnecessarily wrongful death at the hands of someone else. It was a way of him paying retribution to her to make sure that her soul was at rest.'

For Ron Schleede, too, there was a poignant postscript to the Japanese disaster. Ten years after the accident, an official from the Japanese Ministry of Transportation visited the NTSB's laboratories and produced a photocopy from Mr Fujiwara of the three business cards that Schleede had written on, with the little drawings of the joint. He'd attached his own business card and a note written in English saying, 'I'll never forget our time on the mountain: Mr Fujiwara.'

Like the JAL crash, the Windsor incident (described in Chapter 12), the Paris DC10 disaster, and that of another DC10 at Sioux City, Iowa in 1989 were caused by a failure of the planes' hydraulic controls. Yet of course, even accidents resulting from the same failure are different. And whereas the JAL accident was caused by faulty repairs to the tail, the Sioux City crash resulted from a failure in the engine. Moreover, thanks to the extraordinary skills of the pilot, also related in Chapter 12, the Sioux City crash caused 'only' 112 deaths, and 184 people were saved.

The tin-kickers get early warning of an accident. 'We heard about United 232 while it was still airborne,' says Bob McIntosh. 'The FAA command post had gotten a call from the folks in the centre in Chicago that the aircraft was diverting to Sioux City. We were informed of the total hydraulic failure and, recognizing a large transport aircraft with hydraulic controls, we knew that was serious trouble. My boss told me to go ahead and mobilize the go team and to be prepared to launch.' Waiting for their flight to the scene in a lounge in a hangar, the team saw the DC10 on TV, somersaulting down the runway. 'En route we contacted a couple of the air-traffic control stations to ask about the conditions, and when they informed us of survivors we were really shocked. From what we'd seen on TV we really didn't expect anyone to have survived.'

Mike Marx found that the hydraulic systems were damaged. When the investigators reconstructed the tail section, they found that they were missing the fan disc, which had literally spun out of the number two engine. The disc had broken off while the plane was flying at around 37,000ft and so could have landed anywhere over a wide area. Worse, the airport was in the middle of the biggest corn belt in the world. As the song goes, 'The corn is as high as an elephant's eye' in Iowa as well as in Oklahoma. When Marx strayed into a field of corn (what the British call maize) off the runway of a disused airfield, it was well over his head – this was July. 'I walked about 50ft into the cornfield, made a left turn and then looked around. I couldn't see anything, the corn was so high.' They even had problems finding bodies.

The investigators were told by the locals that the disc would be found fifty days later, when the corn was harvested, but they couldn't wait. They calculated where it might have landed and searched for it with infrared cameras, but to no avail. The engine manufacturer, General Electric offered a reward, a gimmick which initially worried the investigators. Mettallurgist Jim Wildey points out that the part should have been easy enough to spot.

The disc itself was a 300lb titanium forging, and on top of that there were these fan blades that stick out. The whole thing is very big, very heavy. You would think that you could walk up and find them. The Safety Board performance engineers conducted an analysis of the possible trajectories of the pieces, and identified a very probable area. In fact this was where the fan-disc pieces were found.

They flew over the suspect areas with helicopters. 'You can imagine,' says Wildey, 'the tops of this corn moving in the breeze created by the helicopter. It wasn't like going to one area where there was a 3ft hole.' The wind from the helicopter blades swished the corn around, and the corn itself had natural gaps in it, so they couldn't assume that any hole they spotted was going to be where the disc piece was.

In the event the locals were right. The disc was found by a farmer who was ploughing up the corn three months after the accident. Janice Sorenson, who farmed in the area with her husband, Dale, was combining corn with the John Deere combine, which takes six rows at a time.

I knew immediately when I saw it and felt it what it was. I backed up and could see it protruding out of the ground. General Electric had been asking the farmers in this area to keep their eyes open for it, and it was great to have found it. They certainly needed it to get to the bottom of the crash. I went back to the house and then Dale came with the tractor. I phoned the sheriff and they came and picked it up out of the ground.

They had the deputy sheriff and everybody here at the gate. Nobody else could come in, because they had it very well protected. They didn't want anybody else there. They took it up to our turkey sheds and washed it off. Then they took it to Storm Lake that night and put it under lock and key, and then next day a jet flew into Storm Lake to take it away.

The incident provided the Sorensons with a classic case of the Warholian fifteen minutes of fame. With all the cameras around, 'It felt like the White House,' said Janice at the time. Much later, Dale was pleasantly surprised when a man in Arizona who had heard the story came up and hugged him.

Jim Wildey was one of the team which examined the disc and visited the General Electric unit responsible in Nevada, and the forger's factory in Ohio, and carried out a number of different tests to pinpoint the source of the problems.

In my profession it is quite an exciting thing. Here you have a large titanium forging that's made into this big rotating part, spinning at thousands of rpm, and it fails. Now it's my job to go in and find out where the fracture started. To find out how the fan disc broke, it's simply a fractographic examination, and that means looking at the surface of the fracture. On the fan disc, the features were very easy to read. There was a radiating pattern that emanated right from the hub of the disc, and in that area we could see there was a pre-existing fracture region that had caused the fracture in the fan disc.

The metallurgical evaluation showed that there was a fatigue crack first of all which stemmed from a pre-existing defect in the material, called a hard alpha inclusion – meaning that a very brittle and very hard defect inside the material caused the disc to fracture. In this case the inclusion was caused by nitrogen during the original melting of the ingot material that is used to create the titanium for the disc. The ingot is then turned into a billet, which is sliced, and each of these slices becomes a giant forging for these titanium parts.

Obviously, the titanium is frequently inspected during the manufacturing process but unfortunately this defect was just under the surface and the inspection techniques used were not capable of detecting it. During the investigation, says Wildey, 'they found some anomalies in the record-keeping.

When the billet is cut up into pieces, each piece is assigned a serial number. When we searched through the records, we found that there were two discs with the same serial number, one of which had been rejected at the time of manufacture. The second disc with that serial number was the one involved in the accident. So the suspicion was that maybe they had rejected the wrong disc, or maybe they accidentally took out of service the one that was good and left the one with the defect in it in service. Records from various sources showed that the one that they took out of service was the one with the defect found during the inspection process, so we don't think that there was a mix-up with the parts themselves. There was a problem with the serial numbers and the way these parts were kept track of. You have to realize that, in terms of the maintenance records, we're talking about something that happened eighteen years before the accident, so I think it's pretty nice that they have all the detailed records they do. But there are glitches in the system. Things like this happen. Now we have computers to keep track of more of this, but at that time it was all done on cards that had to be stored, filed, and kept for eighteen, twenty, twenty-five years, so there are going to be some problems.

Once the fan disc was assembled into the engine, it should have been inspected by the airline involved. As it turns out, the disc from the engine that broke had been inspected by United 760 flight cycles before the accident occurred. The Safety Board concluded that there was a detectable crack in the disc at the time, but that it was not detected. Part of the reason was the manner in which the disc was inspected and the simple difficulty of manipulating a large disc. There are other factors, too: at the outer rim of the disc, into which the fan blades are inserted, they move and create little disturbances along the surface. When the disc is inspected, sometimes these create what appears to be an indication of a defect and the inspector has to go in and verify every one of them, so he has to spend a lot of time on the rim of the disc. But this defect was on the inside of the bore, in an area that you really have to look right into. One of the problems with inspecting is that you have to do this over and over again, and there's always a possibility that certain defects might be missed.

One of the things the Safety Board would like to see is a requirement for fewer inspections. We'd like to see parts replaced with new parts instead. There are always going to be problems with the human factors issues associated with inspections. Did the inspector get enough sleep? Are the lighting conditions correct? and on and on, because frankly it's a pretty tedious job to go down a whole row of rivets or to look at every single square inch of the surface of a fan disc to make sure there are no cracks.

And indeed, since then greater automation in the manufacturing process has reduced the need for inspections, which have themselves been simplified. But what remains is a sense of amazement. 'It's a bit mind-boggling,' says Michael Marx, 'when you think of the size of the engine, the size of the airplane, the magnitude of everything that transpires there, that something as small as a metallurgical flaw the size of even a small grain of sand could bring it down. But that's the reality.'

More generally, the JAL and Sioux City crashes resulted in an attempt to preserve the hydraulic systems in the case of a catastrophic failure by introducing a fuse into at least one of the hydraulic systems to preserve it in a pressure blow-out or a severance of all the hydraulic lines. At least one of them would then be preserved so that it could be used for operating other hydraulic systems to maintain flight. And since these disasters, NASA has been experimenting with methods of controlling planes purely by using differential engine power.

Of all the accidents caused by maintenance problems, the one that sticks most persistently in the public's mind, as a result of the pictures and TV images beamed round the world, occurred on 28 April 1988, when an 18ft section of the top of the fuselage of a Boeing 737 belonging to Aloha Airlines ripped off at 24,000ft, just like the top of a sardine tin. Miraculously, only one person, an unfortunate flight attendant, was killed, and the plane managed to land safely at Maui Airport in Hawaii.

At the NTSB, the first reaction was one of sheer disbelief. Tom Haueter remembers thinking, this person can't possibly be reporting this right. 'We thought it must be a much smaller hole. Then they started describing this huge hole in the fuselage through which passenger rows were clearly visible. It was unbelievable. As we got more reports back, it was clear that this was something very unusual.' At first there were rumours, as so often, that a bomb had gone off, but this theory was soon ruled out because there had been only one fatality and a bomb, however small, would have caused far greater damage.

When Jim Wildey and his colleagues arrived in Hawaii, they found the plane was sitting there off the runway for all to see.

Of course, they had painted out the name of the airline – the operators often do that because they don't want an advertisement for their broken airplane – but you could see that the roof was ripped off. It was sitting there just like in the pictures, and we all looked at it, just as all the tourists did as they landed and taxied down the runway. I was wondering what the tourists must be thinking when they landed and saw this airplane. It's something you never usually see. You think of airplanes as these nice, gleaming white bodies and here's one with its guts ripped out, or in this case the roof ripped off.

Wildey, who was responsible for examining the structure, and his colleagues from Boeing and the FAA started going over each portion of the fracture in detail and making notes.

You can see rips in the skin and all kinds of rivet pull-out patterns and things like that. We were trying to find where the structure was broken and where the fracture might have begun. First of all, we were a little bit worried that because almost all the structure from the roof area had been lost, we might not be able to determine the cause of the fracture, but the big breakthrough came as we were looking around the perimeter of the break. We found a string of rivet holes that had fatigue cracking in them and we could also see that the lap joint in that area was disbonded and there was corrosion there. This gave us our first big clue as to the conditions that might have caused the accident.

Of course, everyone was pretty excited, and eventually we all started to learn about the history of the cracking problem. With the people from Boeing we talked about the airworthiness bulletins and service bulletins issued by the manufacturer and the FAA, and eventually we got where we could understand what happened in the Aloha accident in relation to previous history, and how this had affected or led to the conditions that allowed the accident to happen.

We also visited Aloha's maintenance facility in Honolulu. We found that a lot of their airplanes had corrosion damage and cracking problems. Once the airline started going through their fleet with a fine-tooth comb, they realized that the corrosion problems were relatively severe. Eventually they took four airplanes out of service, including the accident airplane – Aloha decided that it was not economically feasible to try to repair all the damage.

Tom Haueter takes up the story.

Around the rivets it looked like a tufted pillow. You could see where the rivets were indented, almost because the corrosion was pushing the metal away. Originally, the lap was designed to be glued together and then riveted, and so it was quite clear that the glue joint had failed and that the metal pushing around the rivet was causing additional stress that would be causing cracking in that area. During the investigation, we found that a lot of the lap joints on the 737s were disbonded and had corrosion. Boeing had made an angled or bevelled hole to have a flush rivet head, and that gave a nice smooth aerodynamic look to the outside of the airplane. But it also created a little knife-edge corner where a recessed rivet hole intersected the inside surface. As a result, when the environmental condition caused the lap joint to become disbonded, all the stress was now being pulled through the rivets, and as the stress was introduced along the rivets, into the rivets and into the skin, the knife edge there created a perfect point for fatigue cracking to initiate. And with each cycle of pressurization, the skin would be pulled again and again, and eventually cracks would develop along a whole series of these upper rivet holes. What we found in the Aloha plane was that there was undoubtedly cracking in a whole lot of these rivets, and that basically they just fractured right along the upper rivet line of the tenth stringer on the left, the whole roof section pulled up and went on both sides of the airplane and fell off away from the airplane.

As the lap joint comes down, this piece of skin has got an edge which should be sealed. There would be another piece underneath here, but this joint could allow moisture and water to get in. In addition, as the airplane climbs to high altitude, it gets cold and you get condensation, so there's plenty of opportunity for very small amounts of moisture to get in. Once that happens the corrosion starts.

But it wasn't the corrosion that was the problem so much as the stress on the rivets which caused the cracks.

Every 10ins, the 737 had a series of crack-arrest members or stress-reducing members. The theory is that if any damage or cracking develops, a crack could run a short distance, enter an area where the stress is reduced, and then turn. This would create a flap of material that could open up and relieve the internal pressure in the airplane. It would depressurize, the stress would mainly go away and you wouldn't have a catastrophic accident. In the Aloha accident, each of these little bays between these crack-arrest members had cracking, and when a crack started to grow and get larger it decided to jump over the crack-arrest member and enter the next bay. It just kept doing that from bay to bay, and so it got around this design feature of the 737. This phenomenon is called multiple site damage. If you have cracking in a whole lot of features in a row, the whole thing can basically unzip along that line.

The team also found that the disbonding problems were known about before the accident and that in fact Aloha was one of the airlines which had found a relatively large crack in the stringer ten left lap joint, and had reported it to the FAA and to Boeing, which had issued service bulletins. These were then adopted into airworthiness directives. Unfortunately, the directives only required an inspection along the top two lap joints, along the top centre of the plane, and did not include the lap joint that eventually caused this accident and Aloha had only done what was required by the airworthiness directive.

Confirmation of their ideas soon came with 'a diamond in the dust'. During the investigation, one of the teams interviewed witnesses, including of course all the passengers, many of whom were in hospital. One short Japanese woman told the investigators that she had seen a crack as she was boarding the plane before the flight below the eye-level of taller passengers. It was not until Jim Wildey was returning from Hawaii that it was finally realized that this piece of evidence might be important. He was asked to drive down to San Diego with another investigator to find the witness. They took her out to an aircraft at San Diego Airport, walked up the steps and asked her to show them what she had seen and what she had done about it. She told them that she had seen a crack about 6ins long with a space in it that was pretty obvious to her. She'd motioned to the friend with whom she was travelling to come back. They had both looked at it and then, unbelievably, had proceeded to get on the plane and sit down. 'We asked her, "Why didn't you tell somebody about this?" and she said, "Well, we thought that this was known and that they knew what they're doing." So they didn't say anything to anybody, and of course just a few minutes after they took off, the roof comes off. We think this was a sign of the cracking that was occurring along the stringer ten left lap joint.'

The heart of the problem lay with Aloha which, as Wildey points out, 'did not have an engineering department, only individual engineers. By contrast a larger airline might have engineers capable of understanding the best way to maintain the airplanes in relation to how they were being used.' Haueter adds:

> Their mechanics came from a maintenance school where many of their mechanics taught, so they were getting an infusion of personnel that were already trained, if you will, in Aloha's practices. They also had mechanics of different nationalities and backgrounds who tended to cluster together a little bit. There were cliques which didn't communicate so well outside their groups.
>
> A couple of weeks earlier, the FAA had come in and conducted an examination of Aloha and their maintenance, and subsequently Boeing came in, at the airline's request, and did another one. We got copies of both groups' reports, and it was almost as if you were reading about two different airlines: one group was looking purely at records and the other was actually looking at the airplanes. From the maintenance records and the forms for the airplanes, you'd find that everything'd been accomplished perfectly, everything was up to date. But Aloha had broken down their maintenance schedule into fifty-two increments, so instead of the airplane coming in for one major inspection, it came in for little inspections over a longer period of time, which made it a little more difficult to track what they were doing. When Boeing came in and did their inspection, they actually went to the aircraft and opened up panels, looking at the whole general condition of the fleet.

When Haueter started to look at the maintenance records, he found that a sister plane with a similar flying record to the damaged one was in the hangar at the maintenance base, providing a unique opportunity to inspect Aloha's procedures. Although the records were in order, when he started looking at the aircraft he could see corrosion around the lap joints, and the massive amount of work that had been accomplished to cure the flap-joint corrosion and to rivet the airplanes.

> They were replacing belly skins on the sister ship for corrosion. The upper lap joints were also being de-riveted, the corrosion removed and re-riveted. An airplane's a tube, and you have to maintain its rigidity, so to keep it from buckling with these skins off, they had constructed a

wooden scaffolding to hold the plane straight while they took them off and put new skins on. I had never seen anything like that before in my life. It was kind of an eye-catcher, this airplane sitting there with these massive wooden beams holding it together while this work was going on.

I was intrigued by this process. I got to watch the cleaning-up of a lap joint where they were drilling out the rivets in a lap area, lifting the middle apart and then using sandpaper and a stick to clean out the corrosion. Spray in some corrosion sealant, then rivet the section. I had never seen this before.

And as it turned out, when the bond broke between the glue joint, the corrosion clean-up was good, but you needed to know how much material thickness you'd lost in the area; you needed to put in larger-diameter rivets with larger heads to get rid of the stress risers and things like that. All these little findings later became critical to the investigation.

The FAA's airworthiness directive for the inspection of the upper lap joint rivets was carried out by literally crawling down the upper portion of fuselage, held by a safety rope, with a high-power light and a glass, looking at one little rivet after another and checking for cracks around it.

This is a very tedious procedure, and very difficult to accomplish, especially if there's repainting over the area. One thing the airworthiness directive did not do was require inspection of the lower lap joints down near the door area, and the subsequent investigation found that the crack that started the chain of events began there. Interestingly, the way I interpreted the wording of the initial airworthiness directive, it said that if you found cracks you had to replace rivets in the entire lap joint area for the length of a panel, which was about 12ft or 15ft long. When they read it other people thought you only had to replace rivets where the cracks were found. Finally, I had to get about three or four different lawyers involved to give me an interpretation of what this airworthiness directive intended.

The NTSB's report naturally concluded that the primary problems leading to the accident lay with Aloha's maintenance. The airline's flight pattern for its 737s was probably unique, since it was using them on a very large number of very short flights – up to eighteen a day for each over the plane's twenty-year life. This accumulated a large number of cycles of pressurization stress. But Aloha was still basing its maintenance largely on the number of *hours* the airplane had flown and not, as they should have done, on the numbers of *take-offs* and *landings*. The damaged plane had accumulated the unbelievable number of 89,680 take-offs and landings, a total exceeded by only one other 737, which also belonged to Aloha. As a result, says Haueter, 'while the airplanes were low on time, they were high in cycles, which are more destructive to an airplane than hours'. After the Aloha accident this factor was obviously taken more seriously, as was the fact that additional inspections to check for corrosion problems were required on older aircraft. The findings really shocked the industry. 'The Aloha investigation was a bit of a milestone in terms of the ageing aircraft issue,' says Haueter. 'Since then there've been massive ageing aircraft programmes to take a look not just at 737s but all transport-category aircraft to make sure that as they get older they're receiving the proper maintenance and inspections. It was not even considered when the 737 was designed that it would be seeing over 80,000 cycles, or flying for over 50,000 hours.'

Boeing, too, took note of the findings. The bonding process they had been using was relatively new, and the NTSB discovered that it was not necessarily being carried out consistently to ensure that the bond wouldn't degrade over a period of time. Even before the Aloha accident, Boeing had found that environmental conditions, especially moisture and salt air, were causing a disbonding problem, which has been solved on later 737s.

9
In the Bleak Midwinter

There's an old gentleman, he's ninety-three years old now, Jerry Leatherer. He wrote a paper more than fifty years ago, and in those days state-of-the-art advice was that ice was going to kill you.

— Rudi Kapustin

The stresses imposed by ice and snow provide the sternest of tests for both pilots and planes, which sometimes, inevitably, they fail, with fatal results. Since Leatherer's time, of course, a number of sophisticated de-icing fluids have been developed, but even they can only protect an aircraft for a limited period. Rudi Kapustin, a former NTSB investigator admits that, 'It's a really lousy subject for me to address, because I get pretty upset about it,' but points out that these are just interim protective measures. 'The bottom line is, when you're in an airplane, you've got to go out there and look and see if the air form is clean. Sometimes at night this is not possible. If you don't know whether it's clean or not, you don't go.' Mike McDermott says: 'There comes a point where you have to stop operations or continue with certain precautions, every once in a while those precautions aren't followed, and we lose an airplane.'

'Every once in a while' happened most dramatically on 13 January 1982, and, what is more, within a few hundred yards of the NTSB's offices. An Air Florida Boeing 737 crashed into the 14th Street bridge over the Potomac River shortly after taking off from Washington's National Airport, killing seventy-four of the seventy-nine people aboard (and, incidentally, in the process breaking a record period of twenty-six months during which American commercial airlines had not experienced a catastrophic crash).

It was snowing, and because of the weather, the two men who were going to end up being responsible for investigating an accident in their own backyard were both hanging around the office, unable to get home. Rudi Kapustin, then in charge of major aircraft accidents, was off duty, but had come in just 'to do some housekeeping work cleaning up the office', which had just been moved. At 3pm the colleague with whom he shared a car suggested that they should leave. Kapustin persuaded him to wait because the traffic was so bad, as is always the case in Washington at the fall of the first snowflake. News of the crash came as they were about to start for home. Kapustin originally assumed that it was 'some little airplane which had decided to take off in snow and ice'.

I never thought it would be an air-carrier airplane. I said, yeah, well it's too bad, as I stood waiting for the elevator. Before we got into the elevator, someone else came out and said, 'We think a 737 has hit the bridge so, don't go anyplace. I said, 'Well, I'm off, I'm not on duty.' It just so happened that the investigator in charge who was on duty, Captain Montgomery, had left early. He lives in Fredericksburg, and he was on a train. They said, 'Montgomery's gone – you'd better take this.' So that's how I wound up being in charge of the investigation. It was kind of a fluke.

Ron Schleede's reaction to the delays caused by the weather was somewhat different, though he too knew that it was going to be difficult to get home. 'That winter we'd already had one four-hour trip to get home seventeen miles.' But he'd decided to go to a local watering-hole called Dankers with some colleagues for a drink.

There were several car pools there, including my car pool from the NTSB, and there were people there from the FAA. It was packed three deep at the bar. As I ordered a drink, I heard something on the television and someone else told me that a plane had crashed in the Potomac. My vision was that it was a Cessna, which was noteworthy, but didn't affect me because I was involved in big airplane accidents. We have a local office that would handle a Cessna. Very shortly thereafter a bunch of pagers started going off, phones were ringing and this fellow was hollering for someone from the NTSB. One of our fellows, Jerry Warhol, got on the phone. He came back and said that an Air Florida 737 had crashed in the Potomac on take-off.

Well, we were two blocks from the Potomac or from the waterfront, so we knew we had a big problem. We didn't have mobile phones or anything with us so we left immediately. Fortunately, Rudi Kapustin got a police escort to the other side of the bridge and started organizing the investigation from there. I was in the director's office handling phones and the vice-chairman came round the corner with a couple of other people and told us we had a train accident in the metro station near the Smithsonian. In those days the metro was fairly new and had never had a serious accident. So now we had two major accidents near us within less than an hour. Several surface investigators then went down into the metro station below our building and walked through the tunnel to the Smithsonian station to work on the train crash. In the meantime, our people got on the bridge and to the command post but at that time there was a rescue going on, so we weren't really conducting an investigation. There were people literally being pulled out of the river and we were just getting prepared for the investigation.

Ron Schleede adds: 'Without the park police there wouldn't have been any survivors. They were out with their helicopters on a day when they shouldn't have been out. It was a life-threatening operation from the time they cranked up the helicopters till they got back.'

The investigators were obviously under considerable strain. Schleede says:

You can't imagine what it's like to run an investigation of this magnitude in Washington, within eyesight of the Congress and virtually of the White House. It was a very highly charged scene. The fact that this airplane crashed leaving the airport where the White House, the Congress and all the senior government officials fly in and out of made it the highest interest. It was a tragedy in its own right, sure, and if the plane had crashed at La Guardia or Chicago it certainly would have had high intensity – the NTSB is always in a worldwide fishbowl on a major accident – but this was right in the backyard of the Department of Transportation.

Rudi Kapustin takes up the story.

One of the first people I saw out there was Drew Lewis, the secretary of transportation. Someone pointed me out to him. I had dirty work clothes on from doing this janitor work in the office, and he came over and said, 'Rudi, I really appreciate the work you're going to have to do on this thing. Here's my card. If you need any assistance from any of the segments of DOT' – which includes the coastguard and FAA, of course – 'call me directly. This is my twenty-four-hour number. You can get me through the command centre.' I said, 'The other number is Weinberger's.' He was secretary of defense at the time. 'That goes for him too,' he said. 'We just came from a meeting with the old man,' which was President Reagan, so I guess they had direct orders to provide absolute maximum support. And the case was unique from that viewpoint. I've never had that kind of technical and logistic support. The coastguard was in there with all the resources, the army, army transportation, navy divers. It was pretty impressive; it was almost awesome, in fact. Some areas had too much support – in other words, too many people. That kind of set the scene for the whole investigation.

Inevitably, there was also intense media interest, with up to forty camera crews at the crash site at any one time. This was where the Safety Board members came in useful. Schleede says:

Frank McAdams was our Safety Board member, and did just a beautiful job of giving daily briefings and took that off my back. Once the story got out that the engine pressure ratio was wrong, rumours came up through anonymous sources that it might have been sabotage, that somebody had put chewing gum in the PTT probes. I immediately turned it over to the FBI, and of course they checked it out, found out who had made the allegations and gave 'em lie-detector tests. It turned out to be just rumours and idle talk by a couple of mechanics, but it could have really disrupted the investigation if it had made the headlines. Fortunately, we were successful in containing it.

Because of the appalling weather conditions, one of the first things Kapustin did was to make sure that he confiscated the security de-icing equipment and got fluid samples. The de-icing trucks were impounded and tested; the logs detailing how much fluid was used obtained. Then his operations group got to grips with the basics: weather reports, clearances, dispatch releases, gross weight of the plane, the qualifications and background on the crew. 'Then of course we had a separate meteorology group. Crash-fire rescue became a big issue because at that time Washington National Airport tried to get boats out there and they got stuck in the ice. My human factors group started interviewing witnesses and ground witnesses, but not the few survivors, because they were in no shape to be talked to.'

Meanwhile, the pieces were being recovered by the US Army, helped by the coastguard, the Navy and the heroic park police. The investigators then turned their attention to the wreckage. The Army engineers made plots of the pieces that were under water. Schleede remarks:

> The press got all excited about the fact that the black boxes were very difficult to locate, but then, as Rudi says, they get excited about anything. We knew it was going to take time – it's mud and silt under the water – but we found them. The one thing that everybody was concerned about was that there was a little baby they couldn't find for a couple of days. They finally found the body. I happened to be out there when the diver brought it up and handed it to another police officer. Everybody had tears in their eyes. It was one year old, I guess or even younger. If something like that doesn't affect you there's something seriously wrong. But you can't get distracted from what you have to do.

The investigators didn't know exactly why the engines weren't producing full power. It took a little more analysis to determine that the probe was iced up. But ice can also affect the wings, and that was a factor here. 'We had investigated similar accidents in the past,' says Schleede. 'I personally worked on an accident in Boston involving a British Redcoat air cargo that had taxied and taken off in virtually the same conditions – heavy snow. It taxied for about thirty or forty minutes, took off, staggered for a while and mushed into some trees north of the airport. So we did have a pretty good idea where we needed to start looking, and what the circumstances and factors might be.'

The sequence of events leading up to the crash was soon established, as Kapustin explains.

When the airplane lifted off, it immediately started to pitch up and increased the angle of attack, which would make it conducive to stall. The airplane never did regain any normal flight attitude, because the only way they could have gotten increased airspeed was to get the nose down. And in order to get the nose down, you have to trade altitude for airspeed. They didn't have any altitude, so the airplane was actually at a high angle of attack – nose high, tail low – and it stayed that way till it hit. Miraculously, it missed the steel beams on the railroad bridge. It went just over the top of that, but at the same time it was descending because it was in a stall, and finally the aft end hit the railing and the concrete structure of the bridge, still in the nose-high attitude. And then the airplane broke – actually broke. The aft end broke off and then went into the water, and the forward section kind of skipped across the bridge and plunged into the river.

The investigators were lucky, says Kapustin, that a passenger on another flight alongside the Air Florida plane had taken pictures. These gave them a slightly better idea of how much snow there really had been on the aircraft. 'So besides de-icing and disruption of air foil, they also had some added weight.' From the pilot's point of view, some deadly evidence emerged later from Joe Stiley, one of the survivors, a former US Navy pilot who recalls looking out of the window at the airport before boarding the flight. The Air Florida plane was sitting out there surrounded by snow. 'Before we finally got on the airplane I didn't see any evidence that the pilots had done a ground check. There were no footprints in the snow round the airplane. It looked undisturbed. That bothered me a little bit. I specifically remember thinking I wanted to see somebody walk round that plane before I got on it'. Nevertheless he and the other passengers boarded. 'After a while they began to de-ice it again. They came down the starboard side of the aircraft and I could hear the progress and eventually I could see out through that side,' Stiley says. 'They never came back round to our side of the airplane, and it was nearly impossible to see out of the window on that side. I saw no indication that the flight crew had done the walk-around that I know FAA rules require. Those guys were sitting fat, dumb and happy in their cockpit and talking about the weather in Florida.'

Kapustin himself used to fly Air Florida, but on this flight, he says, the captain, Larry Wheaton, came from a little outfit that operated DC3s, had very little jet experience and obviously did not understand turbine-engine operations. By contrast, the co-pilot was highly qualified, a former fighter pilot who had been a general's aide at one time.

He knew that something was seriously wrong and he tried to tell the pilot, but having been an aide to a general, I think he just didn't have it in him to question authority. Of course, you can't look into a dead person's mind, but unfortunately, I had to listen to the CVR. One of the last things the co-pilot said was: 'This sure doesn't look right.' The captain answered, 'Yeah, here's 120,' or, 'We've got 120,' which means that he was looking at the airspeed. The co-pilot's response was: 'I don't know.' When you read that on the transcript, you could interpret it to mean he didn't know about the airspeed, but when you listen to it you can hear the absolute desperation in his voice.

Understandably, Joe Stiley was more brutal.

Larry Wheaton should have never been in the left seat of a commercial airliner. He wasn't qualified for the job. He was the product of the deregulation era, and he got there by virtue of belonging to a union at the right time. Roger Pettit, the guy that was on the right-hand side of that airliner, was an ex-F15 jock. That guy knew how to fly. He knew what was going on. He tried to tell Wheaton, and Wheaton overruled him in a sense. If Pettit hadn't had that military training he probably would have done something about it.

The pilot's partial responsibility was emphasized by the fact that another plane, which had been properly cleaned, took off safely shortly afterwards.

Eventually the black boxes were recovered. As Kapustin and Stiley assert, conversations confirmed that the co-pilot was desperately and rightly worried throughout the take-off. Indeed, once the investigators had established that the de-icing system was off, they were able to establish from tests on similar engines that the engines were providing less than three quarters of the power they should have done. This was confirmed by the CVR. 'By going to the background noises and ignoring the conversation,' says Mike McDermott, 'one is able to pull out the engine sounds and determine what the power settings were. In this case, when you go through the formulas, it translates to about 80 per cent of the engine performance power for the take-off of the aircraft.' In other words, not enough for a proper take-off.

The CVR also revealed the unease of the crew. There was a lot of joking, but, as McDermott says, it seems to be a way of coping with the difficulty of the situation.

Their nervousness about flying in snow might have been due to their lack of experience. These Air Florida pilots were not used to flying in ice and snow. They were joking about the fact that certain aircraft they passed on their way to the take-off runway looked like they were up to their knees in the snow. They say, 'Well, they're just doing this de-icing to cover themselves or to keep the feds happy.' In particular they were jocular about one of their major concerns: that they were heavy. They had a lot of passengers and a lot of weight on board, and the snow only added to their weight.

One major controversy that developed from the CVR evidence was whether the anti-ice equipment had been turned on or off, a point it took years, and more sophisticated equipment, to iron out. 'It's ambiguous when played in its normal state,' says McDermott, 'so it's hard to hear when they're going through their check list and one pilot asks about the anti-ice and the other responds, whether he says "on" or he says "off". The first question on the list is pedoheat, and the response is on; the second is anti-ice, and all you hear is a click and a thud sound.'

This muffled thud became a major issue in the subsequent inquiries. At the time the tape was even sent to the FBI's lab, the best in the country, if not in the world, for analysis to see whether they could determine what that last statement was, and even their decision was not accepted. Today, says McDermott, 'the equipment is sufficiently advanced to enable words to be compared side by side'. He isolated the response to the pilot's pedoheat query and the answer 'on' is clearly audible. Then comes de-icing. McDermott says: 'After you've listened to this for hours, literally hours, on end, it becomes very apparent that the second word is actually "off". Due to the shortness and sound of the word, it could have been missed by the other pilot or misinterpreted. But I believe he says off.'

Yet even without the new techniques, says McDermott, the CVR provided vital information.

> If the black boxes had never been recovered, the most likely verdict on the case would have been the fact that the pilots took off too long after they were de-iced. As it was, it was about thirty minutes from the time they were de-iced to the time that they departed, and on that particular day, in very heavy snow, heavy wet snow, I think that would have been the only thing they would have had to go on. There would not have been any of the engine performance, any of the comments by the pilots showing their uneasiness with the weather, or any of the comments questioning the engine gauges that you hear. They would have had to just guess on these things. They would not have known that the engine gauges were not performing properly, there would have been no basis to determine that the aircraft was not functioning up to speed, and so they would have had to blame it on the timing of the de-icing. And they would probably have been wrong.

Ice once again wreaked havoc, with fatal consequences, years later, this time without warning. On 31 October 1994 – Hallowe'en – Greg Feith was preparing to go out trick-or-treating with his nephew when he heard that an ATR72, a Franco–Italian twin-engined turbo-prop operated by American Eagle airlines, had crashed at Roselawn, Indiana killing sixty-eight people. Next morning they found what Feith describes as: ' total catastrophic destruction of the airplane'.

> In this 20-acre field, all you could see were stakes that indicated people, or what remained of people, and airplane parts. We had several hundred people walking the accident site assisting the local sheriff and police

department in gathering what was left of the victims. We had several big-impact craters that had filled up with water. The weather was just atrocious that night, and early into the next day, so a lot of our ground evidence was going to be spoiled, not only by people walking around but also by the elements. We knew that the weather was involved; we knew that it had been windy, that it was raining. We also found out that there were icing conditions in the area.

The airplane had taken off from Indiana, heading for Chicago. It was a normal commuter flight. The air-traffic controllers had put the flight crew into a holding pattern because they were flow-controlling into Chicago Airport, and the plane had then gone into several circuits of the holding pattern. Because of the icy conditions, the crew had activated all the ice-protection systems, and so when they looked out the window and saw that the system was handling the ice, it is likely that they didn't perceive it as a threat. While they were flying in this holding pattern on their last circuit, they had the autopilot on but they were monitoring the systems as required. The captain had just returned from the back of the airplane, where he'd used the restroom, and got back into his seat. The conversation between him and the first officer showed that they were checking to find out how much longer they were going to be in the holding pattern. At this point there was still no perception of a threat from the weather. They knew that it was bad, but for the most part the airplane was handling it OK. But after air-traffic control had given the crew an altitude change and the crew had started the descent, the autopilot kicked off and the airplane rolled substantially to the right. It was first corrected by the first officer, who was able to regain control of the plane momentarily. Then there was a secondary roll and then the airplane went into a severe nose-down attitude, from which the flight crew was unable to recover, and eventually struck the ground at about 475 knots, or about 500mph on an attitude that was almost semi-right-side-up. But it was moving at such a high speed, and they were coming down from 8,000ft, that there was no real chance for the crew to recover.

The problems with the ATR72 started with the fact that it was a turbo-prop. Modern jets have what is called a 'hot wing', where hot air from the engines heats the leading edge of the wing and melts any ice that has accumulated there or on the engine itself. And in any case, these planes operate well above thunderstorms and icy conditions. Turbo-props, which fly at lower altitudes, don't have the luxury of a lot of excess hot air and so they use pneumatically driven air to blow up what is called the leading-edge boot, the black boot along the leading edge of the wing, and the horizontal and vertical stabilizers. When the boot expands, it breaks off any ice that may have formed on the leading edge of the wings or round the engines.

The ATR not only had de-icing boots, it also used hot air to melt some of the ice on different parts of the plane. The plane was certified by the FAA to fly in icy conditions on the assumption that the DGAC, their French equivalent, would have ensured that it could be operated safely in similar weather. Indeed, subsequent tests by the NTSB showed that the plane did meet the FAA's requirements for certification. But they also revealed that the ATR72 was susceptible to what Feith calls an 'ice ridge that built up behind the boot along the leading edge'. While some pilots were aware that this could occur, it was not widespread knowledge. 'We didn't know what effect this ridge of ice building up behind the boot on top of the wing, where the pilots couldn't see it, could have until we had done the tests after the accident,' says Feith.

The designers of the ATR72, like their compatriots on the A320 airbus, had taken aircraft design to its logical conclusion. Steve Fredrick, a pilot who sacrificed his career to campaign on the issue, maintains: 'The designers of the ATR took a standard airplane wing and tweaked it. They made it more fuel-efficient; they made it smoother, slicker through the air.' The airlines loved its fuel-efficiency and the fact that it could carry heavier loads than its competitors, but, as Fredrick says, 'They crossed a fine line and inadvertently made a demon of a wing which is much more efficient at collecting ice than any other wing on a turbo-prop regional airliner that has been tested in the United States.'

It did not help that the original certification process was overlaid with political factors. According to Fredrick:

> It was certified by the French government, which actually owns a piece of the manufacturer. So you've got people who are part of the owners' group certifying the airplane, and it passes into the United States under a bilateral treaty with very little FAA oversight. Because turbo-props fly at lower altitudes than jets – 'in' rather than 'above' the weather – inevitably, when you've got an aircraft such as the ATR which is particularly susceptible to that type of situation, you're placing it in harm's way on a constant basis. The certification requirements for the aircraft to fly in icing conditions go back to the 1940s, when it was thought that only one in 1,000 exposures would exceed that level. Unfortunately, later research led to the conclusion that aircraft like the ATR72 operating below 10,000ft, would encounter such conditions more frequently.

Indeed, the frequency is greater in the Great Lakes in the midwest of the United States, which enjoy conditions during some of the year conducive to what Feith describes as 'this freezing rain, freezing drizzle, icing-type phenomenon'.

As early as 1981, the NTSB recommended that the FAA should change the certification requirements for the aircraft. This started a thirteen-year exchange between the two agencies which culminated in a letter written six weeks before the Roselawn accident by David Hinson, the administrator of the FAA, in which the Agency refused to change the specifications. The result of the delays was a series of incidents which foreshadowed Roselawn. Feith says:

> We knew that there was some previous history with this type of aircraft from previous incidents that had occurred over the previous ten years. We investigated an incident in Wisconsin from which we were able to determine that icing conditions were a contributing factor to an uncommanded roll. After that we had information we were able to obtain from other incidents back in 1993 and 1994 in Newark, New Jersey and Burlington, Massachusetts, in which the flight crews also had encountered icing conditions which led to an uncommanded roll of the airplane. When the investigators looked back at the flight-data recorder information from these fortunately non-fatal incidents, they found very close similarities to the information from the flight-data recorder at Roselawn. Now we had a history.

Fredrick is less compromising, drawing attention to the fact that in 1987 an ATR72 flying from Milan to Cologne crashed near Lake Como, killing everyone on board, when it stalled in conditions very similar to those which prevailed six years later at Roselawn – though senior NTSB investigators believe the pilot was at least partially responsible for the Lake Como crash and that there is no real comparison between the Como crash and the disaster at Roselawn.

Fredrick's own concern was sparked by an incident in which he nearly crashed while flying an ATR72. Fortunately, he managed to regain control of the aircraft and climb above the ice. He immediately reported the incident and a month later had a meeting with the FAA and pilots who had survived other ice-related incidents with the ATR. At the time Fredrick kept quiet – 'played the good soldier', as he puts it – but after Roselawn, he appeared on television to give the pilot's side of the ATR story. He was promptly suspended on full pay for his pains. His book on the subject, *Unheeded Warning*, was published in July 1996, though it received a mixed reception from the investigators.

'The more we got into the investigation,' says Greg Feith, 'the more we found that, while the manufacturer had made some changes to the airplane and had put out some new procedures, the flight crews who were operating this airplane were not fully aware of what would happen in this type of conditions.' Feith and his colleagues could tell from tests in any ice tank how and where the ridge of ice had developed, and how the consequent disruption of the airflow had caused the aileron to move all by itself. 'And if the pilots weren't anticipating it and didn't have their hands on the control yoke, this would then cause the airplane to react to the movement of the aileron.' At Roselawn the plane rolled 77 degrees in the blinking of an eye. 'By the time the crew realized what had happened, the first officer had got on the control yoke to manipulate the airplane back to upright. But when he did so, all of a sudden this phenomenon happened again, and the disruption of the airflow over the wing, over the aileron, caused the airplane to roll a second time. That was what led to the loss of control.' The crew could have regained control if the plane had been flying any higher, but at low altitude there was simply no room to recover.

In theory, at least, the conditions in which the Roselawn accident occurred were pretty unusual, as Greg Feith explains.

Typically, if you have a build-up of ice crystals on the leading edge of the wing, when you expand the boot on these turbo-prop airplanes, the ice crystals break off, shatter and leave the airplane. Freezing rain and freezing drizzle is a little different. You have a raindrop, called the super-cooled drizzle droplet or super-cooled rain droplet. This starts as an ice crystal or snowflake. It may fall in this cold band of air, then warm up and turn into a liquid state again, but it never refreezes. So you have a drop that is well below freezing but still in liquid form. The airplane flies through, and this raindrop strikes it. Depending on the size of the drop, it may instantaneously freeze or it may be big enough to start to run a little bit. Then it'll trail back until it loses all of its energy and heat and it'll freeze.'

Research meteorologist Marsha Politovich:

The larger droplets, about the size of drizzle droplets or larger, don't get carried around the wing quite so easily. It's very much like a ship going through water: there's a ball wave that carries the droplets around it. If the droplets are big enough, they don't get carried around, they slam right into the wing, hitting the wings further back from the leading edge than the smaller ones. Also large droplets don't tend to freeze at the point of impact. They'll remain liquid and flow back along the surface of the wing for some distance before they fully freeze. The result is that you get ice accreting away from the forward edge of the wing. If you have de-icing equipment it's usually confined to the leading edge, because that's where icing usually happens, and the pilot is able to remove that ice during flight. However, when you get the ice away from the leading edge, you can't get rid of it in flight unless you find some warm air and melt it off. The second reason is aerodynamic: you have a bigger penalty for ice forming further back from the leading edge of the wing than at that forward point, which is called a stagnation point, where the air separates to go around the wing. So in the large-droplet environment, any wing will suffer icing farther away from the leading edge.

There is some evidence to show that the ATR-type wing may be more inclined to suffer a greater aerodynamic penalty in those situations than other types. There's been some further research done on that with wind-tunnel tests, tanker tests, tests where they glue ice shapes on to the airplane and run it up and down a runway, just taxiing at high speed. Based on the results of that, the company which built the airplane has come up with a better de-icing equipment design which they feel will make the plane very safe in those sorts of icing conditions.

In this particular instance, these raindrops actually struck the leading edge of the wing and ran back across the top of the boot, only to lose their energy and their heat and freeze just after they had left the protected surface, according to Feith. 'The more they streamed back, all of a sudden you start to build up the ridge, and that's what we found when we were doing the icing tanker tests,' he says. 'Using that information, we went up with a tanker. We were able to duplicate the size of those droplets behind the tanker and then fly the ATR in behind it and actually ice up the wing. We saw this ridge of ice start to build up.'

Within a week of the accident, the NTSB sent five recommendations to the FAA which stated, in effect, that the ATR72 ought not to be flown in icy conditions. The FAA didn't actually ground the plane, but in response it did impose operational restrictions to prevent the aircraft from flying in such conditions until the NTSB had investigated further. The FAA then put out an airworthiness directive requiring operators to fit their planes with an expanded boot which the manufacturers had developed to prevent the possibility of an ice ridge forming on the top of the wing.

Such directives naturally create a climate in which pilots and operators alike become only too aware of potential problems. They are therefore highly unlikely to expose even the modified version of a plane to risky conditions. The restrictions on the ATR72 set off the most almighty diplomatic row. Over the years Feith and the NTSB have become accustomed to the arguments their reports can generate, so Feith made ultra-sure that the French knew immediately what was in the report. He carried it personally to France, delivering it as soon as he landed. But nevertheless the row rumbled on. The French accused the Americans of acting unfairly, complaining that this would never have happened with an American-built aeroplane; that it was the pilot's fault ('We still believe,' said one official French statement, 'that the ATR meets the existing requirements. Pilots only need to be vigilant if they encounter ice on wings'). There were, even though not directly from the French, veiled threats that they would take their revenge by refusing to certificate the new Boeing 777.

The international authorities responded with eighteen new requirements for turbo-props, devised at a conference in May 1996. On 9 July the NTSB held a full hearing and stated that: 'the probable cause of the control loss resulted from the failure of Avions de Transport Regional (ATR), the plane manufacturer, to completely disclose adequate information about previously known effects of freezing precipitation on the plane's stability and control characteristics, autopilot and operational procedures.' This vital safety information, the Safety Board said, was not included in the ATR flight manual, flightcrew operating manual and flightcrew training programmes . . . The NTSB also pointed to an inadequate oversight of ATR-42 and ATR-72 aircraft by the French aviation regulatory agency, the Directorate General for Civil Aviation, and its failure to take 'necessary corrective action to ensure continued airworthiness of the aircraft in icing conditions.' The NTSB also said that the French authorities had 'failed to provide the FAA with timely airworthiness information' and that another contributory factor had been 'the FAA's failure to adequately oversee the continued airworthiness of the ATR-42 and the ATR-72 aircraft.'

But, as Feith says, 'Freezing rain and freezing drizzle is a phenomenon that happens all over the world. It's been happening since the world was created.' But let Rudi Kapustin sum up the whole complex situation:

Frankly, I don't know how much more often you can tell people that you have to have a clean airplane; you can't have ice on it, I know the operations are complex – traffic situations, airport traffic, clearances, weather conditions that delay airplanes. Those are all facts of life. These things happen. But the bottom line is, when you've got ice on the airplane you don't go; when you're in it in a certain type of airplane, you get out of it. I don't think we need any more conferences. I think we need crew members to be aware of the fact that if you load an airplane up with ice, you're probably going to die.

10
Dropped From a String

Texas weather can change within a matter of minutes. It can be beautiful one second and then two minutes later, it can be dark, cloudy, hailstorms, hailstones as big as soft balls. It can happen within minutes, and that is your typical Texas weather.
— Paul Reese, station sergeant, Dallas Fort Worth Airport

Ice and snow are obviously not the only severe weather conditions which test aircraft and their crews to, and often beyond, the limit. The list of potential hazards is seemingly endless, ranging from fog and thunderstorms to clouds of volcanic ash clogging the engines. The problems are compounded by the carelessness of pilots, or, more often, their ignorance of bad weather through the failure of meteorologists either to forecast conditions or to convey their warnings to the pilots. Apart from such universal terrors as hurricanes, every region in the world seems to have its own problems. Many are winds: the Foehn, a warm, dry mountain wind that suddenly springs up over the Alps; 'funnel winds' like the Mistral, intensified when it passes north from the Mediterranean up the Rhône Valley; 'ravine winds', common in valleys, which affect Genoa Airport, among others. Or common-or-garden winds which are simply too strong for an aircraft to cope with. In 1975, when a Boeing 727 crashed while approaching Kennedy Airport, the NTSB reported that even if the crew had recognized that they were plunging to earth, 'The adverse winds might have been too severe for a successful approach and landing.'

Duststorms are common – among the worst are the *haboobs*, the sandstorms of the Sahara – while fog can prove equally fatal. It was fog, or rather the pilot's attempts to disperse it, that was responsible for the fire which destroyed a Caravelle at Kloten Airport in Zurich in September 1963. The disaster killed forty-three citizens of the small Swiss town of Humlikon, a disaster with uncanny overtones of the one which afflicted the British town of Axbridge in the accident, which also took place in Switzerland, described in Chapter 13. The pilot of the Caravelle had tried, with some success, to clear the fog from the runway by running his engines at full blast. But in doing so he so grossly overheated the undercarriage that a wheel fractured.

Many parts of the world are subject to frequent thunderstorms. One highly influential accident was the loss of a North-West Airlines Boeing 727 near Miami in February 1963, whose wreckage proved almost as difficult to retrieve as that of the Valu-Jet crash in the same swamps in early 1996. After an unprecedentedly thorough re-enactment of the tragedy, the investigators found that the whole plane had disintegrated. But although there were strong vertical upcurrents while the plane was climbing and during its fatal dive, these were not in themselves forceful enough to have destroyed the plane. It was simply that the pilots had not been taught that their natural reaction to strong updraughts, to point the nose down, could simply intensify the effects and magnify the strain on the aircraft.

The advent of pressurized airliners, starting with Boeing's Stratocruiser in 1940, and followed by the development of jet airliners in the late 1950s and early 1960s, merely complicated the problems associated with the weather. For the first time, planes and pilots now had to cope with the extreme conditions prevailing 'above the clouds'. The normal working environment of jet aircraft is 30,000ft in the air, where temperatures are below freezing and the jetstreams stronger. The jetstream over the Atlantic, for example, normally blows from the west, so it takes much longer to fly the Atlantic against the wind. At that point, writes Macarthur Job in *Air Disasters*, 'the long-sought ideal of "above the weather" flight was finally seen for the myth it was . . . turbulence could be encountered at these levels in every way as severe as that afflicting flight at less ambitious altitudes'.

In turn large jet aircraft can create their own 'weather', their own turbulence, which can be dangerous for smaller planes. Air-traffic controllers use the term 'heavy' to warn pilots of big jets that might cause problems for the smaller aircraft in their wake. The cause of one of many such accidents through the years, the crash of a DC9 on a training flight in Texas in 1972, was traced back to the way it had become trapped in the extremely powerful but totally invisible vortex generated by a DC10 which had approached the runway a minute before the DC9 tried to land.

In recent years, as improved training, better radar and improved forecasts have reduced the problems caused by extreme weather conditions, two other types, the 'rotor zone' and 'windshear' have emerged as the cause of many nightmares. Identifying these dangers has helped the pilots, and not only by warning them of likely problems. Charles Phipps of Delta Airlines asserts: 'Many accidents which were in fact due to windshear were wrongly attributed to pilot error before the problem was identified.' But with the proper warning – and more powerful modern engines – pilots can cope.

Back in the old days I remember that any time your airspeed got low, you would say, 'Oh my goodness, let's lower my nose to gather airspeed.' Today we use what I would call the rocketship approach. We have beautiful bypass large engines and we raise the nose on the 757–767-type aircraft to 15 degrees, which actually gives us our best rate of climb to counteract the wind coming down. The aeronautical engineers say that if we can do that for thirty seconds, we will be out of the microburst downdraught that is forcing us to the ground. We actually turn the auto throttles off so that we can get maximum power, because the autopilot cannot handle this severe amount of turbulence in downdraught and the pilot himself is the one who has to fly out of it. So it's maximum power and auto throttles off, and autopilot off, and it's all up to you. That's what we train for.

The 'rotor zone' is caused by strong winds battering on one side of a mountain range and creating turbulent zones in the lee of the wind, like those under the crest of a wave crashing on to a beach. It seems to act like the undertow which traps an unwary bather. Such a zone was responsible for the crash of an Uruguayan airliner in the Andes which led to the cannibalism so graphically recorded by Piers Paul Read in his famous book *Alive*.

Mount Fuji, the most sacred of Japanese mountains, was responsible for a similar crash in which all the members of a party of seventy-five American executives on an outing to view the mountains in a BOAC Boeing 707 died in March 1966. The aircraft was not fitted with a CVR, and the fire after the crash was so severe that the FDR was destroyed. Miraculously, an 8mm cine-camera was recovered and the film showed something of what had happened. The wind was blowing hard from the Asian mainland to the west of Japan, and the air was clear and dry, giving unusually good visibility, and, less happily, what Macarthur Job calls: 'mountain wave' systems,

a disturbance of the airstream broadly analogous to that of a river flowing over a rocky bed, the ripples and 'breakers' on the surface of the water corresponding to the standing waves and turbulence found in the airstream above mountainous terrain. The higher the mountains and the faster the airflow over them, the greater the resulting air disturbance. The worst turbulence in such conditions is found in a 'standing rotor', a highly agitated body of air rotating about a horizontal axis downwind from and parallel to the mountain ridge producing the air disturbance.

The pilot, Captain Dobson, had inadvertently exposed his plane to the worst of the conditions when he swung the 707 towards the mountain so that his passengers could get a better view. He hit 'an unseen cauldron of fiercely boiling air – the vicious rotor zone of the severe atmospheric turbulence the 70 knot wind was creating in the lee of the 12,000ft mountain . . . The shock would have felt something like colliding with an invisible wall . . . in this case sufficient to immediately snap off the tail fin, together with all four engines in their mountings beneath the wing.'

The other potential nightmare, windshear, was probably first identified when a Braniff BAC111 crashed near Falls City in eastern Nebraska in August 1966, an accident witnessed by hundreds of local spectators who had rushed outdoors to watch the approach of a thunderstorm. They testitifed that the plane never reached the main line of the storm, but that there was a 'boiling roll cloud' nearby. The FDR was destroyed, but the CVR showed that the pilots were talking of a 'hole in the cloud' just before the plane came down. The investigators used the different noise levels recorded by the CVR at different speeds to establish the aircraft's speed at the time of the accident, and found also that it had broken up within two seconds of the initial shock caused by a sudden encounter with an exceptionally powerful gust.

It also became clear that an outflow of cold turbulent air from the advancing storm front had reached as far as the accident site, producing severe low-level turbulence which became known as 'windshear'.

This analysis was confirmed by Professor T. Fujiya, a leading meteorologist who had been working on a region in the Rockies known as 'tornado alley'. Macarthur Job quotes his report in *Air Disasters*.

A well-developed line of thunderstorms pushes ahead of it a mass of cold air. Storm cells force down the cold air from high altitudes to balance powerful updraughts of warm air within the cells. On reaching the ground, this cold air spreads out to form a cushion or 'cold dome'. As the line of thunderstorms moves forward, pushing the cold dome ahead of it, warm air at ground level is forced up, forming more thunderstorm cells. The leading edge of cold air becomes the windshift line and may be invisible . . . sometimes the line is marked by a roll cloud, but windshear at the line can be vicious even if there is no cloud.

This phenomenon is well known not only in the Rockies, but in other regions as well – in the lee of the Alps, the Aleutian Islands and Greenland, for instance – which are subject to the same conditions. According to Charles Huettner of NASA windshear is rare but can occur where there is downburst-type activity near the end of the runways. 'If you then have a headwind and you're trying to maintain your airspeed, you have to reduce your thrust. You then enter the downburst section of the thunderstorm, which hammers you towards the ground, and if you do that at low altitude, you're obviously in a situation where you can strike the ground.'

Over the past twenty years, a great deal of research has been carried out into the causes and consquences of windshear. In the late 1980s the FAA required aircraft to carry windshear-detection equipment. Thanks to work carried out by NASA in conjunction with the FAA, there is now a specialized radar system that can predict any windshear the aircraft is likely to encounter ninety seconds ahead. But it costs over $100,000 an aircraft to instal the new radar, which replaces equipment introduced only a few years ago, and by 1996, not all airlines had incorporated it as standard equipment.

Rotor zones, windshear and wake vortices from other aircraft have figured in a number of accidents in the United States in the past fifteen years. As we see in the next chapter, two of these, at Colorado Springs in March 1991 and at Pittsburgh three years later, remain unexplained to this day. Another disaster where shear played a probably underestimated role was that of a Lockheed TriStar belonging to Delta Airlines at Dallas Fort Worth Airport in 1985 – a dreadful year which saw twelve other major crashes in the United States as well as the appalling JAL disaster in Japan.

The Dallas crash showed how easy it was to blame the pilot for a disaster in which the treachery of Texas weather played an unquantifiable but important role. Indeed, Professor Fujiya wrote a book about the accident which was entitled *Microburst at DFW*. Paul Reese, a station sergeant at Dallas Fort Worth Airport, remembers the fatal day, 2 August, as 'hot and windy, not a cloud in the sky, just a typical beautiful Texas day'.

> Around six o'clock in the evening, while we were preparing the meal, the weatherman came on and told us of some severe weather at the north end of the airport. On our side of the airport it was beautiful, no sign of any bad weather. We thought that he must be mistaken, but on the other side of the airport it was a whole different story. On the east side there were winds exceeding 100mph; there was sideways rain that was blowing so hard it felt like it was going to penetrate your skin; there was thunder, lightning, dense, dark clouds all the way to the ground; there was hail the size of golfballs. There were hurricane conditions on the opposite side of the airport whereas on our side it was calm, clear, blue sky.

When flight 191 crashed, hitting some large water tanks, Reese immediately drove out.

> The rain was so hard I couldn't see past my windshield. The rain and the wind were holding the windshield wipers back – they wouldn't even wipe the windshield. I tried to roll the window down to see and then it was like somebody standing outside with a bucket of water hitting me in the face with it, it was that bad. As I got closer to the scene I still didn't see the aircraft because it was so dark and gloomy and the clouds were right down at the ground. You could not see the crash scene. As I got closer and finally figured out where the site was, I wasn't sure if all the blackness was smoke from fire or if it was clouds. Then, as I finally approached the scene and saw the devastation there, it was just unbelievable.
>
> As I approached and actually got to the tanks, I was not ready for what I saw. From all my years of firefighter's training, I really expected to see an aircraft sitting there on the ground, but there was no aircraft, just

unrecognizable pieces. It was raining so hard that there was nowhere for the water to go. It was just building up deeper and deeper and deeper. And then the tanks were also busted, so we had 4 million gallons of water pouring out of them. When I got out of the vehicle and tried to protect myself from the lightning and the hail and the rain, the water was actually coming up almost to my chin. I could see the aircraft debris looming out of the water and fire and smoke and fuel burning on the water, and I could actually see bodies wedged in between the debris.

When Rudi Kapustin first saw the wreckage, he was amazed that there were survivors, and that in the first place the plane had managed to miss a fully loaded 747 belonging to United Parcels Services. 'If it had hit that 747 full of fuel, there would have been no survivors.' In fact there were 30. When the investigators got to work it was immediately obvious that there was severe windshear. By 1985, air-traffic control centres had meteorologists on the staff, but, says Kapustin, the one at the Dallas Fort Worth centre wasn't there and the back-up weather facility wasn't functioning. 'Real-time weather was never disseminated to that flight crew.' He flatly disagrees with the apportionment of the blame.

They pretty much left it all with the crew, based on the fact that one of the crew members said there was lightning. They knew there was bad weather out there, but you don't know where the lightning was in relation to their position. On the final approach to DFW, the crew knew from visual evidence that there was some weather ahead of them. Speaking strictly from a safety viewpoint, if you're not sure what you're going to encounter, you go around – severe thunderstorms usually go away in ten, fifteen minutes. But there's always a reluctance to do this, particularly if someone has landed just in front of you. Everybody is saying, American or TWA just landed, how come you couldn't land? The passengers don't like to be late, but of course they don't know the seriousness of the decision-making process. Anyhow, these guys saw some lightning but apparently they didn't perceive it as a threat and continued to land.

On the very final phases of their approach they encountered a severe microburst. The downburst velocities were way, way beyond the capability of the airplane to climb out of. The airplane was just short of the runway, on the other side of a major highway, and they simply could not arrest the sink rate because of the downburst velocity of the microburst. The plane struck a car and decapitated the driver, bounced on to the airport, hit the water tank and broke up. The speed was so great that it actually overturned a dump truck in the general area. When I first heard of that I didn't believe it and sent one of the investigators out to try to verify it. It actually turned over a heavy dump truck.

The air-traffic controller or the tower controller saw what this guy was flying into, what he was going to fly into. At the public hearing, I specifically asked him, 'Why didn't you tell the flight crew?' He said, 'Well, I felt they could see it just as well as I could.' That was not true. They were on the other side of it. It was a very, very severe weather system. There were forecasts, but again, in that particular case, the county round the airport had better forecasts as far as localized flooding and things like that were concerned than the people in the airplane did, and state of the art really, really shouldn't have permitted this to happen. Later, there were lawsuits filed against the government and a long trial in Fort Worth without a jury. I don't know whether it was the first time it was used or not, but video animation was used to portray this flight going in and the lightning. But that's a little bit of Mickey Mouse. I mean, you can put the lightning anywhere you want to on an animation. Of course the government got off scot-free in the litigation too, but that's how it is when it gets to litigation. I think whoever tells the most convincing story, right or wrong, wins. I wasn't very happy about that.

Indeed, so unhappy was Kapustin about the allocation of blame that he left the NTSB when its report into the crash was adopted.

A more recent accident was that in July 1994 of a DC9 belonging to US Air over Charlotte, North Carolina. Before crashing, the plane's speed dropped by 80mph and the captain described the sensation as like 'being dropped from a string'. When they cleared the rainstorm, the crew realized that they were flying below the treetops. A few seconds later they came down on a suburb of Charlotte, killing thirty-seven of the fifty-seven people on board.

Windshear was immediately suspected and was confirmed when the FDR data showed that at a critical point, when the crew had decided to abort the landing and were going around, the aircraft pitched over 20 degrees and then flew into the ground. However, once all the data was available, the investigators, led by Greg Feith, found that 'It was not particularly the windshear that caused the accident, it was the actual operation of the airplane by the flight crew. They just happened to be in an environment of a windshear at the time of the accident.'

Even so, it became clear that the windshear was greater than that in Dallas. The manufacturer, McDonnell Douglas, did some simulations and told us that in fact when this airplane had been properly configured, the power had been set and the crew had done operationally what they were supposed to have done, the airplane would have transited through that windshear with minor problems. They would not have struck the ground. So what it brought us back to was the operation of the airplane. The captain had said 'down – push it down,' and on the FDR we were able to see that there was a reaction to that statement of a 20-degree pitch, from 15 degrees nose high to 5 degrees below the horizon, and, at only 300ft, the airplane actually flew into the ground.

11
Every Billion Hours

At the end of the day, I have no qualms at all about flying on the Boeing 737. Its history of twenty-five years and 65 million flight hours speaks for itself. It's one of the most tested airplanes out there.

– Greg Phillips

Occasionally – fewer than half a dozen times in the past four decades – the investigators of the NTSB have had to admit that they have not been able to establish the precise cause of an accident. Despite unusually prolonged and intensive inquiries two such 'no-shows' occurred in the first half of the 1990s, with weather as one of the suspects. To further complicate the equation, both disasters involved the world's most popular aircraft, the Boeing 737. The result is unfounded public unease about the 737, and a feeling of frustrated misery at the NTSB. As Haneter puts it: 'You'll always be the one who didn't do it.'

The first accident, on 3 March 1991, involved a United Airlines flight from Denver to Colorado Springs, and killed all twenty-five people aboard. On such a short flight, the aircraft climbed only to 10,000ft en route before beginning its descent into Colorado Springs. The weather had been clear; there were no clouds in the area, but, as quite often happens in the Rockies, there were very strong westerly winds, which come across the peaks and begin to cause what is called 'mountain wave'. The Rockies, like other long mountains, can cause long waves of air movement and also wind rotors accompanied by severe turbulence and up and downdraughts. Ron Schleede, who had worked in the region before, had known many days when moderate or even severe turbulence on the eastern slope of the Rockies would be predicted because of the high winds at mountaintop level. 'And there were times when you had 100-knot winds at the top of Pike's Peak or Mount Evans. The way that wind blew over the top of those peaks was going to cause a lot of turbulence on the eastern slope.'

Fredo Killing, an amateur pilot at Colorado Springs who knows the vagaries of the local weather, defines a wind rotor as 'a very turbulent cloud that's usually right under the wave. You can only see it because it's a very fast wisp of condensation, and it appears and disappears, so only the trained eye usually pays attention to it. But there's extreme turbulence in there. In a small plane it

136

can actually turn you upside down without any notice.' George Bershinsky (a retired pilot who had flown weather trials in the University of Wyoming's atmospheric science aircraft) says: 'In real time it's very difficult. It's kind of like riding a horse across the prairie with one gopher hole. If you miss that gopher hole, everything's OK, but if you step in it you're in real trouble. It is invisible, basically. It'll change, it moves around with time.'

Killing describes the day of the crash:

> The conditions were unusual because the rotor was very, very close to the ground. Normally we're used to seeing that at about 12,000ft or 13,000ft, but the rotor was right on the ridge, maybe 100ft or 200ft off the ground. Also, the night before we had had extremely high winds. The cement tiles were blowing off the roof of my home, so I knew that the westerly winds had been very strong. Another unusual thing was that the rotors went way out into the east. I could look out into the distance and the rotors were as far as the airport, which is unusual. That indicates that there was probably a secondary and tertiary wave fifteen to twenty miles from the foothills. I knew that that day there was going to be a lot of turbulence going through the rotor into the wave.

According to Greg Phillips, the NTSB knew that a Boeing B52, the world's largest bomber, flying in the area had lost a portion of its vertical stabilizer some time earlier. 'And we had glider pilots talking about weather conditions of mountain rotors and waves, so the strong push early on was the fact that the weather could have been a factor.'

Ron Schleede notes that the flight crew were aware of the turbulence. 'It had been forecast, and from listening to the CVR, you could tell they were encountering very significant bumps. The airplane was being jostled. They spoke in generalities about how rough the flight was. Naturally, the first thought of the investigators was to examine the flight controls to find out if the aircraft had been controllable.' Flight 585 began its descent and approach to Colorado Springs and everything was routine during the turn to the final approach.

> But as the airplane was approaching about 1,000ft above the ground, beginning to align with the runway, it was in a right bank and it rolled over and went straight down. It crashed almost vertically in an inverted attitude. From 1,000ft it was something like nine seconds from the time that the airplane was OK until it hit the ground. In such conditions, with good weather other than the turbulence and high winds, it was highly unusual for an air-carrier airplane to just roll upside down and go straight in. The wreckage was confined to a very small area, whereas most airplane accidents make a big swathe and pieces are scattered along the ground. In this one it was obvious from the outset that it was

virtually a straight-down impact. All of the wreckage, and, of course, the bodies, were in one big crater.

Phillips summed up the problem: 'The airplane hit the ground in a vertical position with bad turning. The parts were destroyed, and we didn't have a lot to work with. We knew it was always going to be a tough investigation.'

Once the wreckage had been moved to a hangar, it was laid out so that the investigators could try to recreate the wings, the fuselage and the engines. The radar data told them where the aircraft had been during its flight but didn't explain exactly what had happened. Ron Schleede:

> The CVR revealed the actions of the crew, and in general everything was routine. Suddenly, they were fighting the airplane. You could tell they were extremely surprised and trying to maintain control. The flight-recorder covered only seven parameters, providing us with very limited information, but we managed to determine the final flightpath. The only additional information we gathered was that during the turn to final landing, as the airplane was descending, it seems to us that it began to roll out wings-level slightly before you would have expected the pilot to do it to align with the runway. We don't know if that was induced by the pilot or by the weather and the turbulence. Then as it began to roll out, it rolled back over.

The investigators initially focused on the flight-control components to try to establish whether the plane had been controllable. They had already learned that on its short final approach the aircraft had rolled to the right and gone into the ground nose first, but they didn't know why. Because of the part the weather might have played, the investigators went into great depth to model and understand the conditions. They took wind and temperature information from every possible source and fed it to a powerful Cray computer at Boeing. With the help of atmospheric researchers in Colorado, they were able to mock up what they thought could possibly be a vortex which might have been generated by these winds. They fed this purely hypothetical vortex data into a Boeing computer and then actually flew the mission on the simulator to see if there could be any type of wind powerful enough to cause the 737 to flip over. But they drew a blank. Ron Schleede continues:

> During the on-scene investigation we isolated components we wanted to examine further. All the hydraulic-system components – those pumps, actuators – are all heavy structures, and no matter how hard they hit they stay fairly intact and maintain their shape. We had previous cases on the 737 of engines falling off the special bolts that hold them on the wings. We looked at those in great detail but found no evidence of that. We examined the engines thoroughly to make sure there wasn't some failure that might have precipitated it. In this type of accident we take all

these components, document 'em in place, take 'em to the various vendors – in many cases they are documented externally – and X-ray them to try to find the position of certain pistons and things. Then they are methodically examined and opened up. We found some anomalies in the yaw-damper system. The airplane had a history of a couple of events involving the yaw-damper, which makes minor inputs to the rudder to help the comfort of the ride.

This last discovery focused attention on the rudder. Fairly early on they realized that the plane had had some kind of an upset involving a roll or yaw and the nose coming down. 'We didn't believe that was something a pilot would normally do, particularly on an approach like this,' says Schleede. 'So the focus began to centralize around what could cause the airplane to roll over. With the evidence we had, we decided to look at the rudder as one of the key systems to evaluate and find out what had happened to it.' Because of the fire damage, they managed to test only one part of the rudder power-control unit, but fortunately it was one of the most critical components – the servo-control valve responsible for controlling the direction and speed of the rudder's movement. In addition, because of the publicity surrounding the accident, they started getting additional reports from pilots and mechanics of things to look at. One of the most significant was from a United Airlines pilot in Chicago, who, during a pre-flight controls check, had noticed that the rudder pedal was binding.

Nevertheless, after eighteen months of intensive work during in which a team of up to thirty investigators had painfully examined and re-examined the thousands of pieces of wreckage, it became clear that they didn't have a clear cause. They took their report to the Safety Board. The Safety Board could only offer options: either 'it was a mechanical failure which we did not detect', or, 'it was weather of a magnitude we haven't ever measured or seen before'.

Three years later there was a similar 737 crash on the approach to Pittsburgh, in which all 132 people aboard US Air flight 427 lost their lives. What Tom Haueter found on his arrival at the scene set the tone for the whole investigation.

When I first got to where the fire department and the police had set up, it was just mass confusion. There were policemen from various different townships, there were state police, local police, city people; there were fire departments from eight different jurisdictions; there was an incredible number of news media. At first it was just total chaos but it was got under control pretty quickly. My first impression on going to the accident scene itself was how surreal and quiet it was. It was very early in the morning, about 7.30, and it had just rained. The wreckage was still smouldering, and we were walking through probably the most incredible devastation I've seen in terms of fragmentation on an accident site, and there was mist and smoke rising. It was very unreal, just taking a look around and then trying to find out where the various pieces of the airplane were, because when we initially walked up to the scene you couldn't see anything recognizable as an airplane. Then, as you look around, you can see an engine, you can see a landing gear; then you see the tail and you start to accept that yeah, there is an airplane here. We had to figure out a way to put it back together to understand what happened.

During the first days of the Pittsburgh investigation there were all kinds of wild theories. There were so many that each one was called the 'cause de jour' as it emerged. I've learned very quickly to discount all initial theories; to start from scratch, start gathering evidence. Visual witness statements, or those broadcast by the media, are usually not from actual witnesses and they're somewhat imaginative, to say the least. Another complication was that the pilots in the Pittsburgh crash had triggered their microphones on the way down and so a lot of their discussion was recorded on air traffic-control tape, which belongs to the FAA. They made a preliminary transcript of the tape, and somehow it was leaked to the press. But it had an error in it. At the same time as the crew said, '427 emergency,' a controller was pointing out traffic to another aircraft. The two conversations got mixed up and in the transcription the crash was described as a traffic emergency. Immediately people said there must have been another aircraft, that there was a mid-air collision. There was wild speculation that the airplane was dodging or doing unusual manoeuvres to avoid some other airplane. That theory took almost a year to finally dispel in a lot of people's minds, and only after it had caused me a fair amount of aggravation.

Another early rumour was that there was a federally protected witness on board the plane. People liked that idea because it has a certain sense of mystery to it, I suppose. As it turned out, there wasn't. There was a gentleman on board who had provided information for a case, but he was never going to be a federally protected witness; he was not even going to appear in the court action or anything else. So a bomb theory persisted for quite some time, although none of the investigations – by us, by bomb specialists from the FAA and FBI – found any evidence of any type of criminal intent regarding what happened to US Air 427.

Greg Phillips continues:

We believed that since it was a very clear, smooth night, there was no unusual weather similar to Colorado Springs. We knew that the focus on flight controls in the airplane was more intense than it had been in Colorado Springs, because we knew that weather probably wasn't a factor. The FDR data showed that the plane had had a sudden bank and had then dived into the ground from about 6,000ft. Again, we had a limited FDR in that we didn't have the rudder position recorded. We had to derive it analytically with aerodynamics, aerodynamic models and simulations. That work led us to the fact that the airplane had to have had some kind of a yaw [the aircraft equivalent of a skid].

The primary job of the rudder-actuator, the power-control unit, is to yaw the airplane, so we started an extensive test programme to see if it was functioning the way it should have. We had worked with them before in the Colorado Springs accident. We brought the servo-control valve into our laboratories in Washington and had metallurgists look at all its surfaces with a scanning electron microscope up to 20,000 power to look for any evidence that marks had been made by jamming of particles which could have caused the rudder to move without control. We also looked at possible electrical problems, misporting of fluid, movements where you thought you would push the right rudder and it would go left, which we call reversal. We found none.

We had the rudder-actuator back intact so we could functionally test it. The actuator rod had a slight bend to it, but once that was replaced it passed all the manufacturer's acceptance tests once again. We've subsequently torn it down, re-inspected it and done some extremely extensive tests on the rudder power-control unit to see if we can determine any failure modes that could have resulted in the accident. One thing we have learned from Pittsburgh is that the best match as to the cause of the accident is the deflection of the rudder. But what may have caused the rudder to deflect remains the question on this investigation.

Very early on it was clear from the flight-data recorder that flight 427 had encountered the wake vortices of another aircraft at the time the upset started. Looking at the radar tapes, we were able to establish that a 727 had passed through just about the same airspace but 300ft higher at the time of the problem, and about seventy seconds ahead. This brought up the theory of what the wake vortices from a 727 could have caused on a 737. We embarked on a very extensive wake-vortex flight-test programme that was completed in September 1995. We took an FAA 727 and put vortex-generators on its wings. US Air provided a 737 that we instrumented with all the parameters we'd like to have for rudder-pedal position and that, and we went out and flew about 120 different wake-vortex encounters at different distances, from four miles up to a little less than two miles in trail, to see how severe a wake vortex could be. We collected a tremendous amount of data, and some of it's quite fascinating. One thing it did show is that the wake vortex would not cause the same yaw motion as caused the upset. It in some respects ruled out a possibility, but it provided a wealth of data for other uses.

Two things came out of it that were tremendous and unexpected. First, on the US Air 427 cockpit voice-recorder tape, there was a thump just prior to the upset and we weren't sure what that was. Collecting cockpit voice-recorder sounds during the wake-vortex flight tests, we found the same thump. Our acoustics engineer was able to determine that it came from about the same position in the aircraft as it did on flight 427, so one little mystery was solved. Also, there's a point where the engine increases in sound level but not in frequency, and once again we found that as the airplane yawed with the yaw input to the rudder, we got a similar type of engine-sound increase. That gave us another piece of data to use in the investigation. It was clear that the event starts at the same time as the wake vortex is encountered. We don't know what factor that may have been, but we are fairly convinced that the vortex itself did not cause the loss of control of the aircraft.

It has clearly proved a frustrating investigation, for the NTSB, which worked on it for over eighteen months without finding a possible cause for the accident, for the relatives of victims, general public, for Boeing, and especially for the operator, US Air, which, like other reputable operators over the years, had suffered a number of unrelated accidents within a relatively short space of time. Part of the problem is that the NTSB has become a victim of its own success: the public expects that the Board will get to the heart of the problem within a few weeks, which it generally does. So the failure here planted a question-mark in the public consciousness about the safety of the 737. As a result – and for the first time in the NTSB's history – the chairman brought in a group of six outside experts to offer a second opinion. But although they came up with a couple of new theories, they don't seem to have helped matters much. Haueter has his own theory.

The 737 has accumulated over 64 million flying hours. There are something like 26,000 aircraft flying about and they're encountering different conditions all over the world every day – a 737 takes off every three minutes somewhere in the world. Therefore what we're looking for is not just unusual, it verges on the bizarre. We're looking for an event that has happened extremely rarely in the life of the aircraft; an event where the crew could not control the airplane, which they were unprepared for, something that is just beyond normal operation. Therefore we're looking for this bizarre little element that can only happen once in every billion hours or so of flight time, and that makes it a very difficult and also in-depth investigation. We're down looking at infinitesimal particles and what they may be doing.

Since Colorado Springs, every time a 737 is involved in an incident, we've monitored it quite closely. So when you initially come up to something like Pittsburgh, it makes you wonder whether it's another

Colorado-type Springs event. Maybe here we'll find the clue that solves Colorado Springs. To a certain extent, you have to treat every accident separately and try to pick up the facts of this individual event. They may help you with a previous one, or bits and pieces from a previous accident may help you with this one, but you don't want to manufacture facts based on what you want to find. You have to let the facts speak for themselves and draw their own conclusions.

12
Supermen and Scapegoats

Let all who build beware
The load, the shock, the pressure
Material can bear.
So, when the buckled girder
Lets down the grinding span,
The blame of loss, or murder,
Is laid upon the man.
Not on the Stuff – the Man!
    – Rudyard Kipling, *Hymn of Breaking Strain*

Throughout the history of flying, pilots – especially if they are dead – have been the easiest people to blame for an air crash. They are also the only factor common to all accidents, so they can never be excluded. The spotlight is particularly bright during the most dangerous moments of a plane's flight, when it is landing. A study carried out by IATA's chief safety officer, Lawson C. White*, found that forty-four of sixty-three crashes which occurred during landing were caused by pilot error. But after analysing the incidents, White became convinced that 'many of the accidents classed as pilot error were the result of human error other than the pilot's. Someone who forgot that pilots are normal. There is only so much information a pilot can receive and integrate at a given time. Anything in excess of this is not conducive to human reliability.' Nevertheless, pilot error is the residual factor, the one that comes automatically to mind. Before any other explanations have been sought, pilots can be blamed for their incompetence, their casualness, or their characters.

This state of affairs has worsened with the general improvement in planes themselves. Pilot error now emerges as, in a sense, the last frontier of accident investigation. John Crum, a Delta Airlines pilot, elaborates.

When the Wright brothers started this whole institution of flying, obviously it was the mechanical part of it that was riskier than the human factor. The wings fell off, the engine quit, or whatever, and it was the pilot who really didn't seem to have any repair problems or

*Safety in the Accident-Prone Flight Phases of Take-off and Approach and Landing (IATA, November 1972).

144

improvement problems. Today, the pilot is the weak link in the chain. Now, conveniently, you have statistics saying that pilots are responsible for most accidents. Well, that's really quite unfair. The reason for it is that the mechanical aspect has been improved, and we really haven't figured a way to improve on the human body. So as long as you have a human in control, you can't get around that limit.

Bob Besco adds: 'Once we got over our learning curve of the jet era in the early 1970s, the accident rate and the pilot error rate remained fairly constant.'

At the same time, the pilot's lot has, in theory, become easier. 'The jet engine is more reliable than the reciprocating engine and the air-traffic situation, with radar and improved navigation programmes, is a better place in which to operate,' says Robert McIntosh. 'The knowledge of weather and how to combat it and the instrumentation in the aircraft have all contributed to an improvement in safety.'

Because of the increasing focus on the problems pilots cause, it is important to put the figures into proportion. 'In hundreds and thousands of cases pilots have prevented an accident by their action,' says Heino Caesar. 'Only in very very few cases have they failed, and this amounts to approximately fifteen total losses a year with an average of 500 deaths. In Germany alone we have 8,000 dead on the streets every year and worldwide we are killing 500 people in jet aircraft crashes.'

Bob Besco was once a professional pilot and has lived among them for most of his life.

I hardly think of them as a breed, although I can see some common characteristics. First, they are probably brighter on average than people in most professions. It takes a lot of cognitive ability to be a pilot. The capacity to stay focused on your primary objective when things are going bad around you, and to be able to operate under stress, are probably the two main characteristics of pilots. Other than that, I've seen happy ones, I've seen sad ones, I've seen philanderers, I've seen bible-thumpers – I've seen all kinds of pilots at all kinds of ability levels, and they're very similar to people in any other profession. I don't think personality characteristics differentiate pilots from any other group in our culture.

Yet there is seemingly no limit to the number of strains to which pilots can be exposed – and not only in the air. Dave Miller believes that the part of the job which causes the most stress is probably the preparations before the aircraft actually leaves the stand, where the crews are trying to co-ordinate the loading of passengers and baggage with the air-traffic slot they've been allocated. 'Problems like late passengers, late baggage, slow loading and late arrival of the aircraft are all out of the crew's control. Once the pilot is away from the local area and climbing up into the cruise, the workload tends to diminish,' he says. 'It increases again once the aircraft starts its descent and approach to its destination. But generally, the problems occur on the ground rather than in the air.'

One of the most common problems for pilots in the air is competition – from the world's enormous population of birds, large and small. Up to 2,000 incidents of birds striking aeroplanes used to be reported every year in the United States alone, and obviously, the larger the plane, the more likely it is to be hit. A 747 averages one hit per 1,000 hours in the air, eight times the rate for its smaller predecessor, the 707. Inevitably, over the years, a few of these encounters have proved fatal to people as well as birds. Some time ago a Lockheed Electra crashed at Boston after hitting a flock of starlings, killing sixty-one of the seventy-two people aboard. In another incident a United Airlines Viscount hit a swan, which lodged itself in the controls and forced the plane into an un-controllable dive. And no pilot knows when a large bird is going to land itself on the cockpit windscreen. The captain of an Indian Airlines DC3 was killed when a vulture burst through the windscreen of his cockpit (luckily, the co-pilot was unharmed and managed to land the plane). Years later, another vulture, weighing in at 20lb, landed in the lap of a Trident pilot, again in India. A more recent case is that of an Ethiopian Airlines Boeing 727. A vulture cannoned off the radome on the plane's nose into the cockpit just as the 727 was approach-ing Khartoum Airport. Before expiring, the bird tore out the co-pilot's rudder pedal, severely injuring his left leg, and the debris damaged one of the plane's engines.

More newsworthy hazards are explosions on board, at least some of which are survivable. 'It's amazing the number of bombs on aeroplanes that have been survived,' says the AAIB's Ray Davis. 'A few years back, on a BAC 1–11 in the Philippines, a chap went into the toilet, pulled the pin from a grenade and blew himself up. He just flew out the side of the aeroplane, but the captain retained control and landed. Nobody else was injured, as far as I recall. A year later, the same captain had somebody else with a bomb on board, and again he landed the plane. Quite incredible.'

Another common enemy is fatigue. This is not a new problem; indeed, it seems that for many years the authorities needed convincing that pilots were not supermen. As far back as 1953, David Beaty wrote a novel called *The Heart of the Storm* which used the long haul across the Atlantic as a setting. The chair-man of BALPA ensured that the air minister read the book. 'By an unhappy coincidence,' wrote Beaty later in *Naked Pilot*, 'a few months later, a fellow captain and friend crashed at Singapore in a fatigue situation similar to the one in my fictional accident. Thirty-three people were killed. He had been on duty for twenty-two hours. A year later, the first British flight-time limitations were brought in.' The concept of jet lag went unrecognized until the Americans imposed the first flight-time limitations in 1953. Initially, the very idea was regarded by management 'as a ploy by the pilots to obtain more money', according to Beaty. 'There was considerable suspicion on both sides until psychologists and doctors began to understand the problems of long hours on duty and the consequent effect on health and behaviour.' And the problem persists, particularly in the small hours. A study carried out by NASA in 1980 revealed that over a fifth of incidents involving air crews were due to fatigue, and another report four years earlier found that during the early morning hours, all five members of the crew on duty displayed brainwave patterns characteristic of sleep or of extreme drowsiness.

Despite the precautions, fatigue remains a major residual factor in incidents and accidents, leading as it does to inattention and loss of concentration. A French accident investigator quoted in *Naked Pilot* commented: 'Our lack of knowledge of fatigue may well prove to be the chief explanation of those accidents which are now put down to "pilot error" or "the human factor", simply because we don't quite understand what makes well-qualified, conscientious specialists like pilots commit unbelievably stupid mistakes.'

Notwithstanding the problems and hazards of the job, pilots have often displayed almost superhuman qualities. Taking only a few of the better publicized cases, let us start with Captain Eric Moody, who in 1982, was flying a British Airways Jumbo from Kuala Lumpur to Perth in Australia. As the plane passed over Jakarta at 37,000ft, Moody was chatting to a stewardess when he was suddenly recalled to the flight deck. He found the windscreens ablaze with a display of St Elmo's Fire, a well-known type of flicker caused by flying through an electrically charged atmosphere. Almost immediately, the plane appeared to be hit by a trail of tracer bullets and dense smoke penetrated the air-conditioning system into the cockpit. Within seconds all four engines had failed – a fate unthinkable in a modern aircraft.

Not suprisingly, the plane started to fall precipitately, the cabin pressurization system failed and Moody was forced to hasten the descent because the co-pilot's oxygen mask had fallen to pieces in his hand. Attempts to restart the engines merely left a trail of fire in the slipstream, giving the passengers the impression that all the engines were ablaze. At this point Moody made the laconic statement: 'Good evening, ladies and gentlemen, this is your captain speaking. We have a small problem. All four engines have stopped. We are doing our damnedest to get them going again. I trust you are not in too much distress.'

Moody now faced one of the most difficult manoeuvres in the book: ditching a powerless Jumbo into the sea. It was a manouevre he had, by a stroke of luck, practised only a few months earlier. Fortunately, he never had to put these skills to the test because all four engines came alive as the plane fell below 12,000ft. As he landed at Jakarta he could see nothing through a windscreen covered with an opaque haze. It was his flight engineer who realized the culprit was dust from Mount Galunggag, a volcano about 100 miles south-east of Jakarta. Although it had been dormant since 1918, it had erupted a couple of months earlier.

Quite rightly, Captain Moody and the crew were fêted as heroes, but none of the citations in the press quoted his vivid description of what was, literally, a blind landing: 'It was a bit like negotiating one's way up a badger's arse.'

In two other cases, pilots managed to regain control by applying differential power to the engines after the hydraulic systems had failed. The first concerned Bryce McCormick, whose emergency landing at Detroit after what became known as the 'Windsor incident' in 1972 should have warned the aviation community of the dangers posed by the design of the cargo door on the DC10 (see Chapter 3). McCormick had always loved the DC10. Even today he describes it as 'a wonderful airplane to fly. I love to fly it, it flies like a fighter. You can control the airplane so beautifully. It's much more stable than the 747 or the 707.'

Nevertheless, he took an extraordinary precaution when he was learning to fly this apparent marvel of the skies. 'The DC10 was the first hydraulically controlled airplane that I'd ever been into. I just kind of wondered, what if you lose the hydraulics?' he remembers. 'So, at the end of the induction course, I asked the instructor what would happen if we lost the whole hydraulic system. He says, "You can't do that," and I said, "Well, I believe in Murphy's Law – that if it can happen, it will, and I would like to know any alternative methods."' By the end of the course he could land the plane – on the simulator, anyway – using only the throttles. He could use the third, central, engine to steer with.

On the near-fatal flight the first sign of trouble was when the cargo-handler 'couldn't seem to get the handle down, so he pushed on the handle with his knee and it closed. The air-vent door to release the pressurization stayed cocked a little bit, which was an indication that it wasn't properly closed, but he didn't realize it.' The cargo-handler called a mechanic over to look but the mechanic, more familiar with the mechanism on the Boeing 707, assured him that it would blow shut. Just as McCormick was taking over from the co-pilot, as the plane was flying over Windsor, Ontario (hence the name the 'Windsor incident'), the cargo door came loose, though McCormick was not aware at the time that this was what had happened. The force was so strong that it threw his knee up to his shoulder. 'It shoved me clear over to the side of the cockpit, my headset flew off, and I was hit in the face with a lot of dirt, dust and rivets,' he says. 'It stung real bad. It hit me in the eyes – my eyes were just plugged up with tears. I couldn't see anything for a few seconds. When I got my eyes open again all I saw was red lights. Everything was lit up like a Christmas tree, and my face felt just like raw hamburger.'

Fortunately, the crucial hydraulic lines attached to the floor had survived the shock but most of the command systems were unusable because the control wires between the cockpit and the tail had been destroyed. With extraordinary cool and judgement, McCormick rejected the idea of an emergency landing and experimented to see what, if any, controls were working, like someone gingerly feeling their limbs after a fall to see if they are still in working order. 'I took the wheel and I just shoved all three engines forward, and immediately the nose started coming back up again. As it came back up, I could see that we were back in control to a point where we weren't going to go into a big dive.'

By then the flight engineer was feeding McCormick with far too much information, so he was sent back to the passenger cabin to get him out of the way. He was so disorientated that he spent some time looking for his cap when one of the stewardesses told him that a girl had fallen down in a part of the floor that had caved in. The matter of the hole in the floor naturally confused McCormick, who had assumed his troubles were confined to the cockpit. Bob Besco, a friend and admirer of McCormick's, says that McCormick was lucky. 'If that floor had collapsed another inch or two, he would have had no way of recovering the airplane.' By then the rudder had frozen, so the airplane was constantly trying to turn right,' McCormick continues, 'and, with the elevators like they were, I had only one elevator left and that was the right one. Every time I pulled back on the wheel the airplane wanted to roll again.'

On his return from the passenger cabin, the flight engineer kept assuring him that the hydraulics were OK but by then McCormick was convinced that whatever the problem, the plane was behaving in the same way as it would if the hydraulics had failed – which, of course, they had. Acting on this assumption, and using all the skills he had acquired on the simulator, McCormick made a perfect landing. 'I was so proud of the landing,' he says, 'but when the nose wheel touched, that's when all hell broke loose. We went off the runway and I was sure we were going to go through the fire station, a big brick building.' It was the first officer who provided the solution by applying full reverse power to one of the engines and shutting down the only other one that was working. The plane swung away from its collision course and came to rest a mile and a half from the runway threshold. Only then did McCormick have the time to look round the aircraft and grasp that the crisis had been caused by the cargo door.

As we have already seen, the failure of the hydraulics on a DC10 was the cause not only of the Windsor incident and the Paris catastrophe, but also of the crash at Sioux City, perhaps the most stunning example of controlling an aircraft through the throttle and without the use of hydraulic systems, which had been rendered useless. What made this extraordinary piece of flying even more noteworthy was the fact that a crucial role was played by a pilot who started the flight as a passenger.

The saga of United 232 also involved a heroic cabin crew, led by Jan Brown. She had been warned of some turbulence: 'But I never expected that kind of turbulence!' As we saw in Chapter 8, when the fan disc broke off one of the engines, all the hydraulic controls were ruptured.

There was suddenly this loud explosion, I mean, a really loud explosion.
I just instinctively sat down on the floor and held on, because I didn't

know what it was. As soon as we stabilized I stood up. I've always realized that passengers are looking at us to see what they can find out, and how serious the problem is. They look for an answer in our faces. So I've always sort of made it a rule, no matter what is going on inside me, that on the outside I always look as if nothing's wrong, everything's fine.

It was only when she went to the cockpit that the tension resulting from the enormity of the situation hit her, 'like the heat from a furnace door', she says.

Al Haynes, the plane's experienced pilot, admits that when the explosion came, the crew assumed they had an engine failure. 'I've been flying jets since 1968, and I'd never had an engine failure, but still, through the training we had, you just follow the procedure.' Which is to shut the engine down. So that is what they started to do. 'We began to realize that the situation was worse than we thought and Bill, the co-pilot, was the first one to catch that because he was trying to fly the airplane,' says Haynes. None of us had any idea. If you read the cockpit voice-recorder transcript, you won't see any orders, because none of us knew enough to give an order.'

Jan Brown returned from the cockpit. 'I stopped looking at people when I went back into the cabin because I did not want them to read the truth in my eyes. I felt that I should keep the mask over my face that everything was normal. I think you could only read it in my eyes.' But one passenger whom she had already recognized and chatted to had read the fear. He was Denny Fitch, a training captain 'dead-heading' – flying home off-duty.

Originally he thought the problem was probably a compressor stall.

Then I noticed that the right wing kept going down, more and more severely, it seemed. Shortly thereafter came an announcement from the cockpit saying, 'Ladies and gentlemen, we have just shut down the number two engine, which was the engine in the tail of the aircraft.' But the resulting yaw didn't make sense to me. The second thing that was unusual was that if you lose an engine and have only two thirds of the power remaining, the airplane can be flown safely, but at such a high altitude it would need to descend to a lower altitude where the air is more dense and the remaining two engines can produce more power. So I was fully expecting the aircraft to go down. Much to my amazement, when I looked outside, I saw the pitch attitude of the aircraft, which indicated to me that we were in a climbing mode. If that is the case, I thought, it's not right. It shouldn't be doing what it's doing. Now we were hearing the airplane starting to suddenly do more wing rocking, and we were hearing more power changes of greater magnitude. This went on for about ten minutes before I volunteered my help through a flight attendant.

Fitch had waited because he had great confidence in the capacity of United pilots to cope with the loss of a single engine, a manoeuvre they practised a lot. But then Jan Brown, whom he described as 'a marvellously bright, vivacious lady', returned from the cockpit. 'Now this bright, vivacious face was long and sad. Because the concern she seemed to have was, I thought unnecessary, when she came back toward my seat I reached out and touched her, and basically I said to her "please don't worry about this. This airplane will fly fine on two engines."' Brown then told Fitch that the situation was worse than that, and when Haynes learned that there was a training captain in on board he welcomed Fitch's help.

Fitch went into the cockpit. 'I can remember the pilots' forearm muscles being enlarged from squeezing and their knuckles were white from working so hard at trying to move these controls, which were now without hydraulic power,' he says 'making the effort to move them was extremely stressful and took a great deal of energy. That would be my recollection: extreme stress, not that they were out of control. They were working their tails off to try to make a difference, and without obvious satisfaction.' Fitch immediately noticed that all the hydraulic pressure gauges showed zero.

The second thing I noticed was that the wheel we use to make the turns left and right was at its full maximum deflection to the left, and yet the aircraft was going to the right. The first officer and the captain were both pushing on the control yoke, trying to get the nose down, because the plane was climbing. They pushed full forward, and I can distinctly remember the first officer, slouched in his seat with his knee placed firmly under the control column to put even more leverage on the forward movement. But it wasn't affecting it at all.

The captain knew of my presence without looking at me. There's an irony here, but he never physically saw me in all the time I was up there. He didn't make any eye contact, if you will, for obvious reasons. He had a tremendously bad situation in front of him. But he knew I was there and he asked me to go back and do a wing inspection to see if any of the flight controls were making any movement corresponding to what they were trying to do. The two ailerons in these two locations were both floating up in the same direction at the same time, and that was distinctly not normal and confirmed what we saw in the cockpit. So I was convinced at that point that we had indeed lost all hydraulics and therefore all our flight controls.

As I got back to the cockpit and reported to the captain, the airplane was beginning another effort to go to the right. They had the controls fully to the left, and were doing everything they could with traditional systems to stop it. As a last resort, and the only thing that seemed to work, was the captain pushing the throttle for the left engine to full power. Because of the location of the engine, this had a tendency to pick up that wing at maximum power. He was having a terribly difficult time doing this because of the explosion and the way the system on the number two engine had failed. It was jammed in the upright position so it became an obstacle for him to operate around the other two throttles. I saw how difficult it was proving for him to do all this, and as I wasn't doing anything at the time, I said, 'Captain, would you like me to do your throttles for you?' Captain Haynes replied, 'Yes, please do that,' and that's how I got involved with the manipulation of the throttles.

When I started working the throttles for him, he reached his arm up over his shoulder, because he couldn't turn away from what he was doing, and he said, 'Hi. I'm Al Haynes,' and I shook his hand from behind. I said, 'Hi, I'm Denny Fitch,' and he introduced Bill Records and Dudley Dvorak. Neither of those individuals made eye contact, because they had their hands full.

For the thirty minutes I was up there, I was the most alive I've ever been. That is the only way I can describe it to you. The time I was in that cockpit operating those throttles seems closer to five minutes.

Because this was a one-in-a-billion situation, the crew we had no experience or information to go on. They were, says Fitch, basically designing their own system as they went along. The plane, still trying to turn to the right all the time, was going into a series of waves, swooping up and down at frightening speeds. 'We were trying to keep altitude for as long as possible to buy time to learn how to do this. In effect we were our own research and development team in the air.'

Meanwhile, Haynes and his two colleagues were dealing with air-traffic control, the passengers, and the flight attendants. 'Denny ended up flying the plane, and as far as I'm concerned, he became the fourth member of the crew. We had a four-man crew once Denny came up,' says Haynes. Bill Records declared an emergency and asked for the nearest suitable airport. Minneapolis air-traffic control determined that Sioux City was the closest runway. 'We needed to get the airplane on the ground as quickly as we could,' Haynes continues, 'and I didn't care where it was. Just somewhere with a runway long enough to accommodate a 10.'

They had no idea where they were. Denny Fitch says:

We had no navigation capability on board the aircraft, the station which should have emitted the signal at Sioux City was out of service that day, so we had no onboard way of knowing exactly where the airport was. We relied heavily on the air-traffic controller to give us our position at all times. We finally started to see the airport in the last six or seven minutes of the flight. We could see where we were going, and we were able to maintain reasonable expectations of making it to the runway we could see. Fortunately, we were lined up toward the runway when we found it.

Nevertheless, Haynes had his doubts that they would make the airport. The crew asked for an alternative place to land – 'if we could get control of it,' says Fitch. 'Otherwise, we were going to go wherever it wanted to go. I believe Bill went so far as to say a road or something, and they began to clear the freeways for us. 'Of course, we'd never have put down on a freeway because we'd never have survived. We'd have torn the airplane apart. We might have put down on a field next to a freeway. Fitch was more confident than Haynes about their chances. 'From years of flying, we all knew we had enough altitude to make it to the airport. For the most part, I always believed we were going to make it. As time went by, my proficiency at flying in this fashion was improving and I believed with my whole heart we were going to make it. That's what made it so disappointing in the hospital when we found out that people had died behind me.'

Brown had, of course, been told to prepare for an emergency landing. 'I never had a personal thought, outside of asking God if maybe I could be someplace else.' Her throat was so dry that she couldn't speak, and she was afraid that her hand would shake as she picked up the microphone. 'I remember one of my flying partners saying that my voice was very soothing, and for that I'm very grateful to whoever up there was guiding me, my guardian angels. I just brought everything down to a very basic point of maintaining overall cabin calm and getting these passengers ready for an emergency. I really wasn't aware of what the airplane was doing as long as I was able to walk up and down the aisle. Part of my mind was just frozen to contain the terror and the rest was totally focused on keeping us all going. You probably could have cut the air with a knife, there was just that tension. We all sort of withdrew into our own thoughts.

The landing was, as was only to be expected, appalling. They were approaching the airport at 250mph, 100mph faster than normal, without being able to put down any flaps or slats to help create more lift and slow the aircraft. Nevertheless, when he saw the runway, Fitch remembers very distinctly 'the relief I had. I said, OK, now we've got this part nailed, we're going to make it.' As they got closer, Fitch was trying to coach Haynes to use whatever means they had to slow the aircraft down, but Fitch had moved to the engineer's seat and so lost sight of the runway whenever he bent down to make a correction to the throttles. 'Then I would sit back up, like a jack-in-the-box. I wanted to keep the runway in the bottom third of the captain's windshield.'

They were descending at 1,800ft a minute, three times the normal rate, heading for a runway that was only 6,600ft long. Fitch was hoping for a relatively normal landing, if necessary in the cornfield at the end of the runway. At around 400ft the captain and first officer asked Fitch to reduce speed. Haynes asked him to pull the power off.

I said, 'I can't pull the power off – that's what's holding your wing up.' When I thought we were close to the runway, I pulled the power all the way off because I didn't want any more mass inertia to cope with on that short runway. I thought we were right about to touch down, and as I pulled the power back to idle I looked down at the captain's vertical speed indicator. It showed 1,800ft per minute, which was intolerable. We couldn't hit that hard. In a desperate effort, I firewalled both the engines and shoved both the throttles up to full power. The time factor wasn't there for us, and we impacted before I was able to get the engines all the way up to power.

The impact was so hard. I remember my hands flew off the throttles, and it was like a giant hand had taken the back of my head and slammed it down into the radio panel. I popped up again and looked left, for some reason, through a veil of blood – my head had been opened, and I was looking through blood going over my eye – and I saw the corn stalks going by Captain Haynes's window. The strangest thought crossed my mind. My God, I thought, they really do grow that tall in Iowa. Of course, a normal DC10 captain sits at 22ft in the air, and I knew the corn didn't grow that tall. So I knew that something bad had probably happened to our undercarriage or our landing gear. I remember the tearing of metal, a very loud shrieking engine noise. We went straight ahead and then we veered to the right into a sleeping field. It was almost as if somebody had kicked you from behind. Your whole body went forward as if you were going over the top and the windshield filled up with green and then bright light for a split second. Then it darkened again into the green–brown mode, and this time I felt heat, humidity and debris. After that . . . I can't begin to describe in words how violent it was after that. The next thing I remember I was in a stupor, hanging upside down with mud in my eyes and ears, blood running down my face, pain in my back from the compression fractures. My broken ribs would not allow me to take a full breath of air. We were like that for thirty minutes before we were found and a rescue launched.

The cockpit had landed upside down, away from the main wreckage, and the crew were seen only when a rescue truck noticed the second officer's hand poking out of a window in the wreck.

Just before the crash, all Jan Brown could think of was a headline for the accident. 'It would be, "And then we hit." It was so enormous, in spite of the fact that Al had told us that it was going to be hard, and to prepare ourselves.

It was just indescribable,' she says. 'I remember just involuntarily closing my eyes and thinking, oh, my God, I can't believe that we hit that hard. And then I just passed out. But I could still hear the shrieking metal, noises that you'd never heard before and you hope you never hear again.' After helping the passengers to cut themselves clear, she heard someone say, 'There's an opening.'

> Immediately I went back to where I had heard the voice, and sure enough, people were walking out into a cornfield. There was all this debris, cables and all kinds of things hanging, and I just held them aside while people who were taller than I walked out. It was almost surreal. I could have been saying, 'Thank you very much for flying with us today.' They were going slowly, and in the back of my mind I kept thinking, this could blow up at any minute, I wish they'd move faster. And then I saw the first flying partner I'd seen since we crashed coming toward me, and I was amazed. She was perfect – her hair was in place, everything. I knew before she spoke what she was going to say. I just said, 'Get out,' I knew she was going to argue and try to go back in, but I just said, 'Get out, keep going.' Inside I was so relieved to see her. As much as we care about our passengers, your first thought is for your flying partners.
>
> Then I saw this thick, grey–black smoke, like a tornado, except that it was rolling along the top of the ceiling, which was really the floor. It was coming towards me. We're taught that when the fire is too hot, the water too deep and the smoke too thick, you leave. There was no question of me going in to look for anyone else, because it was deadly. That's when I left.
>
> My nylons were melting to my ankles. I was standing out in the cornfield. You could see exactly where my blouse ended, and it was like a light sunburn, but when the sun beat down on it I started getting feeling back, and I realized that I was burned. It was frustrating, because the corn was taller than I was – we're taught to gather passengers away from the wreckage.

Once the rescuers arrived Jan left the scene with some national guardsmen. 'My first personal thought was when some of the helpers were trying to put us into an ambulance to go to the hospital. I thought, I guess they don't need us any more, let somebody who's hurt go, and I suddenly realized that I had to get in touch with my family and let them know I was alive before they heard about this.'

Al Haynes was knocked out in the crash and recovered remarkably quickly, but Denny Fitch suffered appallingly. He told fellow pilots afterwards: 'Hopefully, I've had your nightmare and you'll never have to see one. I've had it for us all, and it's hell on earth. I think I cried for three days on and off – it was just terrible. The survivor's guilt was incredibly bad. I really wanted to die so that the others could live, I would make a trade-off with God so that they would survive. It meant everything to me. But I can't play God, I guess.' This common reaction of survivor's guilt afflicted Fitch until he felt forgiven by a survivor, a woman whose husband died in the crash. They fell on each other's shoulders and she said that God had meant to take her husband that day. Fitch felt a great weight lift from his shoulders.

The survival of 184 of the 296 people aboard the plane amazed the whole aviation community. Haynes says they had all kinds of luck.

> First of all, just keeping the airplane in the air; the fact that it was daylight, and we could see what we were doing, and find the runway. It was shift-change time on the ground in Sioux City, which allowed the hospitals be double-shifted with their own personnel when it came to treating the injured people. The crew; the training they'd had at the airport on what to do if a crash happened there, which had them all keyed up and prepared to react. The fact that the National Guard is stationed there, and there were 250 trained national guardsmen waiting to respond to the crash. It's just unbelievable how these things all fell into place for the 184 of us who survived. Had any of those things not been there, I'm sure the fatality rate would have been a lot higher.

The miracle was confirmed when the accident was replayed dozens of times on a simulator. Only one crew out of thirty managed to get the 'aircraft' down. And even then it was just as difficult to stop the 'aircraft' once it had had touched the ground. Consequently the crew of the United flight realized that they had brought in a virtually unlandable plane. One survivor, Tom Eilers, marvels at his escape.

> It is incredible that this group of unique individuals was in the air in this airplane. If the flight attendants had not been professional, and had displayed their anxiety about the severity of the situation to the passengers, there might have been a much more panic situation. For Captain Haynes to have managed this process like he did, with Denny Fitch being there and being brought into the management team, and Captain Haynes not rejecting his help, is astounding. This crew being in this place at this moment in time in this airplane, saved my life.

As another survivor put it: 'God had placed someone on that airplane that was real special that day. For everyone on board it was fortunate that he was there.'

So much for the supermen: now to the scapegoats. Many countries' authorities are only too happy to blame the pilot. We have looked at the French in this respect, but they are by no means alone in their attitude. Pilots are simply too tempting a target. After a Boeing 727 crashed on a flight to Taipei, it took the threat of an international pilots' ban on all flights to Taiwan to get the authorities to release the pilots of the 727, held on a trumped-up charge of manslaughter.

The A320 is not the only case in which problems with new planes have been blamed on pilots, if only because the manufacturers, and the governments which, in most instances, have financed the aircraft, are extremely unwilling to admit culpability. This was shown very clearly when Captain Foote, the pilot of the Comet which came down on take-off at Rome in October 1952, was blamed for an accident caused by peculiarites, later remedied, in the Comet's configuration. But national pride is not confined to the manufacturers. On 6 February 1958, a twin-engined Elizabethan crashed on take-off at Munich Airport. The accident received huge publicity because it killed seven members of the Manchester United football squad, nicknamed 'Busby's Babes' – the greatest football team ever assembled in Britain. The tragedy was immediately blamed on the pilot, Captain James Thain, even though the runway was covered in slush and the aircraft had exploded on hitting a house which was far too near the runway for safety. Thain's licence was removed, even though two airlines, Air Canada and KLM, had already circulated warnings about taking off in such conditions – warnings ignored by BEA. Eventually, pressure by the pilots' union led to a public inquiry which cleared Captain Thain of blame, even though its terms of reference were limited – incredibly, in order not to offend the Germans. But the German authorities refused to concede any responsibility for the state of the runway or the presence of the house and the verdict of pilot error stood. Thain, worn out by the whole affair, died of a heart attack when he was only fifty-four, prompting David Beaty to quote in *Naked Pilot* the old adage: 'If the accident doesn't kill the pilot, the inquiry will.'

A similar desire to deny what one can only call a national sense of guilt underlay the explanations for the terrible accident to a DC10 owned by Air New Zealand, which hit Mount Erebus in the Antarctic on 29 November 1979. The plane had been on one of the sightseeing flights organized by the airline to the continent's ice and mountains. The route took planes too close to the magnetic pole for magnetic navigation to be employed, so they relied on the Inertial Navigation System, which provides an exact position for the aircraft by detecting the rotation of the earth from a gyroscopically stabilized platform within the plane itself. Unfortunately, different co-ordinates had been entered into the system the night before, putting the plane on a course closer to Mount Erebus – a change made without telling the crew. When the DC10 reached the area of Mount Erebus, the weather worsened, culminating in a white-out, which meant that it was impossible to distinguish between land and sky. So the crew, which had never previously flown this dangerous route, were relying entirely on the reprogrammed INS. The plane flew into Mount Erebus, killing all 257 people on board.

The chief inspector of accidents immediately concluded that the accident was probably caused by 'the decision of the captain to continue flight at low level towards an area of poor surface horizon definition when the crew was not certain of their position'. After the pilots' union kicked up an almighty fuss, and some crucial papers connected with the accident mysteriously disappeared, the pilot was cleared. A royal commission set up by the New Zealand government eventually found that the alteration of the setting on the INS by groundstaff, without informing the crew, was 'the single effective cause of the crash'.

Very occasionally, the exact opposite occurs and it is a pilot's guilt that is established only years after his death and even then only after every other possible explanation has been offered. The most famous instance of this rarest of events, again involving the INS system, is that of Korean Airlines Flight 007, an off-course Boeing 747 flying from Anchorage to Seoul shot down by Soviet fighters shortly before dawn on 1 September 1983 over Sakhalin Island in the Soviet far east with the loss of all 269 passengers and crew. Although the cause of the crash itself was not in doubt, the mystery surrounding the reasons why the plane was in the wrong airspace makes the story of Flight 007 (what a gift that number was for the conspiracy theorists) one of the most fascinating in airline history. The belated release by the Soviet authorities of the tapes from the black boxes nearly a decade later proved what many had suspected all along: that the crash had come about as an indirect result of a banal mistake by the pilots. The many and varied explanations put forward between the incident and the release of the boxes provides a unique insight into the absurdity of the theories that will abound in the absence of such data and thus emphasizes its importance in air-crash investigations.

The incident naturally set off an explosion of Cold War rhetoric. President Reagan, then in full 'evil empire' mode, denounced it as a 'terrorist act to sacrifice the lives of innocent human beings', while the Soviet authorities claimed that the aircraft was on a 'special mission' of espionage on behalf of the United States. Within a year the true explanation had been unearthed by Murray Sayle, a brilliant Australian journalist living in Japan, who had the additional advantage of a certificate of competence in navigation. He focused on the aircraft's navigational equipment. This consisted primarily of an INS. If the proper co-ordinates had been fed into the system it had never been known to fail. If, for one reason or another, the INS system was not connected, then the aircraft would have been guided by its magnetic compass. Sayle's hypothesis was that while the captain was greeting an important passenger and some KAL colleagues in the first-class cabin, the co-pilot had accidentally disengaged the INS and gone over to the magnetic-compass setting which overrode the instructions coming from the INS. The result was a steady drift, caused by the wind and by variations in the magnetic field, away from the correct course. Their error meant that the plane strayed hundreds of miles off course into some of the most sensitive and heavily defended air space in the world. According to Sayle's calculations, the drift would have led the plane to more or less the exact spot where it was shot down. Such a mistake is not unknown, and Sayle's hypothesis was reinforced by the fact that there was a fault in the instrument that should have warned the crew that they were flying on a magnetic heading and not, as they assumed, by INS.

Sayle's explanation, first put forward in 1984 (It can be found in its fullest form in *The New York Review of Books*, 25 April 1985), naturally did not satisfy the horde of conspiracy theorists who, consciously or not, were following the Russian line that it was all an imperialist plot. This notion was first advanced in 1984 in an article by David Pearson in the American magazine *The Nation*, suggesting a conspiracy between the American government and the Korean pilot, Captain Chun Byung In. 'The most persuasive theory,' wrote Pearson, 'is that the airliner made a deliberate, carefully planned intrusion into Soviet territory with the knowledge of US military and intelligence agencies.' This hypothesis was reinforced by the presence near the scene of the incident of an American RC135, a 'spy plane' based on the Boeing 707. Sayle believed that the Soviets confused the two planes, and assumed that it was the spy plane, not the hapless 747, that was heading directly for an area containing some of their most sensitive defences. The problem was compounded by the inefficiency of the Soviets, who could not get their fighters into the air quickly enough to simply buzz the 747 and therefore found it necessary to shoot it down.

This simple explanation was scoffed at by the conspiracy theorists, of whom the most distinguished was an Oxford don, R.W. Johnson who devoted a whole book *Shootdown – the Verdict on KAL 007* – to the explanation of a conspiracy between the CIA and its Korean equivalent, the KCIA, to use 007 as a civilian 'cover' for an intelligence operation. He scorned Sayle's explanation, and dismissed Sayle's painstaking analysis, relying simply on the mathematical improbability of pilot error. Instead, he made much play of the undoubted links between the CIA and the KCIA.

In 1991 the truth began to emerge when a Soviet journalist discovered that the black boxes had been recovered by the Soviet authorities. Two years later they were handed over to the Bureau Enquêtes Accidents, the French equivalent of the NTSB, in their capacity as impartial, technically qualified observers. They confirmed Sayle's explanation. Perhaps the most chilling aspect of the whole story is not the unfounded conspiracy theories but the phrase in the ICAO's report which guessed, correctly, at the real reason for the crash: that '[it] assumes a considerable degree of lack of intention on the part of the entire flight crew, but not to a degree that is unknown in international civil aviation.'

13
The Wrong Stuff

We have no effective screening methods to make sure pilots are sane.
– Dr Herbert Haynes of the Federal Aviation Authority

Between the few rogue elements like the crew of Flight 007 and the many superheroes like Captains Moody and McCormick come the various shades of grey, some of them cases still being debated. In many accidents the blame can be, and is, apportioned fairly widely. A typical example was the case of Captain Ho, the veteran pilot of a China Airlines 747 flying from Taipei to Los Angeles in February 1985. When he found that the inner right-hand engine of his plane was misbehaving shortly before landing, he and the crew closed it down. They became so absorbed in discussing the problem that the autopilot proved incapable of handling the excessive roll caused by the engine shut-down. Captain Ho became disoriented, lost control and, after a terrifying series of inadvertent aerobatics, the plane managed to land safely at San Franciso, though not without seriously injuring two of the passengers. In the event the pilot was held responsible only for the delay in attempting to recover from the original problem.

But the most famous cause célèbre in recent aviation history is Captain 'Hoot' Gibson, pilot on a TWA Boeing 727 which suffered a hair-raising near miss in April 1979 and had to make a forced landing at Detroit halfway through a flight from New York to Minneapolis. This incident led to all-out war between the NTSB and the pilots' Union, and remains a matter of debate to this day. The mystery behind the arguments is based on the control of the front slats and rear-edge flaps used to provide vital extra lift on take-off. They are controlled by the same lever, but there are times – notably when the pilot is trying to get extra lift to climb faster when he wants to use the rear flaps, and disconnects the mechanism which normally prevents them from being used while at cruising altitude – when a disconnection can be made by pulling an electrical circuit-breaker on the engineer's panel.

A few minutes into the flight, the plane started to vibrate, and then went into a steep spiral dive, creating havoc in the passenger cabin. Miraculously, at 8,000ft, Captain Gibson felt that the plane was beginning to respond to the controls and managed to steer it down to a safe landing. There he found that the cause of his problem, an extended slat on the right wing of the 727, had suddenly been ripped off by the high-speed airstream engendered by the dive. Patrick Foreman wrote that 'the massive forces that could have been expected to tear the plane apart during its gyrations had, ironically, finally served to save it from destruction'. But Foreman's reasoning is disputed by Stanley Stewart, author of *Emergency*, an ex-pilot and staunch defender of the breed. He believes that it was Gibson who saved the aircraft by lowering the landing gear, resulting in a terrible shock to the plane but slowing the dive sufficiently for him to regain control.

But this disagreement was no more than a sideshow in a row that rumbled on for more than a decade. After Gibson had been hailed as a hero, an NTSB report argued that, like a number of other pilots, he had deliberately extended the slats at high altitude to improve the performance of the aircraft and that the controls had subsequently become muddled, an action Gibson had already denied under oath. One NTSB member, perhaps significantly, the only one with flying experience, expressed his disquiet at the finding. The union, and Stanley Stewart, retorted that such a manoeuvre was highly unlikely, and that the real cause was a broken piston in the slats' actuator shaft; that this problem was well-known – indeed, it had been the subject of a Boeing directive some years earlier and had resulted in a number of other unreported incidents. The whole affair has left a sour taste and a smouldering resentment among pilots, who feel that they are always held responsible for accidents.

The whole question of slats and flaps can remain a matter of dispute even when the case against the pilot seems clear-cut, which is what happened after the 1987 crash of North West Flight 255, a McDonnell Douglas MD80, when it was taking off from Detroit Metro airport for Phoenix. Obviously, before take-off, the pilot and crew have to check that the high-lift devices – the leading-edge slats on the front of the wing and trailing flaps – are in the proper position. 'Immediately after take-off', says Robert Kadlec, a consultant called in by McDonnell Douglas after the crash, 'there was a sign of trouble. You can hear on the cockpit voice-recorder almost straight after the ground roll and the nose-up of the aircraft, the vibration of the stick-shaker, which is a means by which the pilot is told that the aircraft is at a high attitude.' When planes fly with the nose too high, they can stall and become very difficult, if not impossible, to fly.

At that point, the pilot has several choices. There is in the pilot handbook for the MD80 a stall-recovery procedure which tells the pilot to do certain things. My analysis of the flightpath of the aircraft showed that it slowly started to climb out – not what it should have done had the proper flight high-lift surfaces been deployed, had the flaps and slats been out. This aircraft climbed at about 3,000ft per minute, a very high rate of climb. That was a signal that there was something wrong.

Immediately after the stick-shaker vibrated, the stall warning was sounded – four times during the course of this flight. The pilots never responded, and finally about fourteen seconds into flight and some way down the flightpath, the plane developed roll. The left wing rolled down and struck a light pole at a railcar facility and that started the crash sequence. The plane came down on a nearby roadway and all the passengers and crew were killed, except for one young girl.

The aftermath was investigated very carefully by the NTSB. They found evidence that the flaps and slats were in the retracted position. Furthermore, damage to the flap handle showed that this too was in the retracted position. When you review the cockpit voice-recorder from the time when the airplane was at the jetway, all the way out to the point of take-off, it's clear that the pilots did not deploy the flaps and slats, and for some reason they did not execute the proper pre-flight checklist. The MD80 has an additional safety system that warns the pilots if their engine speed goes above a certain level and their flaps and slats are not deployed, and that system didn't sound on the cockpit voice-recorder on this particular flight. There was a careful examination of the circuit-breaker that would have supplied electrical power to this warning system, and the evidence regarding whether or not it was disabled was inconclusive. However, because sometimes audible warnings can become a nuisance, there is an opportunity for the pilots to remove that warning by just turning off the electricity and removing the circuit-breaker, and that was one of the speculative comments by some people about what might have happened.

Kadlec was called in when the parties involved – McDonnell Douglas, the airline, North West and the Airline Pilots' Association – could not agree on the division of blame. The whole thing was thrashed out in a federal court in Detroit. In the end, after Kadlec had spent a week in the witness box, the jury found that the liable party was the airline, and that the pilots had made a mistake. McDonnell, they concluded, had no fault in the accident and were not responsible in any way.

Inevitably there are many cases over the years where the pilot has been unquestionably the major cause of an accident. Sometimes the sequence of events resulting in the crash can be so bizarre as to be unbelievable and to greatly increase the fear of flying. Take the instance of Ariana Afghan Airlines flight 701 travelling from Frankfurt to London on the last leg of a flight from Kabul. The pilot, Captain Rahim Nowroz, was considered perfectly competent, except for a tendency to concern himself with routine matters rather than the controls. The weather over Britain was curious: Heathrow was clear, but there was fog at Gatwick. The pilot has the last word on whether he chooses to fly and to where, and the air-traffic controllers were unable to persuade Captain

Nowroz to follow the decision of other planes and land at Heathrow rather than Gatwick. On the approach to Gatwick, the aircraft descended into a bank of fog at 500ft. Nowroz was taken by surprise because he had been concentrating on something else rather than on flying the plane. After a fatal six-second pause, he tried to get the nose up, but the plane was too nose-heavy. It brushed through treetops and knocked a chimneypot off a house. The tail careered into the bedroom, of another house, killing the occupants, and the plane finally broke up completely. Forty-three of the fifty-four passengers died.

Captain Nowroz survived. He was recalled to Kabul, taken off flying duties and employed as an operations training superintendent. Yet, as so often in stories in which the pilot seems guilty of monumental errors, there was at least one mitigating factor. Precision approach radar would have warned the crew of their predicament, but the PAR system had been withdrawn a few months earlier on economy grounds.

Captain Nowroz suffered from what is probably the single most prevalent – and most fatal – of pilot problems: he was indecisive. He had never really decided to land at Gatwick. The recorder picked up the telltale remark: 'We'll try Gatwick . . . er . . . if we cannot make it at Gatwick, will it be OK if we go to Heathrow?' And this is not the only time when indecision on the part of these supposedly supremely decisive beings has proved fatal. Even more extraordinary was the crash of a Saudi Lockheed TriStar at Riyadh on the evening of 19 August 1980. Seven minutes after take-off, the crew was alerted to the fact that fire had broken out in the cargo hold, which, since it is inaccessible during flight, is monitored automatically. It took the crew four and a half minutes to find the right place in the checklist and the corresponding course of action, an abnormally long time explicable by the fact that the captain had psychological problems in adapting to changing circumstances, the first officer had initially failed his training programme, and the flight engineer suffered from dyslexia.

Eventually the plane turned back to Riyadh, but not before the engineer had returned from the passenger cabin declaring that there was a fire there as well. In the agonizing seven minutes before the plane landed, the flight engineer, in a classic state of psychological denial of reality, became obsessed with trying to find out if the smoke-detector was really working while the captain seemed unable to advise an understandably worried flight attendant whether or not an emergency evacuation should be instigated after landing.

Half a minute before the landing, the pilot finally decided to tell the cabin staff not to order an emergency evacuation. But when he landed he did not halt immediately to give the fire trucks a chance to douse the fire. Instead he behaved as though it were an ordinary landing, coasting to a taxiway some way up the runway. The passengers were finally doomed by the failure of the cabin staff to open the doors from the inside and the inability of the airport rescue services to reach the doors and open them from outside. The subsequent inquiry found that their knowledge of aircraft doors ranged 'from the limited to the non-existent'. It was all of twenty-three minutes after touchdown before the doors were finally opened by the rescuers and by then the 301 people on board had all died from burns or smoke inhalation.

The reasons why a pilot fails at a certain moment are as varied, and as difficult to categorize, as those relating to mankind in general (just consider the case where a Russian pilot allowed his small child to fly his plane). On a long flight – and sometimes even on a short one – the pilot can easily become inattentive or absorbed in an unrelated passion. In September 1988, a Brazilian pilot on a routine domestic flight became so obsessed listening to a football match between his country and Chile that in the end he had to make a crash landing in the jungle after having flown in exactly the opposite direction to his supposed route. It was said that his first question after he had hacked through the jungle to meet his rescuers was 'Who won?'

But however unpredictable pilots may be as human beings, they are trained to follow a set or a series of set procedures to which they should, normally, adhere precisely. This training, however desirable in itself, creates problems in an emergency when quick, independent thinking may be required. Many Gestalt psychologists (significantly, a term derived from the German word for 'pattern'), emphasize the need to avoid what they call 'functional fixity' and to overcome the mechanical responses instilled by the pilots' training. For this fixity can lead to obsessional concentration on the irrelevant. The pilot of a DC9 which crashed into the Caribbean in May 1970 after running out of fuel had become so preoccupied with his efforts to land at Juliana Airport on St Maarten in the Dutch West Indies, that, in the words of Macarthur Job, he 'lost the plot' on the matter of the aircraft's remaining endurance. At times pilots can even ignore the many warning signals manufacturers install, in the form of lights, horns or the shaking stick for preventing jet stalling. In one landing at Orlando in Florida, the crew ignored the horn warning that the landing gear was not down. Engrossed by the problem of 'other traffic' in the vicinity, they simply silenced it. On other occasions crews have reacted wrongly because they have been anticipating a different instruction. 'I was expecting an order to reduce power,' explained one first officer of an emergency when the pilot had in fact given the order gear up – in other words, to retract the undercarriage. The plane crashed.

The classic case of a problem created by a crew's obsessional attention to an apparent glitch leading them to ignore the real one is the story of United Airlines flight 173, a DC8 flying into Portland, Oregon on 28 December 1978. The captain became preoccupied by the failure of the green light which was supposed to indicate that the main undercarriage wheels were down. For the next half an hour he and his colleagues wrestled with the problem. As a result the captain became confused about how much fuel he had left and in the end the plane crashed into the suburbs of Portland, killing the flight engineer, a flight attendant and eight passengers. When investigated, the fault in the under-carriage proved to be simply a burned-out lightbulb.

I have already cited many instances in which pilots have been asked to do too much, to react like robots in situations of extreme stress. As the director-general of operations of the CAA put it : 'There is no field of human activity immune from the occasion when, once in a while, all the adverse factors pile up together to create a situation no one would want to see.' In other fields the results are not necessarily fatal; where aircraft are concerned, they only too often are.

Pilots, like ships' captains, or indeed anyone in authority, need (or feel the need) to behave according to certain preconceived ideas, which include remaining calm and in control. Even, indeed especially, during periods of stress, they have to conceal their doubts, their fears, the unavoidable strains of the job. According to one British expert, L.T.C. Hayward: 'There is some reason to believe that many pilots, at the peak of their physical health and outwardly calm and composed, are inwardly suppressing a seething sea of emotional turbulence born of domestic worries, administrative frustration, technical hazards and operational fatigue.' Dr Hayward could have added the permanent strain of the regular checks made on their health and competence. Worry about being grounded, combined with a tendency towards machismo, leads to a refusal to admit to having problems. As Dr Hayward puts it in *Assessment of Stress Tolerances in Commercial Pilots, Flight Safety, I*, pp12–18, 1967: 'Pilots with self-perceived problems of a patently psychiatric nature are therefore reluctant to disclose them to the flight surgeon, until the seriousness of the developing situation forces his hand.'

The latent strains sometimes show through, even though I tend to disregard most stories of pilots going berserk (my favourite, recounted by Brian Moynahan in *Airport International*, concerns the pilot of a 707 who 'suddenly wrenched the plane into a steep climbing turn, yelling: "Damn Japs down there are putting up a lot of flak. Guadalcanal will always be a tough target." He was over Oklahoma City at the time. The crew had to knock him out.')

Equally apocryphal are most of the stories concerning crashes caused by overindulgence in sex, drink or drugs. Lord Trenchard, founder of the Royal Air Force, is alleged to have told his pilots: 'Gentlemen, you cannot both fuck and fly.' Fortunately, pilots accept the need for a gap of at least eight hours between drinking and, as it were, driving (an interval known in the trade as bottle-to-throttle time). There are, of course, instances of drug-taking leading to fatal crashes. After one pilot died, his lady friend heaved a sigh of relief, 'I'm sure glad we buried him right after the accident,' she said, 'because the night before we had done a bag of cocaine.' I need hardly add that this particular pilot had passed his previous medical test with flying colours.

Fortunately, or rather thanks to continuous efforts in training and selecting pilots, cases of sheer technical incompetence are becoming rarer. Back in 1965, a training board recommended that a United Airlines pilot, Captain Gale C.

Kehrmeire, be taken out of the cockpit because of 'unsatisfactory performance in the areas of command, judgement, standard operating procedure, landing techniques and smoothness and co-ordination'. Despite this comprehensive list of faults, he continued to fly, and crashed at Salt Lake City in 1965 while at the controls of a Boeing 727. A year later a Lockheed Electra on a charter flight was lost after the pilot, Captain Reed W. Pigman, died at the controls. It later emerged that Captain Pigman, who had founded the airline concerned, American Flyers, had a very serious, longstanding heart condition and also suffered from diabetes. He had only managed to keep his pilot's licence by falsifying his medical record.

This was not an isolated case. In April 1973 the Ladies Guild from Axbridge, a small town in the west of England, planned a very special day out: a trip from Bristol Airport to the Swiss City of Basle. Only thirty-five of the party returned. One hundred and thirty-five women died, leaving fifty-five motherless children, after their Vickers Vanguard turbo-prop crashed into a Swiss hillside. As so often there was a variety of problems for the pilots: repairs to an important landing instrument had been botched; navigation equipment had been soldered in the shoddiest of fashions and neither the radio beacons nor the radar at Basle were up to scratch.

However, the extentuating circumstances did not greatly diminish the responsibility of the pilot, Captain Anthony Dorman, a Canadian ex-military flier. He had become hopelessly disoriented, misidentifying two vital radio beacons on the ground and missing another. When his older and more experienced co-pilot, Captain Ivor Terry, took over, neither of them realized that they were a long way south of the airport. Terry's final run was based on a wrong beacon and an inaccurate fix.

Dorman should never have been allowed into the cockpit. In *Flying into Danger*, Patrick Foreman sombrely records:

> Swiss accident-investigators claimed that Dorman had faked his pilot's licence by making false declarations about his qualifications. Before his civil flying career, he had been suspended from the Canadian Air Force for lack of ability. He had failed no fewer than eight times before finally passing his British instrument flying ratings – the cornerstone of airline piloting competence. As the chairman of his pilots' association put it: 'God knows how he slipped through the net for so long. I've never heard of another pilot failing his instrument test eight times.'

He would not have slipped through under the tougher regulations that were introduced as a result of the crash. The most frequent cause of accidents is not incompetence but overstrain, usually due to overlong hours and the eternal adjustments required to the body clock. Given the stories of pilots falling asleep after delays have extended their working hours the wonder is not the number of crashes, but their fortunate relative infrequency, a tribute to the sheer professionalism of the world's commercial pilots.

Let one case, recounted by Patrick Foreman, represent the thousands of similar incidents, for every pilot reading this account will say, 'There but for the grace of God go I.' The flight was from Gatwick to an unnamed African destination. 'The jet's departure was scheduled for early afternoon, but the engineers had found a snag which, they said, would be fixed in an hour. It wasn't, and the crew kicked their heels for the rest of the day before finally making a midnight take-off.' Unfortunately, a fault in the yaw-damper, which prevents the tail of the aircraft from oscillating, meant that the autopilot could not be used and the plane had to be flown manually the whole way. When the pilot radioed his employers, they simply told him to carry on, and that they'd fix the yaw-damper on his return.

'After a refuelling stop in North Africa,' wrote Foreman, 'the co-pilot found himself flying over the starlit Sahara in the relaxed atmosphere of the warm, dark cockpit.' Not surprisingly, he fell asleep. The captain woke first. He and the co-pilot exchanged notes, and promptly fell asleep again. In the end,' The three crewmen managed to keep themselves awake for the rest of the flight by switching on the cockpit floodlights and they finally landed safely.'

Most flying is now done on instruments. This brings its own problems, since the pilots are flying blind within their own circumscribed cabin space. Flying 'blindfold' produces giddiness, loss of balance and total disorientation, especially in bad weather. 'In non-visual flight' says Foreman, 'the sense of balance is not only useless but worse than useless, because it becomes a compelling liar. Without instruments to put matters right, it is said that the average time for an untrained pilot to lose control and kill himself is between one and one and a half minutes.'

As even experts admit, this disorientation can be simply a matter of mis-interpretation of increasingly complex flying systems leading to an inability to distinguish left from right. The most famous consequence of such an instance was the crash of a British Midlands Boeing 737 on a motorway at Kegworth, agonizingly only a few hundred yards short of the runway at East Midlands Airport, on 8 January 1989. There had been a fatigue failure on the port engine, but the pilot had mistakenly shut down the starboard engine instead, thereby leaving the plane without power. Forty-seven of those on board died in the resulting disaster.

The complexity of attaching blame to a pilot, or indeed to any other single cause of an accident, was never better illustrated than in the case of the world's worst aircraft accident. With any luck the deaths of 583 people at Los Rodeos Airport on Tenerife in the Canary Islands on 27 March 1977 is likely to remain a record for many years to come, because it involved two Boeing 747s. The main undercarriage of a 747 belonging to KLM hit a Pan-Am Jumbo which was taxiing along the runway and immediately burst into flames. All 234 passengers and fourteen crew members aboard the KLM plane died, as did 335 of those aboard the Pan-Am jet, although, miraculously, sixty-one Pan-Am passengers and crew survived.

Behind these simple statistics is an extraordinarily complicated story. It started earlier that day when a bomb was planted at Las Palmas Airport on Gran Canaria, the biggest island in the group, by a group of Canary Island separatists. While the airport was being cleared and searched for further bombs, aircraft were diverted to the smaller airport at Los Rodeos, which was consequently overcrowded with traffic. Moreover, its facilities, particularly its taxiways, were not designed to cope with Jumbos. The Pan-Am plane, captained by a veteran pilot, Victor Grubbs, was en route from Los Angeles and New York carrying a group of elderly tourists to join a cruise ship. Captain Grubbs was denied the permission he requested to remain airborne until Las Palmas was reopened, and was forced to land at Los Rodeos.

But the main problems arose from the KLM plane, a charter being flown by Jacob van Zanten, KLM's chief training pilot for 747s. Despite his seniority – he had been flying with KLM for over a quarter of a century – he had not flown recently but had instead been instructing. Indeed, his co-pilot was a former pupil of his.

Van Zanten was seemingly obsessed by the exceedingly strict restrictions on flying hours newly introduced by KLM and the need to unload his passengers at Las Palmas, which had just been reopened, in time to enable him to return to Amsterdam. So he arranged to refuel, and owing to the lack of space on the airport's aprons this delayed the Pan-Am flight. Then the two moved off, the KLM plane to take off, and the Pan-Am Jumbo to a taxiway.

Then came a series of misunderstandings. The air-traffic controller, who had been on duty all day, was under considerable strain because of the rush of aircraft diverted from Las Palmas. Nevertheless, it is clear that he never actually gave Captain van Zanten clearance to take off. In the event neither the co-pilot nor the flight engineer dared query very bluntly with Captain van Zanten the fact that they had not received express permission to take off. By then visibility had worsened, fog was setting in and both planes were relying exclusively on radio communications.

In the confused jumble of radio messages involving both captains and the control tower, the KLM plane tried to take off before the Pan-Am Jumbo had cleared the runway. When the pilot, by now highly impatient, started to take off, the first officer said, according to Paul Roitsch, a senior Pan-Am pilot who flew in afterwards to investigate the crash, 'No, wait a minute – we don't have our air-traffic control clearance.

The captain replied, 'Yes, I know that.' He pulled the throttles back and added, 'Now, go ahead and call for it.' The first officer called for the air-traffic control clearance. The controller then called back and gave him his clearance to Las Palmas, adding an instruction that after take-off he should turn right to such and such a heading. It's possible that after the first officer had asked for take-off clearance and air-traffic control clearance he could have inferred that any answer in the positive indicated that he had been cleared for both events, which was not in fact the case. The additional directions in the clearance didn't help, either, because it reinforced the impression that they were cleared for take-off. As the first officer was reading the clearance back to the controllers, the captain again commenced the take-off, pushed up the throttles, said, 'We go,' and the aircraft started to roll. This happened while the first officer was still repeating back the clearance. He sensed that this was not right – he knew that they hadn't been cleared for take-off – and so, after he finished reading back the clearance, he said either 'We are taking off,' or 'We are at take-off.' It wasn't even that clear: the words are difficult to comprehend and the tone of the voice changes. It's obviously very tense, but the first officer felt that he had done his part in letting people know that they were commencing their take-off. The words that he used were also ambiguous to other people. The tower thought he had said, 'We're at take-off position,' but the controller wasn't sure. He said, 'OK' – a long pause – 'Stand by for take-off.'

He felt he had covered the situation in any event. Unfortunately, the Pan-Am first officer had also heard that blurted statement about taking off and he came on the frequency and said, 'we're still on the runway, Clipper 1736.' The first part of that statement interfered with the tower's transmission back to the Dutch airplane instructing it to stand by for take-off. In the cockpit of the Dutch airplane, the words to stand by were changed in timbre, lowered in volume. It sounded like a different transmitting station, but it was capable of being heard. The Dutch airplane heard the words Clipper 1736, and then they heard the tower say to the Pan-Am airplane, 'Roger Clipper, advise when you're clear.' The Pan-Am first officer replied, 'Roger, we'll advise when we're clear.' All this time the Dutch airplane was accelerating down the runway, gaining velocity very quickly. The flight engineer in the Dutch cockpit heard the response from the Pan-Am and he questioned the crew, the captain and the first officer. He said, 'Is he not clear, then? They said, 'What?'

'Is he not clear then, the Pan-American?' Both crew members said, 'Ja, ja, he's clear.' At that point they were just entering the heavy cloud on the runway. The Dutch felt they had covered the situation by announcing their take-off, they didn't hear anyone warning them not to take off and they proceeded. It was only, I believe, just after V1 [the speed at which a decision has to be made whether or not to take off] that they saw the Pan-Am aircraft desperately trying to get off the runway. The Americans had spotted the Dutch airplane bearing down on them; they could see the landing lights coming toward them. The captain of the Pan-Am airplane shoved the throttles up and tried to turn the aircraft, but there was not enough time. The rest is history.

Later events served only to complicate the tragedy. The investigation was a joint one, involving the Spanish, the NTSB, Pan-Am, Boeing, the engine manufacturer, KLM and the Dutch government. It started amicably enough, but it soon became apparent that the Dutch were trying to pin the blame on the air-traffic controller. As Roitsch described it, 'The Dutch had decided to circle the wagons. They were searching for something to fasten on to that would divert the blame from their own countrymen.' They suggested that the air-traffic controllers were listening to a football game in the tower at the time of the accident, a slur based on the flimsy foundation that 'someone thought they heard the Spanish word for football in the tower'. They even tried to blame the Pan-Am crew, a suggestion hotly refuted by Roitsch.

The disaster was eventually attributed, rather vaguely, to 'human factors'. But in fact it was the result of a series of appalling coincidences, listed by Macarthur Job:

> If the bomb had not gone off at Las Palmas; if the Pan-Am Boeing had been permitted to hold instead of landing at Los Rodeos; if the KLM crew had not decided to refuel; if the Pan-Am aircraft could have squeezed past its KLM sister ship without having to wait for it to move; if the weather had not deteriorated; if the Pan-Am crew had not bypassed the number 3 taxiway; if they had not transmitted at the moment they did, when they feared the KLM aircraft was about to take-off; if the KLM captain had taken more notice of his flight engineer's doubt . . . Any of these factors could have altered the whole course of events as they unfolded.

14
Call Me God

I think every pilot would like to have an open cockpit with a helmet and scarf flying in the breeze and beautiful women applauding our every move. Do I miss the helmet and scarf? Sure I do. Will we ever go back to that? No, only recreationally. The difference between a professional pilot and an amateur pilot is that you try to leave your ego in your car in the parking lot. Your professionalism, you take that into the cockpit.
                              – Captain John Crum, pilot with Delta Airlines

The pilot's role has changed enormously over the past few decades, but not all of his breed have accepted the transformation with as good a grace as Captain Crum. Above all, they are finding it difficult to abandon their previously un-challenged power in the cockpit. Traditionally, the pilot has been a figure of unquestioned authority, and it is only in the last twenty years that the nature of his authority has been questioned, leading to considerable, and not entirely resolved problems. When David Beaty joined British Overseas Airways after the war, many of the captains lived up to their nickname – the barons. As a con-sequence: 'Communication on the flight deck could be very strained. First officers did not correct the captain or his mistakes. I had my hand smartly smacked when I leaned over the throttle box to put a captain's VHF on the correct switch after he had complained of not being able to hear anything. He would give the order, he said, when he wanted me to do anything. Otherwise I was to shut up and do nothing.' When Norman Tebbit, later Lord Tebbit, was employed as a co-pilot with BOAC, he 'rated captains not least according to how often they were willing to play the co-pilot's role to their first officer,' according to his autobiography, *Upwardly Mobile*.

The nature of the co-pilot's fear of interfering with the captain is known in the trade as the 'Captain God complex', and it leaves the co-pilot psychologically helpless in emergencies. The basic question, which remains difficult to answer, is at what point, and in what extreme circumstances, can a junior member of the flight crew justify even questioning the captain's judgement, let alone trying to interfere with or overriding the captain's actions? The term 'captain' provides a vital clue to the problem. This is a relationship which concerned writers about seafarers for centuries before the first aeroplane ever flew. Captain Queeg in *The Caine Mutiny* was the model for the situation in which many crews have found themselves over the years. Too often pilots have behaved like the one in an incident recounted by David Beaty in *Naked Pilot*. A co-pilot told his captain that approach control had told them to slow down to 180 knots. 'His reply was something to the effect: "I'll do what I want !" I told him at least twice more and received the same answer. Approach control asked us why we had not yet slowed. I told them we were doing the best job we could and their reply was, 'You almost hit another aircraft."' And when the co-pilot reminded the pilot that he had disobeyed an instruction to descend only to 3,000ft the pilot replied, 'You just look out the damn window.'

This exaggerated respect for the pilot is greater in a hierarchical society, or (as happened in the Air Florida crash recounted in Chapter 9) when the junior member of the crew has been schooled in automatic obedience to his superiors in the course of military training. I believe that Qantas's success in remaining virtually accident-free through the years owes a lot to a peculiarly Australian factor: the willingness of Australians to stand up to their bosses. In their non-hierarchical society, subordinates are culturally encouraged to feel free to challenge their superiors. In airline management terms, this leads to a healthy tension between air crew and management, who cannot impose their ideas as easily as they can among more obedient races. If an Aussie crew member thinks a plane is potentially unsafe he will not hesitate to say so, loudly and frequently. This could do more than any conditioning to save lives.

The most obvious potential crisis is physical: when the pilot falls suddenly ill, or, worse, dies at the controls during take-off or landing. It then takes an iron nerve, combined with extremely quick thinking, to save the situation. In 1966 the pilot of a KLM DC8 died of a massive heart attack a mere thirty seconds before touchdown, when the plane was already down to 150ft. The co-pilot, Cornelius de Jager, managed to put on full power and go round again, dragging the dead pilot from his seat while the automatic pilot flew the plane, thus eliminating any danger that the pilot's body might interfere with the controls.

But the key event which led to a transformation in the relationship between pilots and their crew, and indeed between pilots and their employers, was the crash of a BEA Trident, flight BE 548 from London to Brussels, at Staines, just after it had taken off from Heathrow on a summer Sunday, 18 June 1972. The story of the crash reads like one of the techno-psychological thrillers which were Nevil Shute's speciality, for it begins with the personality of the pilot and his relationship with his fellows.

In charge was Captain Stanley Keys, a highly experienced, fifty-one-year-old pilot. He disagreed vehemently, even violently, with his fellows in the British Airline Pilots' Association on the question of their militant stance towards their employers, British European Airways. Strike action was threatened, and a crucial meeting was due to be held on 19 June. The previous day, that of the fatal flight, Key had a violent row in BEA's crew room over his view, one shared by other senior captains.

One consequence of the simmering dispute was a hiccup in BEA's plans to train new Trident pilots to act as 'monitoring pilots', the third man in the cockpit, seated behind the pilot and co-pilot and able, as the name implies, to monitor any unusual actions by the other two members of the crew. Keys' co-pilot on BE 548 was a twenty-two-year-old novice with only forty hours under his belt as a co-pilot. Moreover, the young J.W. Keighley had just witnessed the full force of Keys' disapproval in the crew room. As Jon Scott, a BA first officer observes, 'The relative inexperience of his two junior crew members meant an increase in the workload which, in any case, was relatively high for a captain due to the way the procedures were written in those days with the new jet aircraft.'

The take-off was normal, despite the blustery weather, low cloud and rain, but within a minute after the control tower had received the message, 'Climbing as cleared – passing 1,500ft,' the plane had crashed, killing the crew and all 112 passengers (the sole survivor died within a few hours of arriving at the hospital). The Trident did not carry a CVR, but the FDR revealed precisely what had caused the crash: a deep stall. This was caused by the premature retraction of the 'droops', a device hinged at the bottom of the leading edge of the wing which provides additional lift while the plane is taking off and climbing to its cruising altitude. If the droops are extended, the speed at which the plane stalls is greatly reduced; if they are retracted, it increases by about 30 knots.

But even before the droops were retracted, the plane had failed to reach the speeds appropriate to the successive stages of take-off and climb. Moreover, even when the droops had been retracted, the pilots had plenty of visual and other warnings to prompt them to take remedial action. They could have applied more power to increase speed and avoid a stall; they could have extended the droops again, or tried to reverse the stall by holding the control column forward. This left four unanswered questions, posed by Macarthur Job in *Air Disaster*.

> Why was there such a serious and persistent speed error in the flying of the aircraft up to the point at which it stalled? Who was responsible for retracting the leading edge prematurely? Why did BEA's much-vaunted in-flight monitoring system fail to avert the stall – and why did the crew not fly a recovery after the stall warnings? Why did the crew fail to diagnose the reason for the stall-recovery system operating repeatedly, and why was the system turned off at such a critical point?'

Because of the lack of a CVR, some of these questions remain unanswered to this day. We are still not sure, for instance, who actually retracted the droops. But by the end of the week, a team of six pathologists had conducted autopsies on all the bodies. The body of Captain Key provided the first important clue. The autopsy revealed a severe case of atherosclerosis. There was a tear in the lining of the wall of one artery caused by a rupture in the small blood vessels in the artery wall, a tear which had occurred not more than two hours before the crash. It seems likely that Key would have been suffering chest pains before he climbed into the cockpit, had dismissed them as indigestion resulting from his outburst in the crew room, that the 'indigestion' had caused him increasing problems as he underwent the naturally high strains engendered by even the most routine take-off, and that this had led this normally most punctilious of pilots to fly at too low a speed.

It is possible that the monitoring pilot was occupied at the time with the flight log, or that he and the co-pilot were too busy coping while Key was suffering with his 'indigestion' to take sufficient notice of the stall-recovery warning systems. These should have been unmissable as Jon Scott explains. 'First an amber light would have gone on in front of each pilot, as well as a 'droops out of position' warning light in the front of the central pedestal, followed by a stick-shaker which warns the pilots by shaking the control column that they are about to stall the aircraft.'

The noise and the suddenness of the shock would have been difficult for even the most experienced crew to handle. The Trident was the first British aircraft to be fitted with droops, and it had two separate levers: one for the wing flaps, the other for the droops. Other aircraft had a single lever. So it is possible that either Key or Keighley pulled the wrong lever. In the absence of a CVR, Scott surmises that the captain might have thought that the co-pilot had made the mistake and barked an order to Keighley which the poor co-pilot misunderstood. Another element in the mix was that the warning system had previously proved unreliable, resulting in several false alarms.

Reflying the doomed flight on a simulator, even the experienced Scott had to admit that it was frightening.

> The more we do it, the more horrific it appears. The time scale is very, very short. It's two and a half minutes from starting the take-off roll to impact in a field in Staines, of which three quarters of a minute is spent on the take-off roll. There were only thirty-six seconds between when the droop lever was moved to impact. There was a whole cacophony of sound and light going on all at once, totally unexpectedly, as well as the aircraft buffeting around in the weather conditions at the time. It's quite understandable how the crew didn't recognize their predicament.

The accident report was a model of its kind. As pathologist Air Commodore Cullen summed it up:

> It all goes to show that accident-investigation is putting lots and lots of pieces in the jigsaw. We put in one piece saying that Key had severe coronary heart disease with an acute change that we believe would have incapacitated him. The psychologists entered other pieces; the operations inspectors who evaluate what has happened put in others, as did the engineers and flight-data recorder people, and the net result, of course,

is that the report comes out saying that the reason the aircraft crashed was because the droops had been retracted. Where the medical and psychological side comes in is answering the question of why the droops might have been retracted.

The traumatic consequences of the crash led to a number of technical improvements; to the immediate acceptance by BEA's pilots of CVRs (which were already mandatory equipment in other countries, including the USA, France and Australia), and to a totally new emphasis, which has continued to this day, on the training of pilots to act a part of a team. The focus on pilots' psychological problems brought other insights, such as the fact that they tend to reject the systemic problems in aviation safety. Psychologist and former airline pilot Bob Besco, now a consultant on pilot performance selection and training, puts it,

> Pilots would like to feel that accidents are caused by a dumb pilot. 'I'm not dumb like that dead pilot is, so I don't make those kind of mistakes,' or, 'I'm not deviant in my personality characteristics like that dead pilot is, so I'm not subject to the same kind of errors.' This gives them a false sense of comfort. For generations, pilots have been willing to accept these partial definitions of accident causation in terms of pilot error because it absolves them of having to face the same kind of risk when they go to work.

The two most significant innovations have been expressed in two acronyms: CHIRPs and CRM, which stand respectively for Confidential Human Factors Incident Reports and Cockpit Resource Management. In the late 1970s and early 1980s, the aviation authorities belatedly woke up to the need to improve communication between the pilots and themselves. In the past the repeated failure of pilots to report a particular fault had often led to disaster. It took the crash of a Beechcraft at Spokane in 1981 because the pilot misread the distance-measuring equipment to bring out into the open five pilots who admitted that they too had experienced similar incidents but had been too embarrassed to report the problem. They had assumed, wrongly, that it was they and not the equipment that had been at fault.

This sort of revelation, and the fact that pilots often dared not report incidents involving them or other pilots; dared not complain of stress, of fatigue, of bad maintenance, of unreasonable demands imposed by their employers, resulted in a new reporting system for untoward incidents. In 1977 a prototype safety reporting system had been introduced in the United States, requiring pilots to report every incident of any significance to NASA. However, it was badly publicized and a great many pilots were unaware of it, or of its British equivalent, Mandatory Occurrence Reporting, introduced by the CAA. Inevitably, too, pilots are wary of filing official reports. Nevertheless, information about 4,500 potentially or actually dangerous incidents is passed on to the CAA every year.

This has been reinforced by a system of confidential reporting, a sort of confessional for pilots, surrounded by all the secrecy that implies. This was introduced in the early 1980s by NASA in the United States, where it was known as ASRS – Aviation Safety Reporting System – and was copied a few years later in Britain in the guise of CHIRPS. CHIRPS is run by the Royal Air Force's Institute of Aviation Medicine, and has proved a great success. One pilot told Patrick Foreman, 'It is one of the few aviation circulars to be read from cover to cover by most pilots.' There, pilots tend to feel, but for the grace of God go I. According to CHIRPS, most companies are compelled by commercial pressures to operate to the legal limits, 'and they can't be held responsible if the limits are too liberal'.

More contentious are the many and various training schemes devised by airlines over the past couple of decades to train crews, and pilots in particular, to work better together; schemes generally grouped under the generic name of CRM. Few have gone as far as Qantas, which runs a course designed to highlight the horrible potential consequences of a crew's failure to act as a team. CRM has many converts, though it is dismissed by some as a waste of time.

As so often, it is the worst sinners who have repented the most thoroughly. United Airlines is the largest airline outside Russia, with 8,000 pilots and 500 planes. Bob Besco recalls:

> In the 1950s United Airlines had the misguided philosophy that they didn't want to hire overqualified military pilots. They felt they'd be malcontent and discontented employees. This philosophy was interpreted in a lot of hangar talk as United only wanting to hire people they could control, to make them into good employees rather than good pilots. Consequently, when we started looking at the types of pilot-error accidents that became defined as CRM accidents, we found that United Airlines was committing a lot of 'em, primarily because the captains had been taught by the airline itself that they couldn't trust their co-pilots; that they had very marginally qualified co-pilots, hired right out of college.

A spate of accidents and incidents led to a revolution. 'To their credit,' says Besco, 'United implemented one of the first programmes in crew resource-management, and they have been one of the leaders in CRM. Today, United's safety department is a sort of mini-NTSB with its own crisis centre and technical experts on tap 365 days a year.'

Another major American airline, Delta, started its own CRM programme in 1988 after a number of incidents highlighted the problems associated with the 'right stuff' mentality. Ray Justinic, the systems manager of human factors at Delta, had been an accident-investigator himself, so he could see the need for reform of pilots' attitudes.

What we thought was the right stuff turned out in an airline operation to be the wrong stuff. We needed people who were more of team players. We're not going to change anybody's personality in a two-hours-a-year or a three-day programme: what we do try to do is make people aware that there are different personalities. It's not so much you're a nice guy, I'm a nice guy, as you're different from me, but we can work together as long as we realize that our primary mission is a safe flight. You may have different ideas – we may disagree on politics, religion or whatever – but the object is still a safe flight. Now, how do we get that done? We give them some skills they can use to make that happen, and to make it happen better.

When it was first introduced it was not warmly received either by the airlines or by the FAA. We started a complete programme to educate a little over 5,000 pilots in a twelve-month period. We brought them all through a three-day programme and introduced 'em to CRM, not trying to do it all alone. We introduced 'em to decision-making concepts, to workload management concepts, to communication skills; we did classroom work on it, and then we took them into simulators and we practised in the simulator what we had preached in the classroom. The way a cockpit or an aircraft is run, compared to how it was, let's say, five years ago, is much safer and much better.

When we first started CRM at Delta Airlines, we did an attitude survey to see how open captains were to input from other people; how much they utilized the other resources on the airplane. We found that most captains still bought in to the 'right stuff', solo type of mindset. At the completion of the initial CRM, we did another survey and found that the percentage saying, yes, I want some input, this is a good resource and it's OK for me to use it, had increased dramatically. Now when we do audits or surveys again, which are just attitudinal checks, we're finding that this attitude is growing. They're more open, they're more receptive.

When Delta started its programme, it was largely confined to the flight crew. Not surprisingly they soon found, as Justinic relates, that information can be gathered from the cabin, from flight attendants – even passengers sometimes become part of the team. So Delta has now extended the resource-management programmes to include flight attendants, and are in the process of expanding them to cover technical operations, maintenance people and dispatchers. 'Recently, one of our aircraft had a smoke problem in the cabin,' offers Justinic by way of example. 'It turned out not to be really serious, but the crew did the evacuation just as they had practised in the CRM class, nobody was hurt and I got separate calls from the captain and the lead flight attendant, who told me it went just as it had in the class.'

Justinic's view is echoed by Robert McIntosh. After years of listening to pilots' conversations, he declared of the CVR of the Sioux City crash that he had never heard so much CRM on a tape before. The result, of course, was 'a disaster miraculously mitigated by the combined skills of the crew and the other pilot who happened to be on board'.

Nevertheless, there's an understandable feeling that there's nothing new under the sun. All British pilots have to be inducted into the mysteries of CRM, and British Airways, in particular, has been at the forefront of the 'all-together' mentality – not surprisingly, given the deep and long-lasting scar inflicted by the tragedy at Staines. But to Dave Miller, CRM is simply 'a new name for an old trick'. He asserts: 'It used to be called airmanship. Somebody has put this name to what's been going on already, but has now formulated what was previously an unsystematic approach to the problem of crew relationships.'

Bob Besco is more cynical.

The pilots have accepted CRM in a very limited way. At least a fifth of pilots have objected to it as being nonsensical, irrelevant and a waste of their time. They've been vilified by the instructors for criticizing the training programme, and so they've kind of gone along with it, though a few of the pilots are still out there actively objecting to the small-group dynamics emphasis in CRM training. If you try to suggest that there are other things you should do in CRM besides the small-group dynamics and personality training, you're declared a blasphemer.

This emphasis comes out of academic psychology, out of research that's been done primarily on college undergraduates in artificial small-group situations. We're dealing here with mature professionals in real-world situations. Back in the 1950s, when they were promoting CRM for executive-development programmes for basically the same kind of learning experiences, the content and the methodologies were almost identical to what is being promoted in CRM under the rubric of small-group dynamics today. It proved ineffective then and was dropped, and in my observation it's been ineffective today. The airlines saw CRM as a way of solving the problem of pilot error, which was a serious embarrassment. When fully accredited academic psychologists from major universities tell them that these techniques will solve their problems, they're willing to try it, and they have tried it in spades. It's become a multi-million-dollar industry. It has also appealed to a lot of the executives in the industry, because they can then say that these problems were the result of something defective emotionally on the pilots' part, and it was not any of their responsibility.

Besco is much more impressed with the so-called command leadership resource management programme run by United, one of the first airlines to try 'to redirect CRM away from the sensitivity training and hot-tub psychology into more operationally oriented training'. He would be enthusiastically backed by Denny Fitch, the hero of United 232.

> Basically what CLR is doing is accepting some synergy. It's saying to the captains, 'Listen, you have all this talent in the cockpit with you, you have all this talent back in the cabin with you. When situations arise, consult with as many of these people as you can – get their thoughts, get their views, get their concerns. You're still the decision-maker, but you'll make such a better decision if you accept all the resources around you. It's not a threat to your command, it is an asset to you as a commander.' Captain Haynes embraced that culture and we practised it every year.
>
> When I arrived in the cockpit on 232, these people did not know me. I could have been the neighbourhood cook. I just said I was an instructor and they accepted me. The strangest thing, one of the most wonderful recollections I have of that time frame up there, was when Captain Haynes reached his arm up over his shoulder to me because he could not turn away from what he was doing, and introduced himself and the rest of the crew. The significance of that for me was that now I was a member of the team.

Inevitably, old habits persist. As so often, for example, in a moment of crisis a co-pilot may revert to automatic obedience to his captain, sometimes with disastrous results. Talking of the US Air accident in Charlotte, Rudi Kapustin observes: 'Despite everything, they were making it and climbing out of there. But the captain shouts at the co-pilot, "Get the nose down! get the nose down!" Well, he got the nose down, and they crashed. If the co-pilot had kept on doing what he'd been doing, they'd have been fine.'

In the end, everything depends on the pilots' temperament. The last word goes to Rudi Kapustin.

> Senator Goldwater used to say that you can't legislate morality, and I think if you've got a blockhead, no matter how much CRM and CLR you expose him to, he's probably still going to be a blockhead. A lot of people disagree with that. But if you've got a lousy personality, one who doesn't like to interact with people, who doesn't take advice, I don't know if he can fix that. As far as arrogance and ego are concerned, I think pilots are essentially people, and we find arrogance and egos in the non-pilot population.

GLOSSARY

AAIB	Air Accidents Investigation Branch
ADF	Automatic direction-finder
ALPA	Airline Pilots Association (USA)
APU	Auxiliary power unit
ASRS	Aviation Safety Reporting System
ATC	Air Traffic Control Centre
BALPA	British Airline Pilots Association
BEA	Bureau d'Enquêtes Accidents
CAA	Civil Aviation Authority (UK)
CHIRPS:	Cockpit Human Factors Incident Reports
CRM	Cockpit Resource Management (later Crew Resource Management)
CVR:	Cockpit voice-recorder
DFDRs	Digital flight-data recorder
FAA	Federal Aviation Agency (USA)
FMS	Flight-management system
GPWS	Ground-proximity warning system
HUD	Head-up display
IFALPA	International Federation of Airline Pilots Association
IATA	International Air Transport Association
ICAO	International Civil Aviation Organization
ILS	Instrument landing system
INS	Inertial navigation systems
NASA	National Aeronautics and Space Administration
NTSB	National Transportation Safety Board
RAE	Royal Aircraft Establishment (Farnborough)
RLD	Rijks Luchtvuart Dienst

NAMES OF INTERVIEWEES

Arthur Almond, retired engineer, RAE
George Bershinsky, research pilot for University of Wyoming
Bob Besco, safety consultant and ex-pilot, American Airlines
Jan Brown, flight attendant
Captain Heino Caesar, aviation safety consultant and former head of safety, Lufthansa
John Cook, retired engineer at RAE
Air Commodore Tony Cullen, pathologist, RAF Institute of Aviation Medicine
John Cunningham, retired test pilot
Captain John Crum, Delta Airlines
Ray Davis, former aircraft accident-investigator, AAIB
Greg Feith, senior air accident-investigator, NTSB
Denny Fitch, training pilot, United Airlines
Steve Fredrick, former pilot, American Eagle Airlines
Bob Graham, assistant chief officer, Manchester Fire Service

Dennis Grossi, national resource specialist for FDRs, NTSB
Sir Arnold Hall, former director, RAE
Jim Hall, Chairman, NTSB
Tom Haueter, deputy chief, major accident investigation branch, NTSB
Bill Houghton, retired engineer, RAE
Charles Huettner, NASA
Ray Justinic, systems manager, human factors, Delta Airlines
Robert Kadlec, Failure Analysis Associates
Rudi Kapustin, former investigator in charge of major accidents, NTSB
Fredo Killing, amateur pilot
Dave King, principal inspector of air accidents, AAIB
Bud Laynor, former deputy director, Office of Aviation Safety, NTSB
Michael Marx, head of materials laboratory division, NTSB
Bryce McCormick, DC10 pilot
Frank McDermott and **Mike McDermott**, partners, McDermott Associates, specialists
  in CVRs
Robert McIntosh, acting chief, major accident-investigation division, NTSB
Chuck Miller, former head of Bureau of Aviation Safety, NTSB
Captain David Miller, senior inspector of air accidents, AAIB
Steve Moss, senior inspector of air accidents, AAIB
Bob Nelson, former senior air accident-investigator, AAIB
Nora Marshall, senior accident-investigator, survival factors division, NTSB
Peter Mellor, Centre for Software Reliability
Greg Phillips, systems specialist, NTSB
Charles Phipps, flight instructor, Delta Airlines
Marsha Politovich, research meteorologist
Chris Protheroe, senior inspector of air accidents, AAIB
Ken Raithby, former stress engineer, RAE
Paul Reese, fire station sergeant at Dallas Fort Worth Airport
Captain Paul Roitsch, former Pan-Am pilot, ALPA
Ron Schleede, deputy director, Office of Aviation Safety
Jon Scott, first officer, British Airways
Dale and **Janice Sorenson**, farmers at Sioux City
Captain Stanley Stewart, 747 captain, British Airways, aviation author
Joe Stiley, survivor of Air Florida crash
Jean-Pierre Stucki, French TV journalist
Eddie Trimble, senior inspector of air accidents, AAIB
James Wildey, senior metallurgust, NTSB
Professor David Woods, Ohio State University
Bill Yantiss, senior flight safety investigator, United Airlines

Index